RELATIONSHIP
The Heart of Helping People

Helen Harris
Perlman

RELATIONSHIP
The Heart of Helping People

THE UNIVERSITY OF CHICAGO PRESS

Chicago and London

The University of Chicago Press, Chicago 60637
The University of Chicago Press, Ltd., London

© 1979 by The University of Chicago
All rights reserved. Published 1979
Paperback edition 1983
Printed in the United States of America

90 89 88 87 86 85 84 83   2 3 4 5

Library of Congress Cataloging in Publication Data

Perlman, Helen Harris.
  Relationship, the heart of helping people.

  Includes bibliographical references and index.
  1. Social case work.   2. Helping behavior.
3. Interpersonal relations.   I. Title.
HV43.P457   361.3'2   78–19064
ISBN 0–226–66035–4   (cloth)
     0–226–66036–2   (paper)

HELEN HARRIS PERLMAN is Samuel Deutsch
Distinguished Service Professor, Emeritus, in
the School of Social Service Administration
at the University of Chicago. She is the
author of numerous books including *Social
Casework: A Problem-solving Process* and
Persona: Social Role and Personality, both
published by the University of Chicago Press.

TO MAX

for the heart's reasons

Author's Note

If you are involved in helping other human beings—as a physician,
      nurse, teacher, social worker, counselor, therapist-
If you are concerned that people who need your services and counsel
      often, somehow, seem to resist it-
If you want your efforts to be used and useful-
      then this book is addressed to you.

The point of reference here is social work with persons struggling with
every kind of personal and interpersonal problem, of every class, of all
ages. But the insights and methods are applicable in any profession's
effort to engage cooperation. That is because the development of a
working relationship is one dynamic force in moving a person from his
request for help to his fruitful *use* of it.

    Thus this book's basic purpose: to facilitate your quest to enhance
your working—and perhaps even your personal—relationships.

Contents

1
Relationship Revisited

THE PARADOX struck me suddenly. Here we are in a time of widespread and hungry searching among the young and the not so young for something called "meaningful relationship." It is a something not clearly defined, scarcely delineated; something felt, in some vague way, as a desire, a need for a human connection that seems—what? Real—in a time of superficiality? Dependable—in a time of rapid change? Sensitively understanding—in a time of depersonalization? Caring—at moments of frustration or discouragement or feeling pressed by some life circumstance?

And here we are at a time when a whole new generation has entered the human service professions, committed to helping other human beings in one of the many areas of human need. There are young physicians (in a variety of specializations), social workers (in an equal variety), lawyers (especially those in public and poverty law), teachers (from preschool onward), nurses (general and specialized), corrections workers, recreation workers, therapists for psychological, neurological, physical or skill disabilities of many sorts, clergymen of all faiths—the range of "people helpers" is an astounding one. They are equipped to undertake their tasks with at least beginning competence by their formal education plus (often) supervised practice experience; or they are essentially beginning learners, partially prepared so as to be able to carry their necessary auxiliary roles as aides or paraprofessionals.[1]

1

Most of them feel that they "like people" and that they want to be of help to them. Most have some concern about the human condition and ideals about wanting to do some good in the world, even if that may be limited to the relatively small number of human beings they will influence in the course of their professional ministrations. Most of them have had very little preparation for what is the first problem to be solved in being of help to another person: how to connect, how to come into some alliance in a vital way with the person who wants or needs help. Many of them are themselves at a stage of life when the problems of finding, forming, developing, and sustaining personally fulfilling relationships have yet to be resolved. And most of them are quite unprepared for what they so often find: that human beings are not always willing or able to accept and use the aids offered, to follow the prescriptions given them; that the compromises people often must make are not always palatable; that the way to a troubled person's head is often through his heart.

The paradox is this: at a time—now—when "meaningful relationship" and "good communication" appear to be highly valued in our society, wanted and eagerly sought for in everyday life by most of us, there has been short shrift given to the recognition of the uses of relationship in the human services. Even in social work, a field in which for many years both theory and practice training placed strong and consistent emphasis upon the need for a sense of bonding between a helper and help seeker—even there—the literature of the past decade has given the subject scant notice, as will be discussed further on.[2]

It is the theme and substance of this book that the phenomenon we call "relationship" is a catalyst, an enabling dynamism in the support, nurture, and freeing of people's energies and motivations toward problem solving and the use of help. Two guiding propositions thread through what follows.

One is that the emotional bond that unites two (or more) people around some shared concern is charged with enabling, facilitative powers toward both problem solving and goal attainment. Thus relationship is vital in the conveyance and utilization of any service given by one human being to another. That usefulness is not at all confined to therapeutic purposes. The second is that, in an increasingly anomic and depersonalized world, there may be potential humanizing value in even brief and task-focused encounters between one person and another. An understanding, empathic relationship contributes to a person's sense of inner security and alliance with his fellowman. If there is any truth to these proposals, the substance and dynamics of relationship within all or any of the human services deserves our recognition of its powers again—or anew.

Very early in our helping careers—whatever our special area of service is—we become aware of some surprising and not always explainable reactions both in ourselves and in the people we want to help. Some of them seem to be or to feel "helped" rather beyond our expectations. Some of them, on the contrary, seem to hold back from us or from the service we offer. Some seem to need but not to want help; some to want but not to be able to get it; some to get but not to be able to use it; and some to need, want, and be able to get and use it. On our part we try as best we know how to adapt what we say and do to the particular persons we are dealing with, and almost from the first we become aware that some sort of relationship, some connecting bonds of feeling seem to be growing out of these transactions, good, bad, or mixed.

What the relationship "means"; how it may influence the person's motivations and behavior; what its powers are in facilitating or hindering the person's use of service and resources; in what ways our own feelings, thought, and actions affect that relationship—these are among the particulars we need to learn afresh or reexamine. They lie at the very heart of whatever we do in the interchange between ourselves and another person. Unless we are sensitively attuned to that interchange, responsive to it, understanding of its meanings, we tend to relate to those who seek our help "just naturally," turned on by some people, turned off by others. And what we do and say follows on those reactions "naturally." But that is not necessarily enabling to the person who is our client/patient/help seeker.

What is needed, if we are serious about helping people, is to raise this experience called ''relationship'' to our conscious and careful consideration in order to be able to use it in competent and responsible ways in the best interests of those we serve. That is what this book sets out to help us do. It might even be possible that what you find in it or take from it may be infused into your own ''natural'' everyday relationships and make them more meaningful to you.

I write as a social worker. But I address each and any one of you who has set out to serve people in one way or another—physicians, nurses, rehabilitation and occupational therapists, teachers, mental health workers (psychologists, psychiatrists, social workers—whether professionals, paraprofessionals, or aides), child care workers of all sorts, family welfare workers and family counselors, recreation leaders, specialists in work with the aged—what a diversity and richness of human services there are! I presume to address you all because as a social worker I have worked in collaboration with almost every other sort of helper and have come to know something of what is involved in the many special forms of human services.

Mostly, though, I presume to address all of you because ''you'' is ''us,'' all of us. We are related to one another, and closely. Not only do we often do some of the same kinds of things; not only do we often invest ourselves in the same person who is now patient, now client, now pupil; not only do many of the same principles govern how we deal with people (even though *what* we do differs by our specialty); but an even more vital tie binds us together. It is the commitment we make when we enter any one of the human service professions, a commitment to do the best we can to promote human well-being. Our motivations may be mixed—as motives have a way of being— but in the last analysis we have some compelling interest in human being and becoming, in the human condition, and we feel moved to take part in bettering it in our own small ways. That is the relationship bond that unites us.

Especially do I speak to newcomers to the human services

because I feel with them, remembering vividly my own beginning experiences and their often bewildering emotional impact. Paramount, of course, was the impact of fully realizing the many kinds of problems to which human beings are subject and the kinds of suffering they endure. But a second intellectual and emotional impact for me was the awareness of how significantly one's relationship with a help seeker (or help needer) affects whatever one is trying to accomplish. I know this is a common experience for most beginners in the work of helping people.

Like many young men and women today who find themselves working in the human services, I stumbled into a job—in a family welfare agency—right out of college. I had as preparation one course in sociology ("rural"—because it happened to fit not into my interests but into my schedule) and one in "educational psychology" (which taught me what I later had to unlearn: interpreting intelligence tests). I decided to take the job until the work I thought I wanted came along. When it did I found I was hooked by social work. I found myself reluctant to detach myself from clients I had come to invest in, to like, sometimes to love, to be concerned about, to puzzle over, to be angry with, to be awed by. In short, I came to understand that it is hard to separate from persons whom you have joined in emotional experiences, even when at times they have been not wholly happy ones.

It was relationship and its mysteries that drove me to graduate school to become professionally prepared, to be able to study and think (two activities for which demanding daily practice leaves a person with little time and energy) so as to understand better some of the things happening between my clients and me that I could not quite explain and often did not know how to manage. I was chronologically considerably younger than most of my clients; they were married, I was not; they had children, I did not; they had coped, well or badly, with many kinds of difficult life experiences, while I had had the relatively sheltered life of a middle-class, midwestern child-into-adolescent, within the stable matrix of solid family life and a set school system.

Yet to my repeated puzzlement these people seemed to want to talk with me, to connect with me, to trust me (and my limited knowledge and shaky judgments), to look to me for approval and advice, to confide in me sometimes shocking things (while I worked hard not to show my astonishment). I had a growing sense that there was something they valued in the close attention I paid to what they told me or what I drew from them, in my spontaneous leap of sympathy or empathy, in my earnest concern to be of help in every way I could, in my (often naive) hopefulness. All these, I was later to understand, were considered to be among the useful attributes of a "helpful relationship." But it was only a "sense" I had then, not an understanding, and I hungered for some more conscious possession of how and why it was that people became attached to and then influenced by others. It was this quest that brought me to study that phenomenon called relationship. My perusal of the scattered but often pointedly insightful writings of psychoanalysts and social workers began to illuminate my daily transactions with the men, women, and children who were or had been my clients.

That was a long time ago, but the quest continues—among all of us, I believe—to understand those unseen but powerful currents of feeling that flow between one human being and another, that expand or extinguish both the sense of one's linkage with another and that of one's own selfhood.

That the subject of relationship in the helping professions has had limited exploration in the past decade or so does not mean that it has not been a matter of concern. The human service professions are the product of the society that brings them into being, and so they share their society's troubled awareness of the often confusing complexities in the too large bureaucracies people encounter when they seek personal help, in the increasing impersonality and sense of anonymity and loneness that today's urban life creates. In response to such social concerns (that strike resonating chords in each of us personally, too), a number of the helping professions have indicated their awareness that some greater efforts at being human to another human being should accompany their service to people.

Concern has been expressed by a number of psychiatrists of late, for instance, about the practice in many mental hospitals and outpatient clinics of treating patients almost exclusively by pharmacological means. It is not that such chemical treatment is either necessarily harmful or uncalled for. It is, rather, that it is often administered by persons—psychiatrists or internists or paramedics—who "relate" to the patient in totally superficial or routinized ways. That personal interest and influence might heighten the patient's favorable responses to their drugs, that the uses to which medication is put might be more effective if some more personal attention to the patient himself accompanied or in some instances even substituted for medicaments has been lost sight of in many places.

From the medical profession and its patients there is the recurrent call for the return of the "family doctor." It is a cry for a physician who will be "related" to the person who happens to be a patient, who will hear out his complaints, show concern for his pain or worry, care about his progress (beyond the bright and brittle "Well, how are we today?" without listening to the answer). But the fact remains that family doctors are scarce. It is not hard to understand why. The proliferation of knowledge in medical science makes specialization all but imperative. Yet— might not even a specialist be more "human"? Might not even a "skin man," say, be taught to reconnect with the human self he was before he immersed himself in becoming a professional expert, so as to relate to his patient who is a person *under* the skin? In the best medical schools such attempts are being made to "humanize" modern medical practice. But the particulars of the whys and the hows of the doctor-patient relationship remain insufficiently identified, rarely regularized in the physician's training.

Schools of nursing have given increased emphasis in their curricula to the connections between the patient's mental-emotional and physical well-being and thus to the nurse's need to relate to the patient "as person" and also to the family members close to him who affect his health or sickness in many ways. But one problem in this branch of the human services is that the professionally prepared nurse is often "promoted" from direct patient care to teaching and administrative practice, and it is that changing stream of nursing aides and other caretakers who need but have not typically acquired sensitization to the uses of relationship in what is called "patient management."

One further example, this time from that diversified group of human services grouped under the little understood title "social work." Social work includes work with individuals, with small groups, with whole communities. Even when limited to the microcosm of casework and group work, its services are fashioned to deal with a tremendous variety of human problems, from meeting basic survival needs of individuals and families to leading socializing activity groups, from child protection to child guidance, from counseling on all manner of interpersonal, interfamilial problems to therapy for intrapersonal conflicts. The professionally educated social worker has from his first day in graduate school been alerted to the necessity of "good working relationships" if he is to prove helpful, and the past literature of his profession is rich in descriptions and discussions of relationship attributes and management.

However, since the mid-1960s there has been a tremendous influx into social work's ranks of a number of untrained or only partly trained men and women. Community colleges and undergraduate programs in liberal arts colleges have developed piecemeal or whole curricula in social work programs, theories, and practice, and their graduates have entered the service mainstream in many places and agencies. Today a very diversified crew carries the title "social worker" ("welfare worker," "child care worker," "mental health aide," "health care worker," "social work aide" are but a few of its varied monikers). All of them work for and with people. All are concerned to help people cope with some parts of the social-economic-health interpersonal problems that beset them in their daily functioning. But few of these workers have been more than minimally exposed to the knowledge of the qualities and purposes of a professional relationship, to consider how such a relationship may significantly affect what the client will or will not do— whether he will or will not go to the clinic, follow a medical regimen, look for a job, go back to school, take more responsible care of the children—and so forth. Many among these helpers may be finding themselves, like many others before them, involved in and yet quite unclear or uncertain about the nature and management of that emotionally freighted interplay —relationship—between them and the people they would help.

Among all the helping professions within the past two decades, clinical psychology, especially its humanistic sector, has given closest scrutiny to the helping relationship, its nature, and its therapeutic values. Its practitioner-researchers have developed some ingeniously designed and carefully analyzed experiments to test some of the conditions that create and affect relationships between helper and help seeker. Their findings have clarified many aspects of relationship that, while long known to experienced clinicians, had been insufficiently identified and articulated.[3] But while there is much in these studies that is illuminating for all of us who are concerned to relate to people in helpful ways, they have their limitations, too. The problems people bring to clinical psychologists are almost always those of intra- and interpersonal unease and stress. The help sought is "psychotherapy." From this definition of the problem and specification of the treatment desired, a number of special conditions evolve.

The person who voluntarily presents himself for psychotherapeutic help, whether to a psychiatrist, a psychologist, a clinical social worker, or some other kind of counselor, is a rather special help seeker in several respects. He is self-motivated for help. He has been self-examining enough to perceive that his problem is within him (although it often manifests itself in his external behavior). He is sufficiently educated to the idea of the "talking cure" that he "believes in" its potential efficacy. For the most part he trusts the therapist. He *wants* the therapist's influence;

he expects and wants to change (though he may resist). He usually has sources of support or stability in his circumstances that make him able to afford the luxury of introspection and self-analysis. Under these conditions the help seeker is primed, and he moves into relationship with his helper from the first. (Of course, vicissitudes may occur further along the way).

Now most of the client/patient/pupils of human service workers in the run of daily life present a number of differences from the typical therapy seeker. Many of them do not voluntarily seek help at all; indeed, some may deny the need for it. Many others seek help with problems caused by external circumstances such as deficits, sudden or chronic, in their own resources: lack of money, of medical care and supervision, of knowledge and know-how, of tangible means or arrangements by which to manage some aspect of their daily life. They need and want, then, tangible kinds of assistance. Many others whose difficulties are created or exacerbated by their personality problems tend to project those problems onto outer circumstances. They often want—and often need—some prescriptive advice or guidance that they hope will swiftly and painlessly resolve the problem they recognize. Many do not trust the establishment which helpers from organized institutions or agencies seem to represent. Often they feel put off by helping preliminaries and processes that they simply do not understand or may find culturally alien.

Relationship is actively operating in all these situations, too, spontaneously weaving between the help seeker and would-be helper, whether one is aware of it or not. In many ways—some of which will be discussed further on—this relationship is even more complex than that between the self-motivated therapy seeker and his therapist. Certainly it has been given less attention than the "therapeutic relationship." It has been either taken for granted or held to be of small account when people's problems seem to be chiefly those of physical, economic, or sociocultural conditions and circumstances.

But the fact is that these problems assault or are created by, and are suffered and struggled with by human beings. And human beings respond emotionally, feelingly, "psychologically'' to what happens to them and to what they try to make happen. They—we—have feelings about the problems that beset them, about themselves, about what they need and want, about what solutions are available to them (or are absent), about the help-promising channels they must locate and navigate, about the helpers they must grapple with—about all these and far more. We know this so well in ourselves: there is no problem we encounter that does not strike emotional resonances in us. Our emotional reactions are heightened when we feel helpless to control or cope with the difficulty. They are intensified when we must turn to a stranger to ask for aid, whether by material means or counsel or both.

It seems to go without saying—and yet it needs once again to be said. If services to human beings are to fulfill their alleged purposes, they must attend not only to the problems people have but to the people who suffer and struggle to cope with these problems.

A person's sense of self-worth (or of being ''not much good'') and his sense of being at one with and supported by his society (or of being alienated and outcast) tremble uncertainly at times when he feels social failure or personal defeat. There is no more telling way of affirming his worth and accepting the validity of his need, no better way of demonstrating that he ''belongs'' than for another human being, representing and sanctioned by the social community, to move out to receive him with attentiveness and compassionate concern. That is what a helping relationship is about. It is not at all a substitute for any of the things—aids, means, opportunities—that must be provided for people's well-being. But it is an essential accompanying condition, because it is the nourisher and mover of the human being's wish and will to use the resources provided and the powers within himself to fulfill his personal and social well-being.

Does that sound too starry-eyed? Does it seem to ascribe too much to that too little understood or appreciated phenomenon? For your consideration I suggest in what follows one partial support of the potency of relationship.

When one thinks about how many kinds of help exist today

(and indeed have existed since time began) for human beings who seek or need "straightening out" or "building up" or "psychological support," who want help in finding themselves or finding how to function and live their daily lives in more satisfying and effective ways, a persistent question arises. It is a question that grows louder as one realizes that gurus, swamis, witch doctors, mesmerists, social workers, psychiatrists, clergymen, psychologists, psychoanalysts, counselors and healers of all sorts, practicing according to the principles and idiosyncrasies of innumerable different modes of treating people, all claim to have helped people in dealing with their sociopsychic or psychosocial problems. More telling yet, their client/patient/followers, of whatever designation and in considerable numbers (allowing for defectors and "untreatables," of course) confirm that claim: that they have indeed been helped to cope, sometimes to resolve their problems fully, sometimes to modify them, sometimes to bear them with greater comfort.

The question is: How so? How is it that, with all the diversities in helping theories and means and modes, large numbers of people feel they have been helped by that particular one they undertook to use? How is it that, despite the often acrimonious debates among help givers about which is the true gospel, which the most respectably scientific, which the most existentially artistic, the feeling—sense, conviction—of having been helped is not exclusive to one helping method or its polar opposite? One speaks here of subjective judgments, of course. Objective data for comparison between one and another means of helping are difficult to secure for many reasons, among which is the obvious one of the diverse nature of the problems for which help may be sought or on which treatment focuses. But the subjective experience of having been freed, enabled, released, steadied, remotivated, reinforced in confidence—these are no small gains to the human psyche.[4]

To the question again: What is the common element, the red thread, that seems to run through every successful effort by one person to influence another in benign and enabling ways? The answer seems to be "relationship."

Again, I remind us, this is not to claim that relationship is the be-all and end-all of helping. It is simply to say that it is a necessary, though not sufficient, condition for one person's taking in, using, learning from, and feeling benefited by help from another. This alone, I propose, warrants our pursuit and further study.

Why, then, one wonders, has this potent influence been given so little attention in recent years as increasing numbers of would-be helpers have been attracted to the human service professions? I can speculate about the reasons in social work, and there may very well be parallels in several of the other helping professions. (And if "cause why" does not interest you at this point, skip over what follows until you find yourself connecting again.)

The turning aside from the subject of relationship in social work may have occurred because in the 1940s and 1950s it was simply discussed to death. To relationship was attributed almost all healing power.[5] It was not that other factors in treatment had been totally ignored, but especially among psychoanalytically oriented caseworkers, relationship had assumed magnified proportions. It had come to be seen not only as one of the mysteries of human life—surely it remains that!—but as a kind of mystique of treatment. Mystiques tend not to be carefully probed or examined; they depend upon acceptance whole, on belief. And, as one commentator aptly put it, relationship had come to be spoken of in the "reverential language of the numinous."[6]

Some polar swing from the extremes to which it was hallowed in some places and practice was inevitable. "What else?" thoughtful caseworkers began to ask themselves. "What in addition to relationship, what other forms of influence or nurture might be found to be dynamic in motivating people to change, to learn, to cope with their social and psychological problems?"[7]

Social events gave a rude but necessary push to the questions that were already being examined in social work. Smoldering in the late 1950s, there exploded in the early 1960s a widespread concern with social problems. The rhetoric of social work bespoke the shift of concern from the individual to the society, from case to cause, from curative to preventive endeavors, from the small world of the troubled client to the universe of social and psychological problems of which he was but one instance.

Economic, political, and social forces combined to compel the attention of all citizens, not just those of us in the helping professions, to the suddenly visible poor, to endemic civil and social wrongs suffered by minorities, to rotting slums and rising crime—the litany of old but freshly recognized problems needs no repetition here. Work with individuals was denounced as futile at best, an opiate to radical reform at worst.[8]

One-to-one or one-to-small-group helping continued, to be sure, if only because the wheels of justice grind slowly and human beings are unreasonable enough to want their immediate problems taken care of immediately; and also because there seem to be few social panaceas that do not carry some new difficulties in their wake, and, further, because one man's panacea is sometimes another man's poison.

But a number of changes took place in the ways and means of helping. There was a wide and concerted effort to bring tangible aids and services closer to the people who needed them. Clinics and counseling centers were opened in neighborhood storefronts; there was involvement of "indigenous workers" to facilitate relationships with those who feared or distrusted the "establishment"; a galaxy of new programs sprang up—work training, early childhood education, free legal services, nursery facilities—these were among the many more ingenious social resources and opportunities brought forth in this period of mixed despair and hope. Many of them died aborning or failed in their promise, for complicated reasons that deserve (but cannot here have) thoughtful examination so that our mistakes should not be repeated. Many others set a precedent and pattern for progressive developments in health, education, and welfare services.

Here, however, we resolutely return to the question, "Whatever happened to relationship?" Those social workers who continued to work with individuals and families gained some new perspectives on relationship. Many of them had turned to reach out to persons who in the past had proved most hard to reach because of their distrust of organized forms of help coupled with their hopelessness and apathy born out of chronic deprivation. Among the hard to reach were "multiproblem" families whose lives teemed with troubles of every sort and whose dependency needs were as understandable and realistic as they were hostile and destructive.[9]

Included in their "new" learning about relationship ("new" for some, revivified for others) were these facts: that when people's experiences with those who *seem* to have power have been chronically frustrating and depersonalized, they will have developed closures against trusting or believing in the goodwill of such people. It must be expected that they will transfer to a new relationship the anticipations and feelings that old relationships have created in them. So a would-be helper must reinforce his goodwill and caring intentions with the determination to understand and accept open or undercover hostility, suspicion, anger. Social workers came to understand resistance more fully, resistance to any source of feared manipulation, and to learn better how to face it out and deal with it. They came to appreciate how much psychological nurture inheres in meeting plain everyday needs, in receiving plain material things, in having someone provide simple concrete services—not as briberies but as tangible evidence of a helper's real concern—particularly for persons whose ability to take in more subtle nuances of caring has been blunted by too much struggle for too little gain. They came to recognize that a sense of relationship in the help needer —that feeling of emotional bonding and alliance with the helper—will often be the consequence, not the beginning condition, of the helper's meeting of basic survival needs or the receiving of some wished-for resource.*

---

* A caseworker friend of mine once got for her client, the mother of a gaggle of little girls, a second- or third-hand sewing machine. The woman was delighted. Not only could she now dress her children for less money but, since she "loved" sewing, she felt supported and enabled in her competence. I thought at the time, "There may be therapy in a thimble."

In brief, in their work with "the poor," "the underclass," the alienated, angry, often meagerly verbal people of our society, social workers (and others) became aware of aspects of relationship which had been only minimally recognized and explored when relationship with self-referred applicants for counseling or therapy were in the center of attention. They "worked at" them—and still must do so (as they deal, for example, with the resistive, often hostile, parents of abused children) because, as will be proposed in detail later on, relationship is a source of hope, a motivator for learning, an underpinning and enabler toward coping.

Of course there were failures. There are "inoperable cancers" of a social and psychological as well as of a physical kind. These and the expectable swing back from the overblown optimism generated by the War on Poverty and its many offshoots aroused appropriate interest in critically examining the outcomes of a whole range of helping services and their modes. "Accountability" became the keyword. "Show us," said the supporters of the human services (as well as the detractors), "show us that what you do brings results." Surely we must be held accountable, responsible for what we claim to do (though it could be and has been argued that the choice of what is being counted and the way it is being measured deserves some critical assessment, too). Along with the "what" and "how much" and "to what outcomes" research, there has developed a growing interest in examining helping processes themselves. How are people most effectively and most efficiently helped with their varied human problems? And here we come back to relationship again.

How to test and "prove" the claims that have long been made for its potency in influencing human behavior? How catch hold of it for exact, precise definition? How observe it directly in action? How measure and quantify its extent and degree? How replicate it from one case to another? It is "there," it is known, felt, attested to by its experiencers. But it is subtly ineffable, and it certainly eludes capture in specified behaviors.

No one has proposed that it does not exist. Its vitality and the probable validity of the claims of its significance in interpersonal helping transactions have not been denied. But for the most part it seems to be unresearchable at the present time, with present instruments. So while a number of styles and modes of treatment are being studied, relationship has been shunted aside, pushed off to the periphery of helping practice and theory. It is the old reality: only that which is researchable is researched. And in an era such as ours when scientific proof, or at least systematized inquiry, is highly valued, that which is (as yet) not subject to such test or management tends to be left unobserved. Thus relationship. With some resultant implication that it is not important.

This is an implication that, it seems to me, is overdrawn. It is overdrawn, perhaps, because some of us have grown weary—or is it leery?—of the not infrequent obliteration of human and humanizing experience by the constricting blinders that some—surely not all—researchers resort to. But at the same time there is considerable emerging evidence that even among the most scientifically oriented helpers—the behaviorists—there is growing recognition and respect for the powers and the "art" of relationship.

By definition, the behaviorist takes externalized, observable, definable, and describable behavior as the focus both for his interventive influence and for his study. In their early practice and theory formulations, behaviorists rarely touched on relationship. Their attention was placed upon open-to-be-heard and seen strategies and techniques aimed at the open-to-be-seen behavior that was to be modified or expunged. In its more mechanistic forms, it aroused indignation and rejection by their fellow practitioners within psychiatry, social work, and psychology who considered themselves to be "humanistically" oriented.*

Admitted or attended to or not, relationship has been "there," in the interchange between behaviorist and his client/

*In all fairness, it must quickly be recognized that behaviorists are no more "all alike" than are adherents of any other treatment "school" or model. So they are not all of one mind about relationship's place in their seemingly technical modes of help.

patient. Why, for instance, would a person continue to go to such a helper unless he received from him the sense that he was cared about or because, at the very least, he believed in the helper's power? Why should he feel "rewarded" or "reinforced" by the nods and becks of his behavior modifier unless that helper held some emotional meaning for him? Why should he feel spurred to try again or try harder, except as he feels enough attached to his helper to take hope from him? (Perhaps in relationship lies the difference between people and Skinner's pigeons?) The answers must lie in the play of emotional bonding between the help seeker and his helper, even if it cannot as yet be translated into behavioral and research specifications. And the reassuring fact is that the more recent literature of behavior modification reveals open recognition of the place of relationship in the facilitation of client motivation and cooperation.[10] (Is it too facetious to suggest that perhaps "humanist" and "scientist" helpers may come to relate to one another more amicably and fruitfully, bonded as they may now become by the emotionally laden concept of relationship?)

A "revisit" to relationship this is, even for those of you who are newcomers to the human service professions. If you are one of these, you may not yet have been inducted in any systematic way into such theories or notions about the powers and pitfalls of relationship that are in operation from the first moment of your encounter with the first person you set forth to help. Volumes await your exploration and study.[11]

But remember first that you already know a great deal about relationship. You have known it experientially from your first moments of life. You have been nourished on relationships; you have tasted them, savored some, rejected others, swallowed and digested them comfortably or with consequent gut ache, learned from them, have been patted (or punched) into shape by them. You have been made tall by some, diminished by others. When you stop to think about it, you become newly aware of how meaningful relationships have been in your life, even temporary ones, and how your sense of self-worth and of belonging with your fellowmen has been their product. And you may become aware, too, of how at times of helplessness, of failure, of loss, of too great stress, the natural appetite for being cared about and connected with others may become an acute hunger.

So now you are prepared to revisit what you have known in yourself, but to view it in some different light. The question now is what have you known about being human that you can translate into usefulness to other people, to those you intend to help? How can you "relate"—which is to say, so act in the helping interchange—that the person you assist may experience some sense of being cared about by another human being and of being allied with him? He will not be asking you for a relationship. He is likely to be asking for some plain, ordinary, necessary life-sustaining thing like money, like medicine, like advice, like action in his behalf. But what he gets from you, whether in material or psychological form, will be "twice blessed" when it is conveyed in such a way as to affirm his personal worth and his social linkage.

As for the experienced helper, especially for you whose practice has had firm theoretical underpinnings, this will be a revisit of another sort. It is at times refreshing to touch home base again, to re-view one's root knowledge, to find what seems still to be true and useful and also what calls for some rethinking, perhaps re-vision.

Two special perspectives about relationship require the senior helper's re-view, it seems to me. One mentioned earlier, is the question of the uses of relationship in enabling and facilitating a person's coping with problems that are not exclusively psychological, those that need more (or less?) than "psychotherapy." Questions of the kind and extent of relationship, of its expectable variation by nature of person and problem, have yet to be systematically explored.

A second revisit value for the experienced helper arises from the fact that he is often given or has thrust upon him the privilege and responsibility of teaching the neophytes in his special field. As anyone who has taught knows, whether in a classroom, in tutorial sessions, or even in informal consultations, teaching another person requires that you become fully conscious again of knowledge that has come to live in your very bones. You face the necessity to lift up and put into words what you have long felt as second nature, as habitual, natural, taken for granted.

Furthermore, if you are to teach effectively, you must convey not simply the facts or the principles of practice but the whys and wherefores, the "how comes," the explanations of what you wish to transmit. So you must go back, dust off, light up by your consciousness your bone-deep knowledge. Perhaps this revisit to the familiar will facilitate that effort.

What and how a helper is able to give of himself in the interests of another person depends heavily upon the kind of relationship capacities he has within himself. To think about relationship needs and powers reopens insights into one's own needs, feelings, and behaviors. Self-awareness is the first essential condition for the use of oneself in the interests of others, so this revisit to relationship may serve that end, too. It may serve to remind us that in respect to our common human needs and common human gratifications we are indeed sisters and brothers under the skin, bound in kinship to those we aim to help.

People who come to all those who make up the human service professions do not come asking for "a relationship." They come asking for a solution (at most) or an easing (at least) of some identified problem or recognized need that affects their present and near future well-being. Those problems and needs may be overlapping, inbreeding, interweaving in the disconcerting ways people's problems operate. At one end the help that may be needed is simply gaining access to available material resources. At the other end the help needed is complexly working through conflict (within the self and between the self and others) and learning more satisfactory ways of (yes!) *relating* to other people and life tasks. In between these poles are all the variations and combinations of needs, wants, aspirations that human beings try to fulfill, well or badly.

When they turn to a helper who specializes in the area of

their problem or quest, they want the resources he holds, whether things or knowledge and skill. Yet their ability to use those resources ably, to increase their own effectiveness in coping, to enhance their sense of worth and mastery appears to be closely associated with the recognition, acceptance, support, and caring conveyed in the relationship between themselves and the human being who is to be their help giver.

Therefore, we set forth on this revisit to look once again at the nature and uses of relationship.

2
What Is Relationship?

WE SEEM TO HAVE the fewest words to explain adequately our deepest experiences. "Love" and "loving," for instance: they all but defy exposition. When we are asked to define or describe them, we unconsciously resort to the use of expressions, gestures, and tones that partially *act* out loving rather than define it. Perhaps this is because the sources from which love wells up and flows are preverbal, premental. In its rudimentary forms love surges up within us inchoate, felt as need and sensation, long before we are equipped to name and separate it from the rest of the experience of our being.

So, too, with relationship, which even precedes "love" in that it is first experienced, one assumes, as a physical connection, a "belonging to" the warming, nurturing body of another. One approaches an effort at pinning and dissecting relationship tentatively, aware of the danger that one may begin to sound high-flown and mystical or become a bull in the poet's china shop. Especially in our present age, when science and fact and proof are held in topmost esteem, it is unfashionable, to say the least, for a professional person to assert the moving quality and therapeutic potency of something one cannot put one's finger on, which is not subject to precise description, itemization, quantification, analysis, or even to verification by one or more of the five senses.* Yet no one would deny that it is *there* in all our

*I am reminded of a client to whom I commented that the fear she was telling me about was really just an old wives' tale. "I *know* it's just a superstition," she said earnestly, "but it's *true* all the same!"

22

lives, from birth to death, in every day's interchanges between person and person, person and group, person and work or play involvements. Universal and commonplace as it is, relationship, subjectively experienced, objectively elusive, is the mover and shaker and propulsion force in human life. Its roots live in the deep inner recesses of our being, and, like those of the banyan tree (among the most ancient of trees!), they are continuously supplemented by new rootlets that thrust down from upper branches back into the soil that gives the tree being. Relationship is there, known to each of us as "true" and "real," and thus it must be taken into account by anyone interested in human behavior, including his own. Whether one's quest is for more personally gratifying or more professionally responsible gratifying and motivating relationships for others, it is necessary to make the effort to lift what each of us knows in the heart (and the viscera) into that more accessible region somewhere above the eyebrows where consciousness and thought are assumed to dwell. Only thus can we come to possess what we know in order to put it to use.

So, to that task.

Relationship is a human being's feeling or sense of emotional bonding with another. It leaps into being like an electric current, or it emerges and develops cautiously when emotion is aroused by and invested in someone or something and that someone or something "connects back" responsively. We feel "related" when we feel at one with an other (person or object) in some heartfelt way. (There is no way, you see, nothing one can do to avoid "heart" or some of those other words that seek to name at least the dwelling place of emotion—"gut"? "soul"? "viscera"? "spirit"? "X"?—so let us settle for that touched and touching "funny valentine," the heart.)

Relationship occurs between persons under several conditions. One person is emotionally touched, moved, roused, and the other (or a number of others) experiences a like feeling. There leaps from one to another, spontaneously, the sense of likeness, alliance, kinship, belonging together because of a mutually shared, emotionally charged experience. Or one person feels, and his feeling is recognized, received, and felt *with* by the other.

They do not necessarily feel alike, but one gives himself over to taking in understandingly the emotions of the other. The emotions felt may chiefly attach to the interchange between the two (or more) persons. Or they may rise up from situations and experiences outside the interchange which arouse spontaneous like reactions from the participants or which are made manifest by one and shared responsively by the other.

Relationship may be "good" or "bad," brief or enduring, complex and heartfelt or superficial and skin-deep, swift and spontaneous or carefully built. But whatever its nature and substance, its dynamics are the presence, recognition, deposit, reception, and responsiveness of emotion between person and person or between a person and an object or activity by which he has been moved. The emotions felt and shared may be joy as well as anguish, gratification as well as deprivation, hope and despair, merriment and despondency, rage and gratefulness, guilt and hostility—any or all of these, when they are shared and responded to by others, unites us in kinship with them.

What is usually called a "good" relationship is held to be so in that it provides the stimulus and nurture by which both persons involved feel sustained, loved, gratified, given to, helped, and freed to experience their selfhood and to realize their potential. The give-and-take may not be equal; even in relationships characterized by mutuality and reciprocality there are moments when one person is heavily the giver and the other the taker. And there are times in even good relationships when snags and snarls appear in its fabric. But on the whole a good relationship is one that respects and nourishes the selfhood of the other at the same time it provides the sense of security and at-oneness. Perhaps this is what is meant when "a meaningful relationship" is spoken of and longed for.

To "feel with" or to "feel like" a mutually responsive other is the essence of a "meaningful" relationship. Its meaning is that "I am recognized" (by someone I recognize), "I am appreciated" (by someone I appreciate), "I am cared about" (by someone whose caring matters to me), "I am understood" (by someone whose understanding matters to me), "I am allied to, in union with" (someone who stands with me). "There is a living bond between me and another."

This hunger for emotional bonding with one and more human beings is lifelong. It is most vividly apparent in little children, whose natural dependency on others for physical and affectional nourishment and underpinning makes them open to and malleable by nurturant or noxious relationships. It is seen most pathetically among the lonely aged, whose loss of meaningful relaters through sickness and death or through the indifference of others leaves them virtually starved for want of the input and exchanges of caring. It is continuously and often obsessively searched for by many neurotics. It has been fled from by many psychotics—but the fact is that their mental life is heavily peopled, often by those whose relationships have been hurtful to them at the same time they have been emotionally potent.

In the usual life of the usual adult, relationship hungers may be gratified in many ways—in love and friendship bonds, in marriage, in parenthood. It is little cause for surprise, for instance, that most divorced people remarry, searching yet again for "ties that bind." Nor is it any wonder (though it is often deeply troubling) that abused and neglected children removed from their parents into the safety and warmth of foster homes still carry yearning in their hearts and images in their minds of their own parents (images often idealized or rationalized), from whom, perhaps in the early months of life and perhaps in occasional recent moments, they took in the sense of belonging, at-oneness, connectedness.

This phenomenon—the binding powers of even destructive relationships—must have at least a note here, though it warrants fuller treatment. It is a phenomenon known to anyone who is a good observer of human relations. Husbands and wives, adult children and parents, parents and little children, adult siblings often seem bound together by ties of hate, spite, guilt alternating with hostility, perversity—what is it? Certainly different situations will have different variables and account for what may be seen as the binding quality of bad, mutually wounding relationships. Yet the potent force that runs through them all seems to be a passionately felt emotional exchange. That exchange says the very opposite of "I am with you," "I feel like you." But hatred, resentment, revenge are powerful emotions. They get under the skin, they penetrate the person's psychic depths just as surely as love, acceptance, compassion. Their recipient may break off the relationship by physically removing himself from the other or by building walls of defense or paths of diversion. Yet that other can rarely be expunged. He rises up in dreams (day and night), in sudden associations, or he gnaws at the edges of consciousness—"Something vital has made an indelible impress, a persisting bond between us." That many human beings find pleasure in pain, that lacerating acts and words may keep people in slavish relationships with one another will not be further dealt with here. Is some sense of intense connection, painful though it may be, preferable to feeling adrift and untouched?

Relationships that are gratifying occur not only between people but also between a person and an object or between a person and some regular or occasional activity in which he is involved. "In which he is involved" is the key: that is to say, in which the person *deposits* his caring, interest, attention, concern about his effect upon the material with which he works or plays. The condition for the sense of bonding is that he should get some gratifying feedback from such activity, some evidence that his efforts are responded to in desired ways. So it is that a man may "love" his work and feel deeply bound to it. So a lonely woman may feel related to her caged bird or her philodendron plants— when they show that what she puts in by way of caring and attention makes them grow healthily and happily; they reciprocate, they affirm her worth. Relationship with an object (an old chest of drawers, a place, a painting) occurs when emotion has been called forth in the person by its memory associations or by its moving (emotive) aesthetic qualities.

Often relationship between a person and those activities or things that he puts himself (his feelings) into may be substitutes for person-to-person relationships, substitutes necessary to any one of us at certain points in our lives when we need but are not able to connect satisfyingly with another human being. But more often, perhaps, they are supplements, enrichments of our lives, expansions of our capacity to take and give sustenance to more than one person, more than one role or activity, more than one object. It is probable that the person who can freely invest himself in, "give out to" a number of people with caring and interested attention, can care about his work and play (when they reward him), can invest himself—his interest and involvement—in ideas, causes, aesthetic experiences, and so on, is a person whose energies are strong and free because, at base, his relationship bonds are or have been largely securing and satisfying.

Relationships may be brief, transitory, even one time. Or they may grow in depth, breadth, and texture, become woven into the living tissue of the total personality in continuous and expanding experiences of feelingfully freighted interchanges. All of us have experienced a sudden kinship of feeling of at-oneness with a person we may never have seen before—at a play, in a classroom, at a party, at a political meeting. Some incident, some statement or idea or action rouses lively feelings in us—and we see or hear a similar reaction in another person, next to us or across the room. That person will be remembered as one to whom we felt "related," connected, if only fleetingly. All of us, too, have experienced brief encounters in which we were moved, finding ourselves close or touched, even sometimes that we had taken that other person into our selves in a kind of indelible impress, even though it was a time- and place-limited experience. This phenomenon of incorporating another—called "introjection," a taking into oneself—which may occur in even short-term relationship experiences when they strike chords of feelingful response in us is of particular interest to anyone who seeks to influence another. Of this, more later.

Just as relationship is not inevitably a product of time span, neither is it inevitably a product of proximity or even blood ties. You may live near another person, see him frequently, know him as one who is part of your family and yet have little or no sense of at-oneness with him. Nothing "meaningful" passes between you—which is to say, you and he connect only at a level of casual, superficial, perhaps pleasant but uninvolved communication. (A family funeral or wedding is a good place to observe this—in yourself and others who are joined in an emotionally freighted time- and place-limited event. The person[s] to whom you will feel most deeply "related," if only briefly, will be not necessarily among those to whom you are closest by blood or daily familiarity but the one[s] whose emotional responsiveness to the event most closely matches yours. He and you are "akin.")

Again one sees that essential condition of a meaningful ("moving") relationship, that like or empathic feelings shuttle between two persons, linking them.

Relationships do not stand still. They develop, in breadth or depth, or they shrink and fade off. They may lose or increase in intensity, may shift from one person (or activity) to another. Nor are they all of a piece. Rather, they are often ambivalent— that is, they are charged with both positive and negative aspects. We know ourselves to be pulled toward and also away from another. We have all experienced the thrust to merge with another and some opposing pullback into separation. Ambivalence does not at all mean that we are held in a continuous shilly-shally suspension, swinging back and forth, unable to commit ourselves to investment in other people and tasks. It is, rather, a balancing mechanism of the personality, one evidence of our human duality. It is a way by which a person maintains his selfhood, his particular individuality, his autonomy, even though he also wants and seeks union with another. There are moments and long-time personal needs that make the one drive—either for selfhood or for complete dependency upon the other— dominant.

Here, however, the importance of recognizing the fact and purpose of ambivalence is to prepare us, whether in personal or professional relationships, for the sometimes disturbing evidence that the person we thought loved us, wanted us, needed us is drawing away, resisting us, asserting his separateness. It is a common unhappy disillusionment in young and not-so-young lovers and married couples that there begins to emerge in the relationship some pullback in themselves or in their partners after the period of "falling in love" (when they lost their balance?). And it is a common disappointment in inexperienced professional helpers when the client/patient with whom relationship has seemed good and gratifying (to both) decides to drop out of treatment or, even when he appears, he seems to have pulled away psychologically. This may be the sign of a healthy restoration of balance. Or it may be a sign that the person is fighting his dependency upon the other, is struggling against being "by love possessed." We all want to "belong" to another; but we do not want to be "owned." How complicated we mortals are!

In brief, whether in daily life or in professional usage, relationships may often need to be carefully examined and thought about. Like love, they may need to be worked on in order to achieve or maintain the healthy balance between a human being's necessary sense of selfhood and of union with another.

The usual words used to describe a "meaningful" relationship as well as a "working" or "therapeutic" relationship—all "good" in the sense of being gratifying and growth promoting —are warmth, loving, caring, acceptance, responsiveness, empathy, genuineness, attentiveness, concern, support, understanding. What a lovely, heart-and-soul-nurturing complex of attitudes that is—the very Eden of human interchange! But, it has seemed to me, there is a further essential aspect in relationship—personal or professional—that has been overlooked or given insufficient attention by those who have studied and analyzed the relationship phenomenon. It is that any change-promoting relationship must contain elements of *expectation* as well as acceptance, of *stimulation* as well as support.[1]

Even that most "unconditional love" that is spoken of (and yearned for?)—the love and caring of a mother for her helpless infant, supportive, accepting, all protective though it is, is permeated by conscious and unconscious inputs of stimuli to its development, and by expectations that what she puts in by way of loving care, physical and psychological nourishment, cooing, cuddling, caressing, comforting, will in turn yield such desired responses as the baby's growth and "goodness," his alertness and attentiveness, his development of physical and interpersonal capacities. When those stimulation efforts yield meager response, when the mother's expectations of what is "usual," "normal" (whether learned via Spock or subliminally) are not met, the relationship between mother and infant is blocked. The "cold" or "indifferent" mother so often blamed for creating an autistic or schizoid child may just be a mother who has been chilled by a baby born with some unseen psychic deficiency, who has thus been unresponsive to the usual relationship-producing stimuli and inevitable expectations.

"Good" parenting from the child's birth to adulthood does not consist simply of permissive accepting, caring, and loving. It includes small doses or inoculations of realistic and age-appropriate challenges to do or to be in ways that are held to be both "good" for the child and for the others whom he lives with and affects; and it includes requirements and expectations that certain norms of development—physical, mental, and emotional—will be reached for and met, supported by love and stimulated by training, education, suggestion, parental modeling, and so on.

Any relationship which seeks to enable a person, child or adult, to feel secure and thus to go forward to risk new learning and new experiences combines a warm acceptance of the person in his specialness and his present being (because he is as he is) with the input of stimulation and expectation of his *becoming,* that is, of his reaching to realize his potentials in personally and socially constructive ways. (Of course, the degree to which "becoming" is expected will vary by age, physical and mental capabilities, and other actualities.) The implications in this view of relationship for help to troubled people will be developed further on.

We become human beings and grow in humanness through the nurture of relationship. Air and light and water and food taken in and digested are the essential nourishments for our physical development. Love and caring and the compassionate responsiveness and steadfastness from other human beings are the essential nourishment for our emotional and spiritual development. When these are missing or scant, or when their opposites predominate—indifference, aggression, rejection, inconsistency—the humanizing of the unfolding person is dwarfed or malformed just as surely as physical mal- or undernutrition will stunt or deform bones, muscles, and nerve development. The humanizing of a person, which is to say the budding and unfolding of his sense of himself as one who can stand upright on his two feet psychologically and, from this, as one whose inner security makes it possible for him to look out from himself to attend to and care for others, to reach out to invest himself in responding, learning, working, seeking, playing, thinking, wondering—all these and other qualities we hold to be attributes of full-bodied humanness seem to be rooted in relationship experiences from the beginning of life onward.

Mothering is the first vital relationship the human young know. At first the union of mother and child is total, but not for long. Even the crib's narrow circumference becomes peopled very soon with a fleeting but growing circle of "relaters." In the myriad gestures of interplay between the infant and his expanding circle of caretakers—the cuddling and feeding, being touched,* stroked, crooned over, restrained, admonished, encouraged, laughed with, played with—and his responsive smiles, cooing, attentive taking in of the mother with his eyes as well as with his mouth as she holds and nurses him, whether with breast or bottle, his crying for food or comfort or company and the swift or delayed response to his cries—from all these interchanges charged with the give-and-take of affection, security, and pleasure (or threat of their absence) the growing child experiences relationship.

The infant comes to know his own powers and needs and to know others not just as he knows his bed, secure and warm

---

*The taking in of relationship by touch is probably a human being's first—and perhaps also at the end of life his last—knowledge of it. When we are moved emotionally, we say, "I was touched by...."

though it may be, or his bottle, sweet and hunger quenching though it is, but as reacting, responsive, feelingful "objects" with whom he sometimes feels merged and from whom he sometimes is separated or separates himself. His sense of trust in himself is based on his repeated experience that he can trust others—that relationships with others are safe and dependable and rewarding. They will come when he needs them, give what he wants, at least comfort him in his inevitable frustrations. It is this basic security that frees his energies for investment outside himself in explorations of his world. The foundations for the capacity to trust other people, to receive them freely, are probably laid down by these early experiences of connectedness, separation, and reunion.[2]

When babies do not have these caring relationship experiences, when instead they are left lonely, their cries for comforting left unattended, or they are treated harshly or inconsistently—now as a cute doll, now as a nuisance—their relationship capacities are damaged. But when infants are cared for generously, they are permeated with feelings of safety, security, basic trust: their world feels "good," and, along with this, there is a feeling that if I am loved I am lovable: *I* am good. From this sturdy foundation it becomes possible to venture out physically, mentally, emotionally to invest muscles, attention, curiosity, and affection in persons and things outside the little circle of self and parents.[3]

Up on his own two feet the baby senses himself as "belonging," yes, to his mother and father, his bed and blanket, and to such other sources of attachment as he has, but increasingly he has the courage to feel himself as separate, too, separate and pushed to move out on his own. Nowhere can the evidence of union-separation flux of relationship be seen more vividly than in that life stage, roughly between eighteen and thirty-six months, when the toddler runs off from his mother on his own (with one eye always cocked to her whereabouts) and then runs back, scared by a stranger or bumped by a fall, to bury himself between her knees or arms. Or when he screams "No!" to anything being foisted upon him, even things to which he feels mostly "Yes." His "No!" says, "I am my own man—I balk at you and assert my autonomy!" Yet again, when he is tired or hurt or lured by love, back he goes to at-oneness with his dependable source of comfort.

These two sides of relationship, the push toward union with another and the pullback to ensure self-ownership, continue throughout our lifetimes. They are of importance in understanding any adult relationship, whether personal or professional. The ebb and flow of ambivalence has already been referred to. An emerging drive for autonomy may temporarily disrupt togetherness, and it is essential to be aware that no love is "pure"; it may contain clashes of dislike, resentment, or other negative feelings and still qualify as love! Of particular import to people helpers is the recognition that even grown adults, ordinary self-dependent, may under acute stress or stripping deprivation fall back into needing and wanting union with another who seems to be a source of love and helping power.

As anyone who has lived with the toddler knows, this is a stage where expectation aspects in relationship begin to be made manifest. There are many "no-nos" from parents to child in this period of his going forth in all directions, and whether they are gently or harshly expressed the expectation is that the child will, for the most part, conform. To generously given love and caring, then, there are added small but often hard-to-swallow doses of frustrating expectation. Aside from the fact that such frustrations are often for the protection of the child from harm, they may be said to prepare him for "real life." They become digestible to him (as real-life frustrations become digestible to us all) when some reward, immediate or anticipated, is won for the sacrifice made. That reward for the little one is the appreciative responsiveness of the parent for his obedience, for his emerging ability to hang on to his impulse or to invest his interests and energies elsewhere.

The whole business of toilet training in this period is a prime illustration of the expectation inputs in the exchanges between parents (usually mother) and child. Desirably there is understanding acceptance of his resistance and unwillingness to conform to "unreasonable" cleanliness and control requirements; along with this tolerance is a consistent expectation that sooner or later he will learn. Patient and loving support of his often halfhearted efforts combine with bits of reinforcement to the positive side of his ambivalence about the bathroom.*

Among all the new and often entrancing things that the ambulatory and mind-quickened child begins to see and watch is the fact that his mother and father belong not only to him but to one another, too. If he is one of several children he sees, often with pangs of jealousy, that his parents belong to the other children, too, and if there are other relatives nearby they belong to them at times. Probably the more others that make up the family, the more naturally diluted and spread out is the sense of possession and of being possessed. Probably the most intense sense of jealousy and anger at the recognition that one *shares* rather than *owns* another occurs in the mother–father–one child triangle, Freud's "oedipal complex." Its sexual involvements will not be argued here. We need only take note of the relationship struggle and the desirable growth that occurs when, wanting all of his mother's or father's love, attention, time, presence, wanting to be the other's be-all and end-all, wanting to possess his most loved parent, the child learns to relinquish his wish for total possession of and attachment to another and to share the most loved one.

The little child learns sharing by the gratifications he receives from reciprocal secondary relationships, from the love and attention he may receive from other family members and friends

*It is a common observation among those who have worked with young mothers, especially those whose motherhood was unexpected and unwanted, that problems of relationship between them and their babies rise high in this period when the child begins to assert his own personhood. Whether out of simple ignorance or their own need, such mothers often love their babies most when they are completely pliable, when nothing can be expected of them beyond eating and sleeping as they should, when they are bodily and responsively "at one" with the mother. Difficulties begin when self-assertion emerges and when expectations on the mothers' part are both too severe and excessive or are far more often demanded than rewarded. Then the child begins to be seen as "bad," "disobedient," needing to "have his will broken" rather than understood as a small being whose selfhood is seeking expression and reinforcement.

as he makes his exploratory forays in their direction. He finds that it even feels safer when all his eggs are not in one basket. In large part, he learns this because his mental and physical capacities in their natural development are now readying him to invest his activities and interests and to draw pleasures—sensual, confidence building, mind stimulating—from other pursuits than just those of seeking love and protection. He is developmentally ready now for many kinds of work/play with persons and things, putting himself in the pleasurable work of reading—or listening and imagining as he is read to—of making things happen (coloring, cutting, monkeying with toys and bits and pieces of material), and so on.

Security begins to come now not just from his relationship with those on whom he has had to depend for survival but from his growing awareness that he, too, has powers. Love input begins to be augmented (when the steadiness and warming care of the parents is still there) by the glowing, expanding sense that things and people are responsive to *him,* to *his* doing and behaving, that transactions between him and others yield results that (for the most part) feel good. Moreover, that they are recognized admiringly as "good" by those he cares about.

Of course, it does not always go ideally. One finds many adults who are still in search of relationships that are possessive. They want to own another totally and sometimes to be owned totally. They are jealous of their love or marriage mate's interests elsewhere, whether of attachments to friends or to their family of origin or even to their work and recreational interests. They seem insatiable in their need for reassurance and evidence that they are "the only" love or attention object. In therapeutic situations—and they often seek therapy because they cannot seem to get enough out of the friendship or sexual connections they have made—they often become clinging, long-time, interminable patients, living off the undivided attention and acceptance from their helper (at least for a fifty-minute hour). They are persons who, for whatever reasons, were probably wrenched rather than weaned from the complete dependency and possessiveness of the early stages of parent-child relationships.

Few of us can remember our early experiences of relationship.

But most of us can consciously recall at least fragments of such relationships after the age of six or seven as were meaningful to us, whether in constructive or destructive ways. They were relationships with schoolmates, with teachers, with camp or playground leaders, with pets, with people or even animals who came alive in books, with parents of friends, and also with such work and play activities in which we invested our interests and caring and from which we drew out pleasure and sometimes pain.

The human need for bonding, for being connected with others, moves the schoolchild into an expanding world of relationships. In classes, on the playground, in backyards, he is thrown together with his age equals. Sometimes they are supportive, sometimes competitive, sometimes openly antagonistic. He and they begin in rudimentary ways to develop the strategies by which interpersonal relationships can yield most satisfaction. "Fairness" and "rules" are stressed. Cooperative and collaborative ventures are set up. All of us remember these early and increasingly effective experimentations. (Do they come "just naturally," out of the need to "belong"? Or the need to augment our strength by alliance with others? Or?) Most of us can remember, too, the left-out child, here and there, who seemed to be afraid, shy, babyish, unable somehow to join with the rest for fun or for study projects. Teachers and school social workers see such children today, too—whose hearts and minds are still absorbed with relationship hungers unsatisfied at home. It is not simply the lack of a nourishing breakfast that causes the young child's apathy or inattention in the classroom. The child who is relationship hungry or who has found conflict-ridden or inconsistent family relationships too indigestible sits in the schoolroom or stands on the playground as a physical entity only. His heart and mind are still at home, and, breakfasted or not, his stomach feels empty or churning.

Back in the family when school and playtime are over, the more fortunate child knows comfortable security again. More, he finds that what he has done or not done in the outside world is of interest and concern to the people who matter most to him.

They will be pleased and admiring when he has done well, will affirm his abilities or at the least his well-intentioned efforts. Or they will try to help him cope more effectively if he does less than well. Parental teaching continues both intentionally and consciously and unconsciously, teaching about the self in relation to other people and to tasks and activities.

At the intentional level are all those "oughts" and "shoulds" that govern the expected and acceptable reciprocal behaviors between the self and others. Singly, many of them are trivial, but in the whole (unless they are too frequent, too many, and too carping) they ready the child for confident and pleasant contacts with others and call forth appreciative responses that accrue to the child's sense of competence in interpersonal relationships. Probably far more important in their indelible impress, however, are those interchanges with people that the child takes in through his pores, so to speak, through his observations and imitations of the people he feels most at one with, his parents or older siblings or sometimes other beloved relatives and friends. He models himself (from the preschool years onward) upon the behaviors of those he loves. Sometimes this occurs by conscious imitation (playing house, etc.) but more often by unconscious incorporation, of attributes and attitudes of those who are loved (thus taken into the self) or who seem to have power.

If his relationship models are fairly competent in their interplay with other persons and tasks, the growing child is bit by bit equipped with a relationship repertoire that is flexible and adaptable. If his models are relationship poor—constricted, suspicious, impulse ridden—the child's preparation for investing in other people or even in putting himself industriously into the work he must do will be limited or impaired.

Adolescence is a period charged with high-intensity emotion. Thus relationships are affected. Passionate attachments to persons, to ideas, to ideals, to causes, to activities through which self-expression can be realized—all these are craved, sought, talked about, experimented with. To "belong," to "be crazy about," to "adore," to "believe in," to be keenly sensitive to

the approval or disapproval of certain others, to take in certain
people and ideas voraciously (or cast them off ruthlessly), to ape
behaviors, to pour feelings, at times almost hysterically, into
union with another—all these commonly observed actions and
attitudes bespeak the ravaging attachment hungers and needs of
adolescence. There are many reasons for the emotional tur-
bulence of adolescence (even that which is experienced largely as
pleasurable), and they include a host of socially induced conflicts and tensions. However, the physiological changes, the
suddenly surging sexual energies seeking direct or rechanneled
discharge and deposit, the heightened mental capacity to perceive the delights and dangers, the promises and pitfalls of the
widening world—these are probably the main forces that drive
adolescents to seek new connections and emotional alliances.
Their relationships are often tempestuous, short-lived, oscil-
lating in wide arcs from "love" to "hate." They may range
from the plunge into sexual excitements or to their careful
detour by the immersion of self in causes or ideals, whether as
activists or ideologists. It is no mystery, for instance, that college
students are, world over, the recurrent revolutionaries. Their
spilling-over physical energies, their passionate espousal of the
rights of human beings (heavily freighted sometimes with true
compassion for the underdog and sometimes mostly with rebel-
lion against those held to be responsible for human suffering),
their swift and plunging attachment to the person or ideas of a
leader—these all combine with the wonderfully sustaining sense
of being united with their own kind, bound together by ties of
emotionally charged beliefs. In quite another kind of situation
one may see some of the same dynamics at work: the attraction
of many young people to lawless gangs may often be due less to
their delinquent predilections or their deficits of conscience
than to their hunger for attachment, for connections that provide acceptance, security, a reason for being. The gang offers
these in ready-made relationships.

Erikson put forth the overarching concept of "identity crisis"
as the characteristic problem to be solved during the period of
adolescence. It is an idea that has unfortunately too often been

oversimplified and vulgarized to the point where an adolescent feels he is out of it unless he ponders and raps with his friends about "Who *am* I, anyway?" As if anyone can know who or what one is except through reflections and affirmations arising from the use of one's self in interchanges with other persons and work and play tasks! The achievement of a sense of identity is in large part dependent upon the knowledge of one's self as stemming from past relationships (a point Erikson makes, though in different words). Based upon this sense of continuity and sameness there must be experienced a sense of one's today's self as part of a network of present-day relationships where one is recognized, cared about, respected and in turn (though this "in turn" may be often forgotten by the introverted young person who desperately seeks to find himself only *in* himself) is expected to feed back recognition of one or more others with caring and respect. Through empathic identification with others (present and known, or perhaps only known about), through feelingful alliance with them, and through the caring investment of one's own capacities in performing daily life tasks—in short, through relationships between oneself and other persons and activities—the sense of "I-ness" and "me-ness" is secured and expanded. "I am not only the product of what I have had put into me (or denied me) in the past but the being-and-becoming product of what I am connecting with, putting in and drawing out, in my reciprocal transactions with people, things, and experiences in the now."

In brief, in adolescence as at any stage of our lives we are, each of us, the product-in-process of sustained and sustaining relationships. Or, less fortunately, of their reverse. In adolescence, we are driven to form new and reshape old relationships, by conscious intent, by half-conscious imitations and incorporations of models or ego ideals, by spontaneous attachments to persons we perceive as loving and lovable and/or as powerful in ways that underpin our assurance and security. Because that period from childhood into youth into adulthood is one in which emotions are powerful, readily excited, freewheeling, it is a time when support and stimulation by constructive relationships can deeply affect the rapidly growing young person's present and future sense of himself and of the world around him. It is thus a time of special responsiveness to persons who are perceived as empathic, understanding, helpful.

Adulthood does not occur by arrival at a certain chronological age. All of us know people who, in enchanting or annoying ways, remain adolescent into senescence. And we all know people who seem gratifyingly to mature quite early, if not totally all at once, at least in some important aspects of their personalities. To "mature," to be "adult," connotes the arrival at a developmental level marked by certain capacities and qualities of relationship. Elsewhere and at length I have written of the growth and maturation potentials in marriage, in work, and perhaps especially in parenting.[4] Each of these roles is heavily charged with emotions; each requires continuous dynamic adaptation to changes that circumstances and life phases demand; each involves input, caring, giving out, concern, empathy, receptivity, respect for the material—person or object—with which one is in transaction. Thus relationship—of self to other, of putting out and taking in, of union and separation, of at-oneness and aloneness—continues to be a condition for growth even in adulthood.

What one sees in "mature" people—young or old—are these relationship characteristics: they are able to give out of themselves—their caring, loving, interest in, and concern for others freely and fully. They are empathic with others, able to feel spontaneously with them and for them. They are tolerant and respectful of differences between themselves and others, whether those differences are of age, race, opinion, values—they do not have to demand of themselves or another that they be, think, or act alike; but, rather, they can give attention to trying to understand the apparent unlikeness and yet to find some common ground on which to stand together. They have a sense of their rights and those of the other and also, in balance, some sense of obligation and social responsibility. When their position or role in relation to the other requires it, they can take on and exercise that responsibility. They are able to recognize and to experience their feelings deeply, whether of love or hate, joy or despair, pleasure or displeasure, pride or shame. At the same time, they can control the verbal expression or acting out of such emotion, can manage their impulses when it is in their own or the other's best interests, because how they act is governed by their thinking, their judgement, their understanding.

Does this sound impossibly ideal? Does anyone really ever achieve this? One must honestly admit that scarcely anyone achieves all of it, and certainly no one maintains it all of the time. Even those of us who pride ourselves on being "grown up" have our childish moments, our wound-licking, self-concerned times, our lapses of judgment or of age-appropriate behavior. Perhaps maturity in its psychological sense is a goal that must be continuously striven for. That is why we are always not just being but having to "become." (Which, because it is so demanding, makes brief regressions so understandable in most of us!) But it helps to know what that ever beckoning goal, maturity, requires of us.

In young adulthood men and women seek to bind themselves in a loving, affectional relationship to *one* other, in legal marriage or in a mutually agreed-upon liaison "without benefit of clergy." The frequency with which such relationships are split by divorce or separation speaks to the disharmonies and dissatisfactions on the part of one or both partners with what had been looked to as the "most meaningful," certainly most intimate of relationships. The reasons for such discord and dissatisfaction have been explored and speculated upon endlessly in recent years and need no discussion here, except to note one that is central to our understanding and management of our vital relationships.

In its bare outline: within the past generation there seems to have burgeoned a sense that there ought to be instant and unremitting happiness in intimate relationships. There is little expectation of stress, pain, frustration, discomforts, and little or no tolerance of them when they occur. There is small recognition of the phenomenon of ambivalence (discussed earlier) and of the powerful pull to individuation that balances the equal pull to merge. There is resistance on the one hand to being "owned," possessed—"I must feel free"—and yet the paradoxical wish to possess the other in the absolute sense that one can bank on the other's fidelity, presence, "thereness," devotion. In the excitements of falling in love there is small awareness in most couples that excitement, like other peak experiences, cannot become regularized. And it is a rare rather than a usual couple who talk together about the expectations of self and other that each of them brings to the relationship.

Whether personally involved in the one-to-one transactions of marriage or lover relationships or professionally concerned as a counselor in marriage problems, the necessity is to understand the naturalness of ambivalence, the presence of some negative as well as the (chiefly) positive feelings toward the other that emerge occasionally, the need to clarify and reconcile expectations, each of the other, and perhaps above all the necessity to understand, as has been said before, that relationships do not stand still. They are not "established" once and for all, either in normal life transactions or in help-giving, help-taking situations. Their intensity, their reciprocality, their demands and rewards will undergo changes—some transitory, some permanent—as the persons involved grow or regress, are sick or well, are pressed by daily frustrations and stresses or enhanced by fortunate life circumstances.

Marriage contains some differences from unmarried living-together relationships. (Perhaps it is these differences that increasingly encourage the latter arrangements as substitutes for the former?) Marriage is a "social contract" in more ways than one. It is a public statement witnessed and (usually) sanctioned by others of the relationship intentions of two people. But more than this, it signifies a responsible taking on of roles that, even in a time of upheaval and role confusions such as ours today, have some socially defined expectations of reciprocal rights and responsibilities. Furthermore, in spite of the frequent protest that "I married *you* and not your family!" entry into marriage means stepping into an often complex network of relationships. Geographically or emotionally remote though the spouse's family may be, there is the expectation (on at least one side) that there will be some sort of relationship formed with another set of parents, siblings, and cousins and aunts. The one-to-one bond with spouse will repeatedly be affected by those others to whom each partner, despite protestations to the contrary, may find himself or herself tied. In some instances these relationships may intrude into and even rupture the intimate cocoon of the twosome; in others it may enrich and expand the sense of being liked, alike, and liking, of being part of a larger security system. So it may have its rewards as well as its sometimes onerous requirements. Both the work of meeting relationship requirements (when they are reasonable, one must add) and the responsive feedback they yield (when reciprocations occur) are growth promoting because they nurture, exercise, and reinforce the capacities named earlier as those of "maturity."

Parenting is probably the most potent, painful, and pleasurable relationship that human beings know. It begins when the newborn opens its eyes and ends only when the parents close theirs. Emotions are roused in parents and then drive roots deeply down into their unconscious layers, emotions that popular speech refers to as parental "instincts" (usually "maternal," though recent years have seen the father becoming increasingly emotionally bound to his baby as he participates in caring for it and in the reciprocations of doing for and responding to). Beyond the growth of love by loving exchanges, there are placed upon parents today innumerable requirements, expectations, responsibilities by a society that is itself emotionally involved in concerns about healthy child development, children's learning, children's socialization, children's self-actualization. Volumes have been written, scientific and popular, to advise, warn, blame, exhort, guide parents about the attitudes and actions they transmit to their children via their ongoing relationship transactions. The gist is that parents ought to have the attributes of person, mind, and relationship capacities that we listed several pages back as the qualities of "maturity," "adulthood." Needless to say, some parents fall short of these some of the time, and some fall short most of the time. Again, as with problems in marriage relationships, there has perhaps been insufficient recognition of the many kinds of life stresses and deficits—lack of money, lack of knowledge, lack of relationship supports from families or friends, too much to cope with and too little psychic or physical energy—that disturb and warp parental relationships, that muddy or choke up the free-flowing stream of caring and attending from parent to child. Nor has there been enough attention given to the changes of relationship feelings and behaviors that must be expected to occur on both sides of the parent-child transaction as both the normal life-stage changes are encountered by each individual family under very particular conditions and circumstances.

In short, the caring, nurturing, empathically understanding relationship that is expected to bind parent and child is the product not only of the parent's innate capacity for responsiveness and giving but also of many factors in the family's social situation and educational background.

The two-way flow of relationship between parents and child is obviously not an equally reciprocal one. When the child is very young, most of the "giving," certainly that which is conscious and intentional, flows from parents to child; when the parents are very old, that imbalance is reversed. Somewhere in between is a wide middle period, potentially a friendship time, when there is a fairly equal balance of interchanges of giving and getting, concern and pleasure, mutual acceptance.

The requirements of parenting are demanding ones, and their outcomes may often be disappointing. Nevertheless, the parent-child relationship holds tremendous potential for growth, in depth and breadth, of the adult personality. The affectionally and mentally responsive child feeds the parents' satisfying sense that they are competent—they have produced and nurtured well. More, they feel reciprocally appreciated by their child, loved and bound together with him by the invisible threads of being for and with one another. These feelings may be supported, furthermore, by all the social approvals that a child's responsiveness brings—from grandparents and neighbors and nursery school teachers—an ever widening audience.

Along with the personality-expanding gratifications of requited love and evidence of generativity (Erikson's word), parents feel knit together with their children. It is expectable, then that parents will suffer their children's hurts—except that their greater maturity and know-how makes them able to view and to cope with them quite differently. And it is expectable too that they will partake of and vicariously experience their children's pleasures and small triumphs. "It is a chance to relive so many parts of your own life," said one mother, "only now you experience them differently." She spoke to her sense of union with her child at the same time she could both differentiate her child from herself and her adult self from the child she once was.

Like adulthood, old age cannot be fully marked by chronology. It does not automatically occur at sixty-five or even seventy-five, and today's gerontologists have begun to divide those called the "aged" into the "young-old" (ages fifty-five to seventy-five) and the "old-old" (seventy-six and over). Sooner or later, however, as Freud remarked in his own productive old age, the mind fails the body, or the body fails the mind. And the emotive powers that were invested in relationships with other people and objects begin to dwindle. The reasons are multiple—as reasons have a way of being. There is, in the old-old, an all but inevitable diminishing of sensory acuity— eyesight clouds, hearing dulls, taste buds wither—and the person seems to his would-be relaters remote and slow. He has been relegated to rolelessness either by retirement rulings or by his physical and/or mental inability to carry out a job (including that of housekeeping). Moreover, death or chronic illness have decimated the ranks of his friends and acquaintances. So the range of people and activities to which he had attachments that mattered to him have shrunk. If the old-old is lucky enough to have a devoted family, he loves his children and grandchildren, but it has become a love more dependent upon than supportive of others. He cares, but in anxious ways, feeling his own fragility and helplessness, needing to harbor his small store of energy. He wants and needs the attentions and connections with others more robust than he, even though, unlike the unfolding child, he cannot fully utilize them.

Even the young-old become aware of relationship changes. Many of them leave their familiar surroundings in search of greater comfort in living. Their common experience, however, is that "it is very hard to make real friends at this age." Acquaintances abound, to be sure, people all eager to connect anew, to pass the time of day with others. But meaningful friendships are difficult to form. When one wonders why, the thesis of this chapter is supported: that vital, heartfelt relationships arise out of emotionally charged experiences that are felt in depth, expressed, received, and resonated to by another. Such experiences, with their concomitant peaks of joy and hope or their depths of anxiety and despair, come less frequently past middle age and at retirement time. The chief hope then is for health and economic security; the chief fear is illness or death. But such fears are usually pushed under, not talked about or shared. Most life events flatten out, or the energy to engage in them fully is depleted. There is more tendency to watch and observe than to participate, whether in sports or in the care of a new grandchild. The probability is that psychological defenses protect the aging from too much caring or involvements that are too psychically costly. So while long-time relationships may still provide nourishment and security for some years ahead, new ones tend to be only skin-deep, casual, and both comfortably and yet unsatisfyingly superficial.

This chapter has dealt with the normal, usual, everyday relationships of normal, usual, everyday people—what needs they seem to meet, how they grow, well or badly, and their vital effect upon the individual's interpersonal and person-to-task competences and gratifications. The needs to be recognized by others as "a special person," to be accepted for what one is, to be believed in as being more and better than a cursory contact might reveal, to be cared about especially at times of trouble, and to feel that one belongs and is allied with some source of strength and support—these needs are known to every one of us experientially, either because at one time or another they have not been met or because by our sense of confidence and stability in movement we know we have been given to generously.

Yet in every life there are moments or months when a sudden crisis, an accumulation of stress, or the loss of essential means make it necessary to turn to some source of emotional support or guidance and/or tangible resources and services. When the help we want seems essential to our physical survival or psychological balance, we are, quite naturally, emotionally roused. We are stirred by what is often a three-pronged hazard: the hurt or threat inherent in the problem itself; the undoing sense of helplessness when one is unable to cope; the sense of unease, perhaps even fear, about what losses of self—self-management, self-respect, self-integrity—may occur if we go to another person for help.

In every life, too, there are times when we need or want to stretch ourselves, to gain some new or greater mastery of knowledge and skills, not because we are facing problems but in the wish to prevent them or in the drive for greater self-fulfillment. Even then, buoyed up as we may be by hope and confidence, we may find stirrings of doubt and unease in ourselves, some pullback to giving ourselves over to something new, perhaps some fear of failure, of falling short of our self-expectation, or of the riskiness of change.

Every would-be helper in the human service professions—whether he attends chiefly to those who are in physical, economic, or psychologically induced troubles or to those who are reaching out to enrich their occupational or personal lives—needs to understand these things: what usual relationship needs people have; why they may be intensified in times of trouble or of personal change; and what part relationship may play in simultaneously supporting and moving human beings. Especially do we need to give our attentions to the usages of relationship in helping people to learn, to do, to cope, to be and to "become" with greater personal gratification and social affirmation. So we look now to the special nature and purpose of "helping relationships."

3

The Helping Relationship

Part I: Its Purpose and Nature

WHAT IS a "helping relationship" for, anyhow? What's the point of it?

If a man who has had a stroke needs to learn to use his paralyzed leg and arm again, refer him to the physiotherapist and the equipment by which he will be exercised and trained. If a young mother needs to know how to feed and care for her baby, take her to the nearby well-baby clinic. If a child seems to be having trouble paying attention and learning in school, talk to the teacher and his mother and refer him to a special reading tutor or to a diagnostic clinic or ———— . If a patient is to be discharged from the mental hospital, take a good look at the boarding homes or halfway houses available to him and settle him in one of them. If a set of parents are neglecting their young children or, worse, actually abusing them, they need to be talked to, explained to, told what the consequences of their actions might be; and the children should be placed somewhere.

Develop or get hold of the resources—deliver the services—do it courteously and decently. What more is necessary? Why must we concern ourselves with the business of relationship? With giving our care and attention to creating a feelingful alliance between ourselves as helpers and those who ask for or need the kind of help we can offer?

Before I go directly to attempting to answer these questions, let me first present an anecdote that is all but absurd, but perhaps no more "absurd" than many other common human experiences.

I am returning a pair of gloves to a department store. It is a big store—and therefore a "bureaucracy"—and I have been sent from the counter where I thought I bought the gloves to yet another counter, then to the section manager, and thence to the adjustment department on still another floor. I must wait in line. The problem is that I bought the gloves on sale, "non-returnable," but I was sent the wrong pair. I am not asking to be "given" anything—except my "rights." I have thus far told my tale to three people, and I feel increasingly indignant, even outraged, that (1) my time and energy is being wasted, (2) the clerk who waited on me was careless, (3) nobody takes responsibility for anything, and (4) now I must stand in line. I spend those minutes recalling all the other times I have been inconvenienced by big organizations, composing acid letters to the management, etc. By the time my turn comes (perhaps in five minutes—but it feels like at least a half hour), I am furious with the innocent and calm girl who faces me at the adjustment window. She is the enemy. I thrust the boxed gloves through her window and tell her (my anger controlled but showing, I'm sure) of my tribulations with this purchase. She listens, blankly unperturbed. She asks for and writes down identifying information. Without a word, she goes off into some labyrinth of offices. After too long (two or three minutes?) she returns, takes the gloves, gives me a credit slip, and the transaction is satisfactorily terminated. Satisfactorily—and yet, why is it I go off still fulminating, thinking, "Big is ugly" and "I'll never go *there* again," and so on? I have gotten what I wanted, and no one has been discourteous or less than civil to me. So why do I leave this department store in a state of annoyance, ready to snap at or complain to the next person I meet (depending on how he "relates" to me)?

For one thing, the transaction was totally depersonalized. I was just another faceless problem presenter. That in itself feels

like a brush-off. But more important: I felt irritated by the
inconveniences to which I had been subjected, and yet the
"helpers" seemed oblivious to it. That I *felt* something (rightly
or wrongly) was of no concern to anybody. This adds to one's
sense of meaning nothing. If I characteristically suffered from
feelings of inferiority or of being victimized, they would have
been confirmed once again. If I had felt I had no retributive
power (such as closing my charge account—a recourse I dis-
missed at once as more harmful to me than to the organization),
my sense of helplessness would have been intensified.

I did not want the department store helper to bleed over me.
I simply wanted a momentary indication that I was seen as a
person separate from the person who preceded and the one who
came after me; I wanted some sign of recognition that my
problem had some feeling content for me and that such feeling
was appreciated as understandable. That's all. But it would
have made a deal of difference in my next ten minutes' physiological and psychological well-being, in my attitude toward the
place (which I then generalized to "all big organizations"), and
in my disgruntled feelings about people who have somehow lost
the human touch. It is quite possible that I was overreacting.
But so do many of us—our help seekers, too—when a problem,
big or small, upsets our usual equilibrium.

To return to examples of "real" and deeply disturbing problems that people bring to human services personnel every day.
The stroke victim may need but not want "rehabilitation"—he
is too weary, too discouraged. The young mother may be too
preoccupied with her marital or financial problems to have the
interest or energy to take herself and her baby to the clinic. The
mother of the child who is already failing in the second grade is
sure that he will "outgrow" his learning difficulties. The mental hospital patient is terrified at facing the prospect of independent living. The neglectful abusive parents deny the accusations
against them, and the juvenile court judge, looking at the clean
faces of their children, sees no reason to issue an order for child
placement.

In every one of these instances—and in thousands of others—

a person has to be helped to understand and, further, to want what he needs, to move in his feeling/thought/action from one attitude or perspective to another. Relationship is a major dynamic in such movement. It is a major motivator of a person's acting, thinking, and feeling in some different ways. This is because relationship is a process (not a "state") of building a supporting, reliable bridge between one and another. When I know that you feel with me, that you care about me, that you understand what my reasons and reactions are, then I am more likely to care about you, to want your approval, to listen to you, to take your hope and encouragement into myself and to open my mind to your suggestions or opinions.

Relationship is an *emotional* experience. We are *moved* when our emotions are touched, *motivated* by the push or pull of feeling. Those feelings may be transitory, of varying intensity, and may, of course, be invested more in the problem situation than in the helper. But if a would-be helper is to influence a help seeker to cope with his problem in some more personally satisfying and/or socially satisfactory ways, he will need to connect with and be sensitively responsive to the emotions with which the person's problem is charged. It is no mere word play to recognize that "motivation," "movement," and "emotion" all stem from the same Latin root, *movere.*

There are several further reasons for the salience of relationship in any helping service to human beings. They will be set down here and will thread their way through all the rest of the book. Beyond its motivational potentials and its never to be underestimated affirmation of the personhood of each individual and the promotion of his sense of at-oneness with others are these further considerations.

Most of the people who come or are sent to human service workers are having some troubles. Some crisis, some loss of money or health or personal supports, some undermining of their personal capacities or social resources, some last straw has broken the back of their usual functioning and rendered them helpless. The problem, and all the additional problems it generates, may be as commonplace as weeds. It may require only a quick reach for ready resources. But the person who has the problem feels it uniquely.* It *does* things to *him*. Such as: he feels overwhelmed, confused, at a loss; he feels angry, put-upon, victimized once again; he feels to blame, inferior, demeaned in his own and perhaps in others' eyes because he has not been adequate somehow.

So he turns for help to someone—you—who he hopes, or has been told, can offer the assistance he needs. And now another cluster of feelings arise. He brings some hopes—but perhaps fears, too. What will you think of him? What will you ask of him by way of gratitude, obedience? What will you do to him? If his experiences with strangers have been largely negative or he has heard lurid tales of "what they do to you," there is likely to be an admixture of antagonism, of readiness to take offense, of determination to reveal oneself as little as possible.

As if having a problem or an unmet need were not enough, there is often the superimposed problem that what the person wants or wishes for is actually not to be had, or it may be had but under conditions that he finds difficult or unsatisfactory. He has feelings about all this, too.

One need not make too much of this. Every client/patient is not always a cauldron a-boil, but it is in the nature of being human that something is a problem not only in its objective manifestations but because we feel it to be, because our internal being—physiological and psychological—is upset and thrown off balance by it.

What do we need and want at such times when we feel helpless, victimized, hopeless, perhaps distrustful? First and foremost we want to be given the means and services that will meet our need. There is no substitute for that. But we also want to be recognized as a person, not just a problem carrier; to be paid attention to, receptively; to be responded to feelingly, which is to say, to have evidence that this stranger understands something of what the problem is doing to me, something of

*When you have "the common cold," it is of small comfort to know that "everybody has it." You still feel miserable, hampered in doing what you want to do, annoyed that this should have happened to *you,* etc.

how I feel, and that he cares enough to feel with me and to try his best for me. We want a compassionate connectedness along with the rent money, even if that relationship is limited to that one contact and that one need.

Play with that idea for a moment. Suppose there were a system of machines (anything seems possible these days!) specialized to produce the solution to certain problems, and by the input of a request and eligibility information a problem solution would be delivered—the rent, a bottle of medicine, the address of a nursery school, maybe even a card that said "Sorry about that!" The feelings brought to the machine would be minimal, chiefly related to having a problem. The receipt of "help" would be completely impersonal (though I have seen people slap and kick a gum-ball machine when it did not deliver!). What the person did with or about the resource provided or the referral suggested, what he might understand or feel about it, would remain unknown. "Better than being kicked around by a heartless bureaucrat," you may be thinking. Would it be better than being caringly attended to by a bureaucrat with a heart?

I would argue that it is the very fact that one brings one's troubles to another human being that provides the opportunity for a humanizing experience. That opportunity may of course be absent or, worse, twisted into a hurtful rather than a helpful interchange. But our lifetime relationship experiences, especially those that drove deep into us at times of our helplessness, need, dependency upon the caring of others, condition us to want not only whatever material or psychological aid we need but also another human being to resonate to our distress. We want the reassuring sense of being connected with and able to call forth human compassion.

The "bureaucrat with a heart" is simply one who, by responding to the feelings of a person, is affirming that person's personal worth and individuality. The interchange between a human helper and help seeker, further, is a socializing experience because it demonstrates (both actually and symbolically) a bonding between one member of society who needs a hand and another member of that society who represents its concern that a hand be available. This is what the human services in all their forms are for—*to meet human needs in ways that deepen and fulfill the sense of social caring and responsibility between fellow human beings.*

Some human service organizations serve people not because they are in trouble but, rather, because they are seeking to fulfill and enrich their lives. People who want to further their education, to improve what skills they have or to explore new ones, who want to engage in some personally gratifying leisure time activities. By and large these persons are confident; by and large they trust; they are not afraid that the person across the desk will think ill of them. But even here some feelings may be involved or may emerge, though they will be of lesser intensity. Any undertaking that requires some change in oneself or in one's usual habits, anything that is new, pulls us by its promised interest, yet it may make us uneasy, too. Change is risky, the unknown both beckons and threatens. So even here, as teachers and tutors and occupational therapists and group workers in many endeavors know, there may be necessary not simply the open opportunity to learn but, along with that, the support and affirmation of the learner and the empathic appreciation of the doubts and obstacles, external and internal, that may interfere with his full engagement of himself.

In sum, a supportive, compassionate working alliance is what any professional relationship is for, an alliance in the safety of which the person copes at once or learns to cope better with his felt problems and/or in which the person is freed to put his energies and capacities into new learning. Thus it is part of the skill and professional responsibility of the helping persons to know what a helpful relationship consists of, what its components are thought to be, and to incorporate them consciously, insofar as that is possible, into his dealings with people.

The relationship attributes that experienced clinicians (psychologists, professional social workers, psychiatrists) seem to agree upon as desirable or even necessary are these: warmth, acceptance, empathy, caring-concern, genuineness.[1] Each of these merits some explication if we are to grasp why they are meaningful and what their helping values seem to be. Without recourse to dictionaries but drawing, rather, upon our common relationship experiences, let's look at them.

Warmth. This connotes some positive lively, outgoing interest in another person (or object or activity), a spontaneous reaching out to take in another with pleasure or compassion. We say a mother is "warm" when she behaves in such ways to her children; likewise a teacher or physician. Warmth is probably a personal disposition, probably the product of early and repeated experiences of having been responded to in pleasurable and confidence-giving ways. Some people helpers are not naturally warm. They may be shy, as yet unsure of themselves, constrained by some personal doubts or the discomforts that certain people or problems arouse in them. But we need not despair!—there are other attributes more readily cultivated that may serve as good substitutes.

Acceptance. This means taking the person as he is and where he is. It means understanding that the way he is and the ways he acts are the product of all that he has known and that they are rarely consciously intentioned or thoughtfully chosen. But it does not mean that expectation will not also be in the helper's mind and attitude. It all but goes without saying that if the ways a person behaves are causing him or other persons trouble, the expectation is that he may be helped to modify or change them. The expectation is that through his work on the problem, aided by the help that can be given him, he will achieve some better personal and/or social functioning. What, otherwise, is a helping service and process for?

How does one walk this fine line, both accepting the person's "being" and expecting his "becoming"? It involves, to begin with, making some judgments. And immediately we must stop to take a careful look at that. So many writings on relationship and on helping adjure us to be "nonjudgmental." I submit that this is a poor term, the attitude is misnamed. Surely we cannot suspend all judgment. What does expertise in any profession consist of if not, among other responsibilities, that of judging that one form of behavior is "better" than another, one decision less likely to bring satisfactory outcomes than another, assessing and predicting on the basis of knowledge and experience? What "nonjudgmental" really means is "nonblaming," "noncensorious." That is more readily understandable because, especially before a relationship is strong and trustworthy, one cannot feel at one with someone who looks askance or criticizes; one must, in self-defense, withdraw from such nonacceptance.

However, even when a person's actions and behavior are judged negatively, it is still possible to accept the person by crediting his *intention,* which happened to be carried out badly (for him, as well as for others), or by recognizing that he did the best he knew how to do at the time (though the action made things worse) or that he was so uncertain (upset, furious, afraid —whatever) that he couldn't put his best foot forward. There is no hypocrisy here. These comments carry the necessary message: "I accept *you* but not your acts." They are honest and true. Most people, when they do or dream foolish, crazy, even cruel things, do so on blind impulse, because they are at the time driven by irrationality often combined with ignorance.

In long-term relationships when client/patient has come to feel trust and safety in his helper and knows in his bones that the latter is with him and for him, it becomes possible to challenge behavior more directly. Such challenge is acceptable to the person only because he has come to trust the helper's consistent acceptance of him.

Rogers, whose formulations and research on therapeutic relationships have set a model for many therapists,[2] speaks of "unconditional regard" for the client. I find this a puzzling concept. No relationship is without its conditions and expectations. In a helping relationship—even one where the problem lies chiefly within the person's intrapsychic life and the material in work is chiefly that of the person's feelings and reactions— even when the respect (regard) for the person remains steady and consistent, there is the expectation that change will occur. Can "unconditional" regard then be genuine? If the person chooses to quit therapy or to abandon his search for healing, one surely must accept his decision, one surely should not censure him for it—but (unless he is proven to be untreatable) the therapist would surely try to influence (thus "condition") his decision? Perhaps one can settle for respect for the individual that includes some belief in his potentials?

Empathy. This means feeling *with* and *into* another person, being able to get into his shoes. It may occur spontaneously or may be a carefully learned "listening with the third ear" and responding in tune with the other person. It may require that the person be drawn out, bit by bit, to describe what and how he feels, so that the helper may respond with accuracy. Empathy differs from sympathy. Sympathy surely involves a bond of feeling between helper and helped. Unlike empathy, however, sympathy rises out of an assumption that "*you* feel as *I* would under the circumstances," that "I understand your feelings because I assume they are like mine." Empathy, on the other hand, says in effect, "I want to be attuned to how *you* feel—I put my antennae out to take in (from what you say, from how you act, from your responses to my understanding-seeking comments or queries) how it seems and feels to *you,* what it means to *you.*" "Let me get into your shoes so I can more fully understand."

A caveat here: there is probably no more annoying or even threatening person than one who "understands" too quickly and too deeply, before you have had a chance to get the words out of your mouth, who reassures too swiftly because of his sometimes erroneous assumption that you and he are on the same wavelength. Such a person may often make a quite different interpretation of what you said from what you meant. Such a person may be quite sympathetic, bent on making you feel better fast. But he is not empathic. This involves giving oneself over to getting the meaning behind the words or, for the person who has trouble expressing himself, making some tentative comments or queries—"Do you mean ... ?" "Is what you're saying ... ?"

Empathy, in short, is leading oneself to another to feel into and take in the moment's essence of the other. Aside from its value in increasing the helper's understanding of the person, there is nothing more gratifying to anyone's self-esteem than for another person to pay close attention to him, to consider him important or interesting enough to want to understand his special feelings and meanings. It is a common experience for all of us that when we speak of being "understood" and of another person's being "understanding" we do not mean that he grasps our words. Rather, it is that he is sensitive to what is *under* those words or actions; he senses and relates to their accompanying feelings.

Some of us are "just naturally" empathic. Whether this is inborn or inbred is a matter for argument.* Happily, however, some recent experiments in "empathy training" of human service personnel indicate that it is possible to learn empathic skills and thence to increase awareness and sensitivity to the feelings of others.[3]

A persistent problem is involved in empathy. How does one retain objectivity? How get back into one's own shoes? This is absolutely essential if you are to be of help to a person who of course experiences his problem subjectively, who feels tumbled about in his thoughts and feelings, and whose involvement may even cloud and distort the reality.

Objectivity is an act of conscious discipline and self-management. Fortunately, its consistent practice entrenches it so that getting back into one's own shoes as the responsible helper can become habitual. But beginners need to learn to do it. First they need to learn that "objectivity" does not at all mean an attitude of cool detachment or complete neutrality.† Neutrality means "I don't really care—either way, any way is acceptable to me."

*One might suggest "a matter for research." But one problem would be that an empathic person's reports of his early experiences would be colored by his already present understanding insights.

†In today's adulation of science and its modes, there is an assumption that scientists are always "objective." Is that assumption valid? It is doubtful that a scientist—even the most careful experimenter—does not at times really care how things come out, does not have some investment in proving a hypothesis, some hope for a certain outcome. Objectivity is attained and maintained not by detachment from the material with which one works—whether it is people or particles—but by awareness and discipline of self in the interests of the quest.

It is inimical to a helping relationship. There is, then, a dilemma here—the need to be warmly empathic, responsive to subjective reactions of the client/patient, and yet the need to be able to move back into one's role as professional helper, expert (one hopes) in assessing the person and his problem and the kind of help he needs. The sensitively attuned helper finds himself in continuous movement between momentary merging with his client/patient and regaining his objective stance as a professionally responsible assessor and actor in the client's behalf.

"Objectivity" is the recognition and then the mangement or control of one's subjectivity.

Whether in working with people or things, the first and most essential step toward objectivity is self-awareness, awareness of your own emotional and reactive responses to persons and situations. Past the awareness that "I, too, have feelings"— sometimes appropriate and sometimes not—the need is for self-management. The helper disciplines himself by the question, "Is the verbal or action expression of my feeling likely to be helpful to my client/patient?" If the answer is uncertain, and surely if it is no, such feeling must be shelved while the helper reminds himself of his purpose and of how he can best further it. Shelved, but not forgotten—as will be discussed further on. With practice this staying of impulse becomes almost second nature. But it requires continual vigilance. Even the most experienced of us are now and then shaken by emotions aroused by this client or that situation. Such emotional involvements may be "natural" and explainable, but they are rarely useful.

Caring-concern. Caring is love in its giving, protective, nurturant aspects. It is concern for the well-being of the other. In everyday relationships caring is one mark of mature love in that it is not solely one's own love hunger one seeks to gratify but mostly that of the other.

In professional helping relationships, caring is concern for the welfare of those one seeks to help. It does not imply that one needs to "love"; it implies, rather, that one cares about the person's hurt and/or about the hurtful consequences of his

behavior, whether for himself or others. This suggests one salient difference between "caring" in professional and in natural
relationships: while the human service worker's concern is for
the individual he is helping, it may also be for those other
persons who are affected by his problem. His concern is for
social as well as individual well-being. Teachers, nurses, physicians, social workers, and others must be concerned with the
contagion potentials in their pupil/client/patient's problem.
"Caring" thus adds to warmth, acceptance, empathy the responsible concern for the "system" of which the individual is a
dynamic part.

Genuineness. To be genuine is to be free of pretension. It is to
have a sense of wholeness, of being put together, of knowing
who and what one is, what one's guiding values are, and, as a
result, of being on fairly good terms with oneself. Genuineness
is the product (again and always!) of life experiences that made
it possible to be self-observant, self-aware (of one's strengths
and one's foibles, too), and self-accepting (as a human being
with some human "badness" along with "goodness"), to be
unafraid of and therefore able to tolerate differences, to be able
to bear conflict and uncertainty—even at times to take pleasure
in not being cut-and-dried sure. That's a tall order, and it
cannot be commanded at will. One cannot wake up one morn-
ing and resolve, "Today I'm going to be genuine!"

However, there are small behaviors that may be learned and
practiced by which you can avoid pretension and convey the
sense to your client/patient that you are for real, sound, and
dependable. Here are a few common ones.

It seems hollow and unreal to a dreading and anxious person
to have someone rush in with excessive or false reassurance. Pats
on the back or "There, there, everything's going to be all right"
are good ways to make the helper himself feel more comfortable. Their effect on the help needer is often that he feels you
do not really understand the depth of his fears or the seriousness
of his situation or what his reality is. Sometimes it feels like a
brush-off—"I don't really want to hear or know all about it." If
one is to feel "genuine" to a person in trouble, one needs,
rather, to be *with* him at the very bottom of his despair—"It is

really one tough situation you're in"—"It's not an easy thing to have to do"—"It'll be a long slow haul." Then, if there is any realistic margin of hope, one needs to convey that. "But it's worth the try"—"Still, from what you've told me, you've gotten on top of things before"—"Maybe we can't make everything all right again, but I know of some possible steps we can take."

It also feels false to a person when he has done or said things to others that he himself knows are socially unacceptable, that may even be unacceptable to himself, and the helper acts as if they don't really matter. Here one walks that fine line of accepting the person and not accepting his act. What is needed is recognition of what feelings or intentions drove the person to do what he did. But also, by question or comment, to indicate genuine concern with the consequences of his act—did it produce the results he hoped for? Did it work? Is it a solution as he sees it? Simply to slide across it may leave a client puzzling, "What's your game?"

One needs to differentiate here between a client's revelations of what he thinks and feels and what he actually *does.* "Bad" thoughts and feelings are quite genuinely "acceptable" as part of the baggage of everyone's inner life; they are of concern when they are acted out against the self or others, when they are actualized.

Genuine relationship with a client/patient requires, further, that the helper be able to admit that he doesn't know something, that he needs to find out, that he needs a little time to think something over. (How gratifying it is to any one of us to know that we and our problem will occupy a place in the mind of another person!) It includes being able to admit having made a mistake—"I realized after I left you last time I forgot to . . . ," "I think I gave you a bad steer, and I wish we could talk that over again today." (How gratifying it is to find that someone in authority also has his weak spots!) Nor does a genuine helper lather up his self-esteem by hiding behind technical jargon, high-sounding labels, or pat interpretations that create an illusion but not the reality of understanding.

"This above all, to thine own self be true, / And it must

follow as the night the day, / Thou canst not then be false to any man.'' So said Polonius, who, in this advice at least, was a very wise old man.

One further note on the relationship qualities we have discussed: as you can see, they overlap. They can be separated, dissected and ordered in our thinking, but in their being acted out live they merge and intertwine in varying combinations and degrees. They are expressed whole, received and responded to whole, felt as whole, with no measuring sticks for how much of which. They are, in their amalgam, the qualities that characterize all supportive and nurturant relationships, natural or professional.

There are, however, some important differences between everyday natural relationships and those formed for the purpose of professional help to people. It is these to which we turn now.

A Professional Relationship Is Formed for a Recognized and Agreed-upon Purpose

The purpose of professional relationships is to enable a person (or group) to resolve or to cope in some more effective ways with some identified problem that is currently troubling or undermining his functioning and/or to enable him to utilize himself and resources to achieve a desired goal.

To say ''a recognized and agreed-upon purpose'' is to say that the help seeker and the helper together are clear with one another what it is the seeker needs, wants, and can reasonably expect to get; and, beyond this, that they come to some general understandings or a more or less formalized ''contract'' about what next steps may be anticipated and what may be involved for each of them.

The kinds of problems we in the human services encounter run the whole spectrum of human experience. The help that is asked for may be as plain and clear as the need for material means or services by which to carry on everyday living (money, medical and nursing care, child care arrangements, special tutoring are all examples). At the other end of that long continuum the help sought may be as complex as the easement of corrosive anxiety and incompetence in the daily interchange between oneself and other people or emotionally invested life tasks and the means by which to learn less destructive, more rewarding skills in self-to-other, self-to-object relationships.

At one end, then, the purpose may be achieved in a relatively short time and in a relatively uncomplicated (though always caring and careful!) relationship. At the other end, relationship may become a highly complex process, shot through with past as well as present emotional needs, potent in its effects upon the person's sense of self and his problems. Somewhere in between these two poles is where most of us work most of the time. What we must always be alert to, however (I risk repetitiveness because it is so important), is that because people's wants or needs often make them feel deeply, though in individually different ways, and because commonplace deficits (of money, of health, of education) are often those that most threaten our survival, there are very few problems that feel "simple" to the problem carrier. So the supportive, responsive qualities of relationship, even in a brief encounter, may have therapeutic value.

The "business" for which helper and client/patient meet is that of working together by discussion and/or provisions of means to deal with a designated problem or goal. They talk about the problem's nature, what it does to the person, how he sees it, feels it, understands it, connects it with himself (or not); about what he wants or would hope for; about what solutions or steps on the way to the goal seem to him and to the helper possible and feasible; about what his reactions are to these, too, since "solutions" often fall short of what we would wish. They explore such means and resources as may be used; they rehearse promising forms of behavior; they take stock of progress or failure; they consider alternatives and come to decisions on choices of action. Sometimes this is short-term, sometimes it is long-term business. But always it is a weaving of the facts of the situation across the loom threads of the person's sentience. Thus relationship grows between helper and the person being helped. Its purpose is not to meet all the love and attention hungers the person may bring with him. Rather, it is to provide the support and facilitation a person needs when he must make some changes and readaptations in himself and/or his circumstances in order to cope more satisfactorily with some part(s) of his here-and-now living.

A Professional Relationship Is Time Bound

Naturally so, if the purpose of a professional relationship is to enable a person to work on some specified problem. The relationship ends when that purpose has been met or has come as close to being met as the client's motivation (what he wants) and capacity (what he is able to do) and the helper's resources (his own ability combined with available services and aids) allow for.

That the enabling-facilitative relationship should end when the wanting-and-using service ends seems obvious. Yet it warrants some further attention on several counts.

When work with a client/patient has gone on over a long period of time, a sense of attachment develops. Some dependency elements play a part (on both sides, at times!), some comfortableness with a known and dependable source of support and understanding. There may be a temptation to prolong contact, to put off ending, especially when relationships in the client/patient's natural milieu tend to be unsupportive or even harsh. On the helper's side there is often the pull to stay with the responsive, appreciative client—it is so gratifying to be needed and wanted!

But why not? Why not continue to be giving to the relationship-hungry person? The most obvious reason is that work loads must be kept open for new cases, within the worker's realistic time limitations. And a second obvious one is that gratification of relationship needs, for all of us, must be sought and met in our natural environments.[4] It is to this end that a large part of counseling, guidance, and therapeutic help is given—to enable people to form and sustain fulfilling relationships with the persons and endeavors that are part of their everyday lives.

There is a powerful psychological reason for time limitations. It is something we all know. When we are aware of "what time it is," we tend to mobilize ourselves.[5] We hate and we want deadlines. The clock and calendar force us to pull ourselves together, to concentrate, to channel and pace our activities. Thus an awareness on the part of both helper and help seeker that there are time boundaries (to the single interview, to our next steps together, and, roughly, to how long or short a span we should count on for dealing with the problem) serves to keep us focused on the work we have to do. Relationship moves that work forward. It may be deeply meaningful to the client while at the same time it must remain realistically connected to the task at hand.

Many problems are self-limiting, and the service asked for may be given at once or over a few times. This recognition provides containment of the client's relationship investment and expectation. There are other problems so complex that only one part at a time can be dealt with, and still others that surface, unfold, and reveal complications as discussions between helper and client go forward. Time limits become more uncertain in these instances, and relationship between helper and client/patient may become complicated, too. Even here, however, the use of periodic stock-taking of planned stopping times—for purposes of taking inventory of where we are, where we have come from, where we are going from here—serves to hold the purposive problem-solving work as the clear and central reason for being together.

Ending a helping relationship occurs ideally when the problem for which help has been sought is resolved. It occurs less ideally but necessarily when stocktaking between helper and client results in agreement that they have come about as far as they can go together for this time, under these circumstances. And it occurs often when circumstances force it—as when the helper leaves the agency or is transferred to another service. (Of course, client/patients often determine their own ending times, sometimes precipitously, leaving unanswered questions of "why" or "what did I do wrong" in the unprepared helper's mind!)

Ending by plan should be a flexible "contract" subject to extension or contraction as both the nature of the problem and the client's motivations and capacities become manifest. And even if the agreement is for ending now, it should be made explicit that further help is available if and when it is needed.

Most important to the preservation of the person's sense of having some part in decisions that affect him, rather than being subject to those made by someone else, is his participation and preparation for ending. This is especially true if the relationship has been meaningful to him (even, one reminds oneself, if it has been shot through with ambivalence). He needs to be given the breathing space to pull back a bit, to express his reaction to the prospect, to talk it over. It is important because if indeed a sense of emotional bonding and even partial dependency has connected him with the helper, its breach may be felt as a betrayal.

"Every separation is a little death," some poet once said. Your client may put this in other terms—"I was afraid this would happen!"—"Just when I thought I could depend on somebody. . . ." Help him to say what he feels. Respond to it, understandingly. Help him to know, to take in why the ending—or transfer to another worker or place—is necessary. Sometimes he will need to deny that he cares for reasons of self-protection. (Look in the next section at Mrs. Green and her controlled "understanding." And at my "heartless" ending with her because I hadn't the heart to taste and bear my own guilt!) Even for the self-defending client it may help to know that it is only natural to feel discomfited (at the very least) by an unwanted change. In short, the binding threads of relationship should desirably be loosened, not sharply cut. You may feel genuinely sorry to leave him, too, and there is no need to deny this. So, even at ending, a feeling between us is shared.

One word of comfort on the always touching business of ending what has been a meaningful relationship. The client may harbor his helper within him for a long time after their working relationship has ended, just as we all carry within us feeling-laden images and memories of persons who, even briefly, took us into respectful and caring account. We carry many clients within us, too. Isn't this what we refer to when we say we have "learned from our clients"?—that we have incorporated some parts of the interchange experience with them that made an impress upon us, sometimes troubling to and sometimes fortifying our confidence?

A Professional Relationship Is for the Client

Does this also strike you as too self-evident to be given further space? But can you tolerate a few "ands" and "buts"?

Ordinary life relationships are expected to be for both parties. Each expects some gratification or reward from the other in reciprocation for what he gives—not in any calculated, carefully measured quid pro quo but on the whole. We tend to draw away from relationships that seem to demand great input and give little feedback. That may be our temptation in professional relationships, too—until we recognize and accept two things: first, that the very *need* for a giving relationship may be occasioned by the person's inability to form and maintain satisfying relationships in his natural life situation; and second, that when a human being is under great stress or deprivation the safety and care of self become paramount. Most of us must tend our own wounds before we can look to those of others. So we must be ready to accept that in many instances the giving of attention and responsiveness is mostly one way, from helper to help seeker.

The professional helper gets money compensation, of course. If he is compensated by gratification, too, by his sense of effectiveness and usefulness, or by his client/patient's verbal or behavioral responsiveness, it is heartwarming. That is all to the good. But his personal gratification is irrelevant to his purpose. If he is, as may often happen, annoyed or frustrated by the unresponsiveness or contrariness of his client, that is tough going. But it too is irrelevant. We cannot deny that spontaneous feeling for or against a client will affect our attitudes and actions in many subtle ways. But the recognition and self-reminder that the client is the one to be served, that *his* needs are to be met, not ours, helps keep our perspectives.

To be for the client means that his needs are held to be central. "Client centered" is the term Rogers gave to this commitment on the part of the helper. "Client advocacy" is the term which has become popular in social work over the past decade or so. "Advocacy" implies more than attentiveness and concern in the one-to-one interchange with the client. It includes intervention in the client's behalf in his environment by efforts to influence and modify not only those persons and circumstances that immediately impinge on him in unsatisfactory ways but also to include reforms or creation of necessary social programs and provisions. This widened concept deserves but can have no space here since it would take us off our course.

Yet "client centered" and "client advocacy" or even being "for" the client raise some relationship questions that cannot be ignored. One is, Who is your "client"? Another: Does client advocacy or client centered mean "my client, right or wrong"? Because surely becoming a client does not absolve a person of his "sins" or responsibilities?

To be "client centered" presents few problems when one's client voluntarily asks for help for a problem that lies largely within himself. Complications occur when the problem is one that in its cause or its cure involves other people, too. Family problems involve, always, several persons, each with his individual needs that are connected with those of others. It is only natural that spontaneous empathy on the helper's part may be for one member rather than another, but purpose will not be served by spontaneous relationship bonds, nor does a decision as to which individual's needs take priority always help. You are a mental health worker and you are *for* your client/patient, a postpsychotic young mother, recently released from hospitalization, who wants now to resume her former living arrangement that includes the return to her of her four-year-old little boy. I am the child welfare worker. I found a foster home for this once badly frightened and anxiety-ridden child. During his mother's six-month stay at the mental hospital he has relaxed, unfolded, and found secure pleasure in his foster home. You are for the mother; I am for the child. Who is "the" client?

Obviously you and I will have to put our heads together, and our hearts too. We will have to begin that process we call "cooperation," thinking, analyzing, weighing together, perhaps consulting with those whose greater expertise gives them greater predictive authority. But underlying all this must be our full recognition of two conditions. One is that "the" client is often a twosome or small group, bound together by an often unwillingly shared (though differently felt and reacted to) problem. The other is that the helper's purpose, whether with one or more clients, is to facilitate their coping with a mutually recognized, if multifaceted, problem. In that sense, we must be purpose and problem centered, not simply client centered. We are *for* them toward their better rather than worse resolution of the problem that entangles them both (or all). Thus the nurture and support we offer by our relationship are to make it possible to do what is often necessary in problems of interpersonal trans-actions: to make the compromise, conciliations, self-to-other adaptations that interdependency with other human beings so often requires.

That sounds too pat, and often it may not work. But it is set before you for chewing on at a time when concepts such as "client centered" and "self-realization" sometimes levitate our feelings but make us lose our footing.

Some of the same hard considerations hold for the client who is manifestly "in the wrong"—the child abuser, the bar-hopping mother, the unrepentant delinquent. Actually, these persons can scarcely be called "clients," since they are usually thrust upon the human service helper by coercion or threats of more severe measures against them. They themselves rarely want help or guidance. Yet they may badly need it because (again) they are harming others. Can one be "for" them?

Again, we must put clearly before ourselves—and them—the concern or purpose for which we are met. If they are to be at all engaged in making some changes in their behavior (whatever their motivation), we shall have to work with and through them. We shall have to remind ourselves that we are for them in the business of some lessening of the problem they help to create and that, while we do not condone their behavior, we are ready to lend ourselves to understanding them as persons and to support their potentials for change. (A later chapter will deal in more detail with this problem of relationship with the nonvoluntary, actively resistant "client.")

Back now to some remaining considerations in being for and with the client: A relationship that is for another person respects his rights to confidentiality. "The confidential professional relationship" has long been deeply valued by several helping professions, but only a few have had legal safeguards to support it. Once a basic foundation stone in the codes of professional ethics, it has of late been given little attention. It is interesting to speculate about the reasons. We live today in a "show-and-tell" society; in autobiographies, on television screens, at social and so-called therapeutic group gatherings there is an astonishing readiness to reveal and revel in all kinds of information about matters that were once considered to be strictly private; tape recorders are carried about as commonly as notebooks, and on and off they go, no permission asked. The right to privacy has become a cause when once it was taken for granted.

For quite other reasons, there has been within all human service agencies—hospitals, schools, clinics, social agencies, rehabilitation and residential centers of all sorts—a marked increase in collaborative work on individual cases. Teamwork, interdisciplinary staffings, consultations between two or more specialists or two or more helpers representing several different agencies—all this putting together of helping expertise and concerns serves many useful behind-the-scenes purposes for patients and clients. But they scarcely assure confidentiality.

What, then, can a helper who is part of a service organization honestly promise his client/patient by way of confidentiality? It is simply not true that "what you tell me is strictly between us." At the very least, he is likely to be discussed with one's supervisor or a colleague; the relevant information he supplies is to be recorded and transcribed; it will be available to a possible successor, and so forth. The helper can, however, promise his client and hold himself to the safeguards which follow.

That he will transmit no information to anyone except as it is to be *for* the client/patient, in his best interests, to further his problem-solving efforts. No sharing of funny or juicy bits of information at coffee-gossip times or elsewhere unless there is a scrupulous anonymity maintained—no names named, no occupational or other possible means of identification. More than this, the client/patient ought to be informed when it seems necessary for his case or problem to be talked over with other professionally responsible personnel, the reasons for it explained, and his agreement or consent asked for. (Of course, this holds only with clients who are able to comprehend and participate in such a discussion.) Certainly if nonprofessional persons are to be seen—members of the client's family or others who have some bearing on his problem—the client must be informed at the very least, the promise being made to him (and strictly observed) that nothing he has said or done will be revealed except as it bears upon help *for* him, in his best interests.

Such open and aboveboard methods are plainly practical. Trust and cooperation are not won when one party learns or suspects that things have been going on behind his back, without his informed consent; and often one cannot move forward with a new plan or new information without informing the client, belatedly, of efforts made in his behalf but without his knowledge. The helper's own integrity is involved, too. One cannot be genuine without acting genuinely. One cannot claim to respect the present rights and potentials of another person except as that respect is exemplified in every possible action. If you are for your client, you are for respecting his right to know and to choose in his own behalf whatever you can.

Exceptions: obviously one does not need to inform one's client every time a regular supervisory conference is to be held or another staff member is to be consulted. Somewhere along the way the client/patient needs to be informed (if he does not already know it) that you are not a free-lance helper who just happens to be occupying space in this agency or hospital; that you are part of a total organization; that the organization's protection of and responsibility to him, the client, is furthered by keeping a record of his problems and their course of treatment; and that you have other sources of knowledge and judgment to draw on when there is need for them. Not all at once, in a lump, of course, but as there is evidence of need for explanation.

A Professional Relationship Carries Authority

"Authority" is a word that makes us uncomfortable because we often assume it means authoritarianism—a dictatorial, bossy attitude of which we want no part. But before your hackles rise, consider what follows.

The essential condition that gives anyone the right to be designated a "professional," as different from a spontaneous, natural helper, is that he has some expertise about the problem and about how it may best be dealt with. Note the qualification "about the problem." It says not that the helper is in all ways and in all areas superior to the help seeker. Not at all. It says that he has experiential and theoretical knowledge about the kind of problem presented, that he has skill in assessing and dealing with it, and that he has access to existent means for its solution or amelioration.

His "authority," then, is that of knowledge and expertise. It is what any one of us wants when we seek out a counselor or physician or teacher or carpenter or dressmaker. We want someone who has power—which means "ableness." We want that ableness to be used *for* us, not *over* or *against* us. We want to retain our right to take, to reject, or to modify the expert's advice or guidance, and we want from him the assurance and demonstration that the power of choice ("self-determination") remains our own, that we will not be forced against our will or even "killed with kindness." With such confidence and reassurance we want to be "connected with," "related to" a person who has the authority of knowledge and ability to command resources.

Authority inevitably carries concomitant responsibility (authoritarianism does not). A major responsibility that accompanies the authority of knowledge is that of making judgments. That is, what one knows, by combination of theory and one's own and others' life and practice experience, enables one to anticipate certain sequelae of conditions or behaviors and to predict, roughly, what consequences might be expected from them. Thus any knowledgeable professional has the responsibility to assess whether given arrangements or actions are likely ("likely," not certainly) to produce better or worse outcomes, to be enabling or disabling, say, to a client/patient.

The authority of knowledge operates in several essential ways: it forces consciousness of why I think or feel what I think or feel; it helps thus to sort out one's purely personal preferences from preferences based on knowing and predicting (within human limits); and it requires of us that we take responsibility for sharing what we understand with our client/patient. That is what advice, guidance, counseling means: placing before a person who may be unknowing or confused or uncertain what his alternatives seem to be and what, in the helper's carefully weighed judgment, the probable outcomes may be, what better and what worse, which more and which less desirable. Placed before him is an "educated opinion," not in any sense a dictum, about which his reactions are encouraged, responded to, supported, or differed from.

Sometimes help seekers tend to impute more authority to the helper than he in fact holds. At times an applicant wants a flat formula, a piece of advice, an answer that will unlock his dilemma. In other instances he assumes that the helper has the right to dictate to him, the power to coerce or to punish him if he is not fully compliant. When these overblown or distrustful attitudes are discerned, it is useful to recognize them together with the client, clarifying not only by demonstrations of respect for his own capacities and rights but sometimes by direct discussion of his incorrect perception of what the helper can or cannot do.

The most difficult management of professional authority is that which actually does involve coercion.[6] It occurs usually when all noncoercive means have been tried and have failed. Thus a school social worker may have no recourse but to report a chronic truant to the juvenile court; a child welfare worker or a visiting nurse must report abusing parents to the police; a mental health worker or psychiatrist may have to commit a patient against his will; parole and probation officers are charged with reporting repeated or serious violations.

Coercion or the use of force feels mean on both sides of the transaction. In the helper (who now feels like the executioner) there is an uprush of emotional discomfort—mixed anger and frustration and anxiousness about whether he is doing "the right thing." Under such stress we tend to harden ourselves against feeling, and this is when cold and severe attitudes may emerge, in self-protection. Yet it would be inhuman to feel indifferent. For a helper's own mental hygiene—and its inevitable transmission to his erstwhile client/patient/parolee—it may be useful for him to remind himself that the coercive authority he must exercise is vested in the professional role he carries and in its legal sanctions and requisites. Anyone occupying his position would be charged with taking this same kind of unpleasant but necessary responsibility. To be clear about this makes it somewhat more possible to maintain objectivity and to be able to act toward the client with some compassion as well as conviction.

A Professional Relationship Is a Controlled Relationship

"Control" is another word that we recoil from. Quickly, then, it must be pointed out that control is not over the client or by the client. Rather, it is by the helper over himself and over his ways and means of helping. Control is in the interest of helping in the most effective and efficient ways. As used here, it is the antithesis of let it hang loose, come what may, "I'll fly by my gut feelings."

Control implies being tuned to one's own reactions and impulses and their management in the interests of the client and/or the business to be done. It implies that the helper conducts himself and the course of what he and the client do about the problem presented or the goal sought by knowledge (not just intuition), by responsible assessment not only of the problem and the ways and means for its solution but of the help seeker's own motivation and capacities. What is talked about, how it is talked about, what is done and how it is done, what attainable goals are put forth and agreed upon, what is required of each participant—all these matters of substance and method control the course and consequences of professional help. They are the helper's responsibility, not the help seeker's.

Perhaps the subject of self- and process control in a professional relationship needs no separate discussion since, as you can see, every one of the characteristics of professionally responsible relationships already discussed exercises control over both the what and how of helping. Certainly purpose controls content and method, time boundaries, client-centeredness, expertise about the problem and its implications, judgment of what is and is not possible, what is and is not desirable—all these shape, fuel, and guide the brief or extended journey we take together with each client. As always, however, the client should be regarded and involved to whatever feasible extent as partner, as decision maker. Sometimes the helper will propose and the seeker will dispose. That is his right: always the helper at a point of having to take charge ought to share the reasons for intervention in order to maintain community of understanding. "I'm going to ask you to hold what you're talking about now—if you can—because we've got to get back to [this or that priority consideration]"; "I'm about to ask you some questions that might seem funny to you, but I do it because . . . "; "I want to explain to you why we think this" (rather than that), and so forth. Not only do these courtesies of control facilitate ongoing communication; they also say to the client that he is seen as a participant, not just as a taker or refuser.

As every helper knows, there are circumstances that control us, to which helper and help seeker both are subject. Some of them inhere in the policies, regulations, and purposes of the organization we represent. Here, however, will be discussed only one area that often necessitates thoughtful management and control, one that is part of relationship. It is the phenomenon of transference and its counterpart, countertransference.[7]

What the terms "transference" and "countertransference" mean is essentially this: there is observable behavior that indicates that one person is not seeing the other as he actually is; the behavior seems inappropriate to what the realistic situation calls for. The indication is that the person's attitudes and reactions are being transferred from some past vital relationship (benign or malevolent) into the present one. It is as if the relater were seeing the other person through a set of lenses on which were pasted images of someone else in another time, place, circumstance. "Transference" refers to this not uncommon phenomenon when it comes from the help seeker. "Countertransference" is the same thing, except that it emanates from the helper.* The reason for our need to be aware of this distortion of perception in either ourselves or our clients is that as a man sees, so he acts. We behave in consonance with how we see and size up a situation.

So it is that a help seeker may be hostile toward you before you have said a word or made a move; that another may be excessively compliant despite the opportunities you offer him to express his opinions or choices freely, because he sees you perhaps in the image of a powerful parent who must be placated. On your side, you may find yourself drawn to or repelled by a person without being able to put a finger on the reason for it—"something about him," "some chemistry."

It is only when there is repeated evidence that feelings are interfering with or distorting the thinking and behavior of the help seeker (or helper) that one needs to take counsel with oneself (and/or one's supervisor or a trusted work mate) about whether something in the here-and-now helping transaction is causing this problem and can be differently managed, or whether reawakened needs and associations with bygone relationships are being infused into the client's (and/or helper's) reactions.

*These terms have been used by some clinicians to name all emotionally freighted relationship manifestations in a helping situation. When everything is identified as "transference," it seems to me, there is a loss of distinction that is of some importance in assessing how accurately and realistically a client perceives himself and his helper or how blurred his perceptions are by his unconscious associations. Therefore, I hold to this differentiation between intense relationship feelings that the reality situation arouses and that which is repetitive of some former relationship, that shows little awareness of the differences between then and now, or of the specificities of this present situation.

For the helper himself there has already been set forth the guiding principle for the control of self: admitting into your consciousness and accepting (maybe ruefully) your feelings; putting them firmly to one side as you conscientiously lend yourself to the client; and then, when you are alone (at last!)— or with a trusted friend, professional or other—examining what your feelings are, and why, and always whether their expression or playing out is likely to hurt or help the client in your joined purposes.

As for manifestations of transference in your client, they may be dealt with sometimes indirectly, sometimes directly. One of the surest means of avoiding or curtailing transference is to keep firm focus upon your purpose, upon the task at hand, the piece of the problem you and he are working to get solved or settled here and now. A reality-and-action-oriented approach holds the past at bay, so to speak, because concentration is upon the present. Alarms and excursions will occur. But with purpose clear the helper may control the skewing of vision or drift.

Transference is more likely to occur when the problem for which help is being asked is chiefly a psychological one, involving interpersonal difficulties. Almost by definition, the problem then is one of relationships—with the spouse or the children or the teacher as well as with the helper. The rise of associations between past and present needs, frustrations, or sought-for gratifications is almost inevitable. Sometimes, then, evidences of transference must be dealt with directly (but never accusingly, or blamefully, or teasingly). The helper's comments must show his acceptance of the naturalness and the understandability of the client's associations at the same time he places before the client some correction of vision. "But you are a very different person now from what you were then—a person with a lot more experience and a whole different life set"; "I think you're going to find that I'm not going to push you. What I want most to do is give you the backing to make up your own mind. And in your own time . . . ." Thus—gently, firmly, drawing the person back into this time and this place and *his* transaction.

Part II: A Bad Example

Out of a long ago past, I vividly recall an experience of my own that may serve to illustrate a number of the points in this chapter. It is a good example of a "bad" helping relationship. It was meant to be enabling, but it proved, instead, to be detrimental to my client's working out of her problem. I suppose I have the courage now to reveal my mistakes partly because it happened so long ago and far away and partly because I was not alone among the social caseworkers (and many other counselors) of that time in my ignorance of what a good working relationship entailed.

Mrs. Green was assigned to me when she came to the family agency complaining of her acute and growing dissatisfactions with her marriage. Married some eight years, the mother now of two little girls, five and three years old, she said that she was feeling more and more unhappy with her husband. In a veiled and oblique way she wondered about whether a woman who would leave her husband "for no good reason" would be awarded child support and whether she herself would be provided for, since her husband, a laborer in a scrap metal yard, was earning barely enough to meet their rent and food needs. I must have looked dubious. So what she went on to say, directly and openly, tremulously, tearfully, was that she didn't know what to do—things were getting worse for her. Maybe for him, too, though he wouldn't talk about it.

Now I must stop to explain the socioeconomic milieu in which this occurred. Try to ignore it as one may, there is no single one of us or of our client/patients whose little worlds are not deeply penetrated by the big world "out there."

The time was the early 1930s. That a woman with children should leave her husband for reasons other than acute physical abuse or physical and economic neglect was all but unheard of. Yes, it occurred among the wealthy, among those women who had independent incomes, or it occurred for reasons of "illicit" love; but it was not "done" or even countenanced by the traditional-minded, lower-middle-class woman or man. The strong conviction permeating the society, including its "helping arms" and including the great majority of its Mrs. Greens as well, was that the family was to be kept together at all costs. Toward that end, there had been the establishment and support of family agencies which could help couples work out their marital problems: reconciling; compromising; coming to better understandings, agreements, and behavior; or, at worst, settling for patient endurance.

It was, further, the time of the Great Depression. Employment opportunities for women, limited as they always had been, were all but nonexistent. Also nonexistent were child care facilities for a mother who chose to work. Also public or private means of financial support over any protracted time period, and even in short-term or emergency situations money grants were available only for those who had no other possible resources. So much for the external (but always internalized) social situation that constricted and complicated Mrs. Green's situation and the helping possibilities, too.

Mrs. Green poured out the details of her unhappiness. In a nutshell: her husband was a "good man"—he did not drink or gamble or run around with other women; he worked "like a slave" and turned all of his meager pay over to her. But they had "no kind of marriage." He came home dirty and tired; he ate silently, "like an animal"—not even changing his filthy work clothes. He fell heavily asleep right after supper. Since sexual dysfunction had not yet become a topic for a gentlewoman's discussion, she touched upon and left the information that she had for several years discouraged sex relations, afraid of pregnancy but also repelled by her husband's uncouthness and by the fact that even in the kitchen and the parlor they were increasingly "strangers." No, she had not told her husband she was coming to the agency. She did not want to do that because he believed people should keep their troubles to themselves; he would get furious, and things would be even worse.

It took no effort to relate to Mrs. Green. She was attractive, intelligent, open, able to express herself, hungry for attention, quick to understand and respond to comments and questions.

Her distress, her wish to be "fair" along with her wish to be free, and her sense of being trapped would have evoked immediate compassion in almost anyone. An emotional bond of understanding leaped and shuttled swiftly between us. I could feel with her and for her deeply and readily, and I was genuinely concerned with helping her in whatever way I could.

"In whatever way I could." I was ready and able to be supportive, caring, responsive; she was eager to talk and be listened to responsively. But what was our purpose together to be?—what did she want or expect of us? Help to leave her husband? Help to remain with him in the status quo? Help to remain with him only if some changes could be brought about in both of them, in their interactions with and expectations of one another? We somehow never really grappled with this question of her hope and purpose—and thus we did not come to an understanding of what work we had to do together.

Instead, there was a tacit assumption on my part—an assumption that was bulwarked by some common theoretical misapprehensions of psychodynamic theory (again characteristic of that period) that if a person was helped to ventilate and explore his feelings, released from their constraints, sustained in a "parenting" relationship, he would come to some better understanding of himself and his situation and thus would be better equipped to cope. Patterning our method on the individual interview of the psychoanalyst, we had lost sight of the fact that in a marriage problem (as different from some intrapsychic malaise in one person) an exchange relationship between two people is continuously in action. It does not stand still, waiting for resolution of the conflict in one of the parties.

Mrs. Green came regularly for her weekly appointment. She came eager to tell about what had happened during the week, details of "what I said" and "what he did." She was tearful at times as she recalled the conditions that had driven her prematurely into marriage and as she picked over her disappointments. Occasionally she expressed pity for her husband, about how hard his life had been, how shy but "nice" he had seemed during their courtship, how he probably saw no future ahead for himself.

I listened responsively, and I encouraged her to believe what I then believed: that once she had talked out all sides of her feelings it would all come together somehow, and she would know how she "really" felt and what she "really" wanted to do.

Mrs. Green would leave our interviews reluctantly, always needing "a few more minutes" to finish. She would express her clinging gratitude for how much better she felt after talking to me, and I would feel a reciprocal glow of gladness at having been "helpful." Several times she had said, "You are like the sister I always wanted." Her loving dependency warmly filled my need to be needed.

Then one day I had a sudden, soul-shaking illumination. It struck me—I cannot remember how or why—that Mrs. Green and I were going nowhere together. Our relationship, I saw, had become the be-all and end-all. By my being all giving, all accepting, all understanding, I was driving a wide wedge between Mrs. Green and her husband. She had less and less need of him as companion, friend—or even as an enemy. She had begun to ignore rather than to quarrel with or coax him, substituting a kind of relished saving up of details that she could safely and gratifyingly deposit in our weekly hour (or its frequent runover) together. The comfort and support she invariably had from me was acting as an opiate for her rather than as a stimulation and underpinning to the necessary problem-solving work we had to do if some resolution of her difficulties was to be arrived at. I was "helping" Mrs. Green to need her marriage less, but what was to be her consciously chosen substitute? Me or my reasonable facsimile?

What was clearly missing were those controls of the helping process that inhere in the characteristics of a professionally able and responsible relationship. To look now at what happened with Mrs. Green within that framework—

On relationship itself first: transference and countertransference ran rampant. Not only did each of us in some way meet personal needs of one another, but my lack of knowledge about relationship left me unaware of what was occurring. I *was* cognizant of what was then believed to be true—that people would "grow" if they were sufficiently nurtured by love and caring. The conclusion was that if you "grew" you would know what to do. But all common sense and common experience reveals that to be a fallacy. It is possible to be quite mature psychologically and still to be in conflict, upset, or lacking in know-how about the ways and means by which some stressful problem can be dealt with.* Overall, the helping relationship was seen as not only a necessary but a sufficient condition for problem solving rather than as enabling and promoting that process.

Had our purpose together, Mrs. Green's and mine, been clarified, specified, agreed upon step by step, and had we repeatedly taken stock of how we might get to it, these in themselves would have exercised a deterrent to transferences and to our loss of direction.

At application, Mrs. Green had said that she did not know what to do about her marriage, in which she was increasingly miserable. "Tell me about it," I must have said, in effect. Thus she was launched, quite appropriately. But beyond "telling about," purpose must include considerations of what the person wants as a solution, and this must be examined carefully in the light of whether such a solution is possible and feasible and what it would involve by way of change, sacrifice, or compromise, what other problems it would create. Ambivalences must be carefully explored and assessed for how the weights of wanting and not wanting balance out. Possible consequences of one versus another decision must be thought over together. And so forth. What such discussions involve is far more than recounting and rumination. They involve the hard work of facing and clarifying one's feelings and thoughts and behaviors and, not the least, what the realistic possibilities are in dealing with the problem. Few problems are "solved" in real life; many are

---

*Chapter 6, "Myths and Misconceptions," deals with this "growth" goal further, since that goal persists in the beliefs of some clinical practitioners to the present day.

ameliorated, lessened in intensity, made more bearable by small changes in the circumstances, attitudes, and feelings of the involved persons or by learned behaviors that bring rewarding results. In such work, supported by the caring encouragements of relationship, the current reality can rarely be lost sight of. Between Mrs. Green and me, however, purpose and feasible nearby goals remained amorphous.

"Time boundaries," as noted earlier, are another control within a professional relationship. Mrs. Green almost always ran over her time. She had so much she needed to say! (And her caseworker found her so interesting!) But quite aside from its being a kind of two-sided dependency, the failure to set time limits may have contributed to Mrs. Green's failure to use the time given her to the fullest. More problematic, however, was the unspoken assumption that our interviews would go on until—when? Until everything came out all right? Until the client got tired of coming?

Failure on the helper's part (do I use the third person to make myself more comfortable, I wonder?) to control the helping process may be seen in yet another instance. Even way back then, social workers knew that marriage is a two-person role transaction, that while each of the two persons may be quite all right in himself or herself, their interchanges may still be fraught with conflict. So even in that dark age it was customary for us to "see" the husband (it was usually the wife who was the complainant) for the purpose of getting his side of the story and to try to engage him in "cooperating," if not regularly participating in the treatment.

Mrs. Green did not want her husband to be contacted. Her reason had some validity, enough (I then thought) to qualify as an expression of her "self-determination." What I did not then grasp was that self-determination is rather different from a decision made on impulse or on insufficient consideration of the consequences of one's choice. The responsibility should have been mine, based on knowing what tends to work best in situations such as the one under attention: to open up Mrs. Green's decision for our joint examination, to raise questions about whether her husband would change in any way simply because she was discussing their troubles, to ask whether she might, perhaps rightly, be seeing herself as the person to help him, and whether then she would not fairly soon need to share with him the fact of her coming to the agency, and—or—but. Mrs. Green would still have had the right to reject the suggestion. But had I been more sure and knowledgeable about the most favorable conditions for dealing with marital disharmony, I might have placed the inclusion of Mr. Green as one condition of our going on. It would not have been pitting my will against hers but, rather, setting a condition that professional knowledge strongly suggested was desirable.

In sum: all the heartfelt qualities of relationship were present between Mrs. Green and me. But the particular qualities that give focus and direction and form and reality orientation to a professional relationship, that differentiate it from natural relationships—these were missing or skewed.

There are more sins of omission and commission that any discerning eye can pick out in this example—but perhaps this much of a postmortem has gone far enough.* One is struck all over again with how relationship affects the problem-solving process and how that, in turn, shapes and guides relationship.

---

*Must I tell how it came out? Badly. My illuminating insight so shook me that I felt I had bungled beyond any possibility of retrieval. I pleaded with my supervisor to let me transfer the case, especially since I was planning to leave the agency soon to go to school, and it was too late to start over. She agreed—whether out of compassion for me or Mrs. Green I do not know. At our next interview I told Mrs. Green I would probably be leaving soon, and I would like to introduce her to her next worker. She was shocked but quietly understanding. But she never returned to the agency. I have often wished I could tell Mrs. Green how sorry I am and also that I could thank her for all she unwittingly taught me. It was my experience with her that gave the final thrust to my decision to undertake graduate professional education. "Someone," I thought, "surely someone knows and will be able to teach me what to *do* with relationship." Which turned out to be true.

Part III: Effects of the Helping Relationship

To this point it has been repeatedly asserted that "good" working relationships have "good" effects upon the people we work with. It is an assertion based chiefly upon the common human experiences we have had and remember, upon clinical observations of unnumbered instances, and, more recently, on some affirming research.[8]

As usual, one needs only to recall the Delphic oracle's counsel to all men who came for guidance: "Know thyself." To know oneself is to know in the main what may be a common human experience; and the answers to the questions about how and why relationship "works" may, as has been said, be found in one's own experiences.

In most present-day lives our many touch-and-go contacts (they may barely warrant the word "relationship") add up or multiply until at the end of any day one may feel either alienated from one's fellowmen or comfortably at one with them. When life is unsatisfying or harsh in some ways and one feels particular vulnerability or need, even a small input of attention or a small brush-off takes on a blown-up significance. Perhaps this needs no further development; the sometimes indiscriminate reach out for a touch of humanness may be seen any day on buses, in waiting rooms, on park benches, everywhere.

When confronted by a problem that we cannot resolve on our own because we lack the inner or outer resources, we turn to another human being for help. In fantasy any one of us might wish for some instant solution—a machine to deliver the rent, an incantation that would raise the dead, a magic potion that would cure, a push button that would reform one's child. But in reality it is almost always another human being through whom we must get what we want or find our way toward it. It is when that other person is "human"—which is to say, when he connects with our feelings—that we ourselves feel "humanized"—which is to say that we respond with a sense of relatedness, of interdependency, of being both gratified and obliged.

Permeating and complicating the actual problems people bring to helpers are these common feelings present in large or small degree: fear, anxiety, and insecurity (about ill health, about loss of income, about threatened changes); anger or guilt that "this should have happened to me"; the sense (frequent among the long disadvantaged and minority or immigrant persons) of being viewed as inferiors and treated as social pariahs; panic (in crisis situations) at the loss of sources of support, affectional and role security; despair (in chronic situations) at one's hopelessness and helplessness; exhaustion of energies (psychic and physical) because of excessive and extensive stress; the sense of being "dumb" and "to blame" or of having been shortchanged and put-upon; dependency pulls and dependency fears.

The beginning and steadfast attitude on the part of a helper that says, "I see you, hear you, accept you as you present yourself" may be variously read and responded to. For many applicants it dispels their sense of anonymity and supports their sense of being somebody worth another's notice. The attentiveness and empathic responses to the help seeker's presentation conveys the sense that "I feel with you; I want to understand how it is for you; I am concerned to be of help to you." The message received from these responses is that this someone is with me, maybe for me, seems to care about how I feel, not just the trouble I'm in, gets what it's like for me. I am not blamed. And this from a person who is a "somebody" (at least he's got a job as a somebody—he "represents" this hospital, this center, this agency). Maybe I'm not so bad—far out—crazy—dumb—unlikable as I thought they'd think?

In short, surely not all at once but bit by bit, over one or more contacts the help seeker begins to see himself in the mirror of the eyes of the helper, and some rise of self-tolerance and even self-esteem is experienced. If I am loved (cared about) maybe it's because I am lovable (worth someone's caring).

Simultaneously the conveyed idea that "I am with you" is felt as a safety bond, the first floorboards of security. When, as is necessary in many cases, it is accompanied by the provision of a needed service, the tangible meeting of some deficit, the sense of being cared about and being supported both psychologically and materially is considerably strengthened.

Simultaneously, too, some subtler effects seem to take place. The helper's receptivity and in-tune responses to the other's feelings creates an increased sense of bonding, of being connected to someone who is for me and who, more importantly, has the power and means to make things actually better. Hope rises, in proportion, of course, to the helper's realistic provisions or proposals about what might be done to deal with the problem. Hope is caught from the helper, is like a lifeline. It buoys the spirit and restores energy. Psychic energy is fiercely consumed and all but extinguished when it must be used in the continuous erection, maintenance, and repair of defenses against hurt and anxiety. When such defenses become less necessary because one is secured and allied with a source of actual or even promised problem-solving help, one's energies are freed to be invested elsewhere—desirably in tackling some part of the problem.

Again we revert to our common human experience that, when one feels cared about, attended to, accepted, helped by such means or kinds of guidance that seem workable, we feel nurtured. When we say of someone, "she has given me a lot," we do not refer to material gifts. Rather, we refer to the giving of interested caring, plus the stimulation and opportunity to feel, know, and try ourselves in new and gratifying ways, and stimulation by the input of ideas, suggestions, advice, when they have been proffered with warmth and respect for our particular mood and makeup.

No one can give out of emptiness. One of the most commonplace and troubling problems that nurses, teachers, social workers encounter is that of mothers (and fathers, too) who seem literally unable to give to their children, unable to extend caring beyond feeding, clothing, and perhaps punishing them for misbehavior. They are usually parents who have known little of loving in their own childhoods and whose current lives hold few if any sources of affectional support or dependable relationships. They neglect and sometimes abuse their children. Reason, coax, advise, scold as one is tempted to do, the fact is they cannot give what they do not have.

Those helpers who have learned to work with them (in the interests of the children) find that they can do so with moderate success only when they consistently give attention and care to the mother's own childlike needs (it is usually she who is dealt with). Often it takes a very long time before the mother can believe that she is respected or felt with. By that human phenomenon that causes us to see ourselves as others see us,* she may long ago have taken into herself a conviction that she is "no good." Yet, by that same dynamism, she may in small part begin to be able to take in, from someone with whom she can feel a supportive bond, some different valuation of herself.

Mrs. Olive offers a miniature illustration. She was a woman of good intelligence who was in mortal combat with her three-year-old Timmy. He was "fighting" toilet training, was "unreasonably stubborn," "deliberately disobedient," hitting and kicking not only her but any neighborhood child who crossed him. As Mrs. Olive detailed her problems and her handling of the child, the caseworker could only feel with Timmy. It was clear that Mrs. Olive was overdemanding, compulsive, overly severe in her punishments. (Later it was learned that she herself had been overly "trained" by an all but psychotic mother and that her present relationship with her husband was at the breaking point.)

Disciplining herself by her beginning understanding of Mrs. Olive's needs, the helper carefully put aside her spontaneous compassionate and protective feelings for the little boy and turned her concern to the mother herself. She drew out how hard the past few years had been for Mrs. Olive; how she had hoped a baby would cement a crumbling marriage, but it had only widened the rift between herself and her husband; how he stayed on the road (as a salesman) as much as he could, leaving her lonely and hemmed in—and so on. To all of which the

*Robert Burns to the contrary, we *do* "see ourselves as others see us," both in our formative years and those moments when our self-assurance is shaken and we look to others for psychological or material supports.

helper was accepting and responsive. At the end of this first interview, Mrs. Olive sighed deeply and said, "Maybe all this has been hard on Timmy, too. I never thought of that." Having been given to, she was able momentarily at least to look outward to her child. It could be hoped that with ongoing nurture she would in turn be more able and willing to nurture rather than manipulate him.

Subsequently, in the midst of the second interview Mrs. Olive suddenly stopped in her recital of "proofs" of Timmy's intransigence and said, challengingly, "How come you're not telling me what to do? Everybody gives me advice."

"Has it worked?"

"Not much. Nothing's worked."

"Now that's how I'm going to be different," said the caseworker. "Between us we're going to try to figure out what'll work best for *you. You* are Timmy's mother, not I. You can't just take on what somebody else tells you. I think you've got to see your own way. . . ." The caseworker records, "Tears welled up in Mrs. Olive's eyes."

One sees the helper affirming the mother's own authority and her potential and relating consistently to *her* (though always in her role as mother). Why the tears? One can only guess. Perhaps because she was swept by feelings of helplessness? Or perhaps because she was touched, moved (thus movable, teachable) by the helper's staunch support of her?

Many people ask for advice; few take it.* One probable reason is that when "advice" is asked for, what is usually hoped for is a magic formula, and life holds few of these. Another reason is that a very wide chasm may exist between wanting-getting advice and taking-using it. When a person trusts his helper, when he feels the helper's genuine concern for him, he is far more likely at least to consider the advice given, to turn it over in his mind, even to try to carry it out. Recent studies of doctor-patient relationships indicate that patients are more

*Josh Billings (one of America's nineteenth-century humorists) was a wise funny man when he said, "When someone asks me for advice, I find out what advice they want, and I give it to them."

likely to follow the directions of doctors who seem to be concerned about them.[9] That likelihood must hold for other helping situations, too. There inheres in any good relationship a safeguard against obliterating the person. Too often advice says, in effect, "If *I* were you, I'd do so-and-so." But you are not I. The relationship-governed approach says, "Since you are *you*, what's your reaction to doing so-and-so?" Good working relationships, even if brief, require that the helper respect the individuality (that is, the wishes, attitudes, capacities, readiness) of the help seeker. At times direct advice may be essential. It will most likely be used if the help giver and help seeker trust and feel allied with one another.

The usefulness of relationship is most clearly seen in situations that involve ongoing transactions between a help giver and a seeker over a period of some weeks or months. Nurses, physicians, psychiatrists, teachers (from nursery school up), social workers (whether in a family and children's agency or in the many kinds of host agencies where social work is used), physical therapists—all such helpers may carry some cases that take prolonged sustaining and/or problem-solving time. There may be regular weekly appointments, or daily contacts, or coming together on call. What facilitates tackling the problematic task is the help needer's sense of a dependable "thereness" of relationship.

Relationship over an extended time may have a number of dynamic effects beyond the sense of backup, and hope, and support. A most important one is that in several ways it provides a climate that both supports and stimulates learning—relearning, unlearning, and new learning, one or all of them.

What may need to be learned may vary from something as limited as how to tend an infant or a wheelchair patient to something as totally involving of the whole self as how to manage and change attitudes, feelings, and behaviors in order to improve one's functioning in transaction with other people or one's daily life tasks.

All new learning involves risk. It requires some change in us, some shifting about of comfortable assumptions or set habits; it means moving from the known to the unfamiliar, and, as all of us know, it often feels easier to stay with a known "bad" than to hazard an uncertain "good." A relationship formed for the purpose of helping a "learner" provides a safety island, a place and person with whom one can risk making mistakes without fear of ridicule or censure, where corrections and directions are given with concern for the person's own individual pace and capacity, where glad recognition is given for trying, even if the effort falls short of the intent. Again we need only to think about our own best learning, whether of school subjects or of how to carry new roles, to recognize that we felt most free, most ready to learn, when we felt allied with our teacher (and wanted what he had to give, of course), when we felt safe with him, and when he showed that he appreciated both our tribulations and our small steps of accomplishment. Relationship warms and energizes the spirit; it is as if both steadiness and forward thrust are borrowed from the helper with the knowledge that if one falls back he will be received and supported.*

Learning seems to occur in several ways. For the person who is

---

*Just at this writing I talked with a friend who is a seasoned reading therapist. She works with children in whom some neurological deficit or twist has created reading difficulties. Which among the many techniques she uses, I asked, contributes most to the child's learning to read? "First," she said, "before techniques: I let the child know that I'm here for him, just us two. I let him know that most kids with his problem have had a rough time and that I've got some idea of how hard school has been for him—maybe home, too. I get him to tell me about how that's been—what his parents have said and done, how he's reacted, what he's figured to do—and where he thinks I come in. I tell him I've been able to help a lot of other kids with his same sort of trouble. Lots of times these kids have been teased by their classmates and treated with a lot of sympathy but also with despair by their teachers. Or their parents have drilled them mercilessly or have been very anxious. So they come full up with feelings of being dumb and hopeless, afraid to expose their usual mistakes.... I try to help them know I understand all that. Then I show them some of the easy stuff we'll begin with—we sort of play at it—they're already sensing that they don't need to be afraid of me...." She then went on to tell me of some of the ingenious techniques that reading therapists have worked out. But underpinning it all, it was clear, was her support and concern for the troubled child-person who needed to relearn but whose earlier learning experiences had shaken his confidence or made him afraid, who needed, therefore, an accepting, understanding climate in order to be able to use the available technical aids.

fairly confident of his capacities and motivated by interest or some goal to be achieved, the task of taking in and digesting new information, ideas, skills is consciously tackled and mastered. For learning that is chiefly above the eyebrows, relationship may be a secondary consideration. Yet every one of us can remember a teacher who turned us off (along with our interest and grasp of the subject matter) or turned us on, to our heightened pleasure and strengthened resolve.

In the helping professions much of the learning our client/patient/pupil must do involves more than his mind. It must start in the heart or spirit—in his wanting to learn and then willing it, and then it must connect with him above the eyebrows, which is to say, with his perception, grasp, memory, mental strategies by which the interior activity we call thought takes place. To feel at one with, liking and liked by, identified with someone who cares and "knows," is the connective tissue that relationship weaves.

One form of learning occurs in all of us unconsciously, by introjection. Its dynamics are again those of relationship, such relationships as have been intensely significant in their combination of love and power. It is a kind of incorporation of aspects of the other, of values, attitudes, behaviors, even personal styles of speech and body language. "Introjection" is a rather steely sounding term, but it can be described as a kind of taking in, as if through the pores. We know it chiefly as we perceive in ourselves (and in others) certain attitudes and reactions and forms of behavior that are "just like" those of other persons to whom there has been felt deep attachment. Learning by introjection occurs chiefly when we are young, when we are most impressionable and malleable. Yet in the lives of most of us there are what Havighurst once called "teachable moments," those times when by some unusual event, traumatic or joyous, our usual equilibrium is shaken, our sensitivities are honed and heightened, and we are as if opened up to taking in another. People who come to helpers often feel themselves at a crucial point and thus ready to take in, to introject a person who demonstrates caring and the power of competence in regard to the problem.

More common in helping situations, however, is learning by conscious model watching or half-conscious incorporations of behavior modes and perspectives. Its reliance on relationship is plain to be seen. Admiration, attachment, belief in another's powers, the wish to *be* like the other are the motivators for taking in or taking on certain attributes or behaviors from him. Said a client, when recounting a set-to she had had with the principal of her son's school, "So when he told me he was going to kick Larry out, I thought, 'Oh yeah?'—but then I thought, 'I wonder what Mrs. P. would say to him.'" So she tried conciliation. It was only mildly successful, alas! But my expressed admiration of her newfound ability to hold her horses and to use a new approach puffed her with self-pride and the determination to try further.

Reinforcing the imitation of an admired, respected, or loved other is the reward of the helper's appreciation or approval of the learner's effort. Whether that try was successful or not, this appreciative recognition encourages further effort. It goes without saying, of course, that the most gratifying reward is the taste of actual success. When what we have tried to do actually works, we claim it with satisfaction as our "own."

At times the helper may actually set up a modeling situation.[10] It is important not only to "show how" something might be done or said or even thought about, not only to rehearse the person himself in anticipatory role-play ("So what if he says . . . ," and so on) but to take it one step beyond. That step is to help the client figure out, to become conscious of, to put into some guiding rule form the *reason why* this kind of action is likely to work better than the other. It is, in short, when heart and head get connected, when a person gets hold of the governing idea, that he may be enabled to transfer what he has learned from one instance to another.

Learning to act differently is learning to *be* different in at least some respects. Self-examination, self-evaluation, self-correction, and self-control is heavy-weather work for anyone. The sense of being "stood under" and understood, accepted, cared about despite one's foibles and failures is basic to the risk and discomfort involved in the work of changing and learning.

This is a tempting ending place. But it would not be quite honest. Because the benign effects of relationship are experienced by those who are able to relate, those who can take in and use the nourishment given by another, who can respond to the evidence that a helping person cares about them.

It takes two to relate. So for all the guiding principles and adjurations that are set down and are then taken up and worked at by a conscientious, caring helper, he may have failures in making and maintaining emotional connections between himself and this or that person or group he seeks to help. You may express warmth, empathy, concern—and all the other desirable relationship qualities—but the one who is to be helped may neither see it nor feel it. Or he may see and feel it almost too acutely and have internal reasons to fear and distrust what he discerns. Or he may seem flat or shallow emotionally, with responses quite inadequate to what you proffer.

At once it must be said that his lack of responsiveness may be due to situationally induced factors. Crises and certain current circumstances may misshape or dull any person's usually adequate relating to another. Excessive stress, intense conflict, sudden shock—these and other conditions of emotional upset or drain may, in any one of us, cause temporary psychological deafness or blindness. Even small, unpleasant experiences on the way to the helper (being kept waiting too long, being passed along like a number instead of recognized as a person) or anxiety-producing anticipations of what will be involved in asking for and getting help, based perhaps upon hearsay or transferred from some past similar experience, may all rouse defensive, self-protective attitudes that temporarily block out awareness of the helper's empathy and attention. (Such difficulties will be dealt with in greater detail in a later chapter.)

More troubling than these temporary relationship obstacles are those that are ingrained in the personality. Many adults and youngsters, too, bring to any interpersonal interchange, including that of seeking help, an ingrained "distancing." They are

people whose earlier and consistent life experiences have been
something like this:

They have been affectionally starved by parents who neglected
or actually rejected and hurt them. They have grown poorly
nurtured in a desolate landscape and harsh climate. They feel
unloved—and thus unlovable. You might be led to expect,
then, that they would be like open, empty vessels, eager to take
in any love or caring poured into them. But nature abhors a
vacuum, whether physical or psychological, and what seems to
occur is that self-protective defenses fill up that emptiness—
defenses of distrust of others, of pervasive doubt about themselves, of guarding against the anxiety that if they give out they
will somehow be cut down again. They have been under- and
malnourished psychologically. When there has been physical
under- or noxious nourishment its effects are clear to be seen.
Psychological mal- or undernurture is just as real, but it is more
subtle, not so easily detected. When persons who have been
emotionally starved or malnourished have adequate intellectual
endowment, they often learn and act out the conventional ways
of relating to others. But there is no body or depth to their
feeling. Many of them may spend an unhappily puzzled lifetime trying to find out "what love is all about." Sometimes
they seek professional counseling or therapy. Sometimes they
can use it fruitfully; sometimes they cannot stomach what they
both want and fear.

Among such persons you will even find little children who
need but fear love.* They may walk a wide circle around an
outreaching adult, watching warily for signs of safety or danger.
They may freeze at an approach that is "warm" because it feels

*For those human service helpers whose chief interest is "prevention,"
there is no seedbed more germinative of interpersonal problems and none
more potentially productive of interpersonal compatibilities and competences
than that of relationships between parents and their young children. Family-
life education, parent counseling, provision of substitute protection, and child
care arrangements are among the socially organized human services that seek
both to ameliorate the child's present-day miseries and to prevent personality
malformation.

too potentially threatening to their brittle defenses of self-"sufficiency." Or they may be indiscriminately affectionate, going from one adult to another to be petted and stroked, but you will notice that it is a shallow, only skin-deep gratification they seem to get.[11]

In the course of your work you will encounter schizoid adults whose senses and perceptions, more fantasy shaped than real, may require a helper's unobtrusive, patient presence over a long time before they can open even a chink in their defensive armor to let him in. You will also find those who are called "sociopathic" or suffering from "psychopathic character disorders." Whatever the label, they are people who have learned self-protection plus self-promotion by manipulating other people (having been themselves manipulated in their tender years), by using, conning, getting the jump on others. Delinquents are among them. Their feeling (if they know it at all) is that they owe nothing to anyone; they trust no one; they were victimized, thus they will victimize. Their capacity for a trusting relationship is expectably minimal.

Just this much, to caution the helper who has given fully of his caring and empathy that he may not always be able to call forth the responses he expects—to caution him—and also perhaps help him retain his confidence. There are all too many confidence-shaking moments in the working day of any one of us who deal with people in trouble. We do not need the undermining of confidence that is the result of expectations of people based more upon our idealizations or misconceptions than upon our knowledgeable appraisal. Moreover, the disappointment in ourselves when, despite all our efforts, the person to be helped cannot seem to relate may, in our all too human need to protect ourselves, be transformed into rejection of the disappointing client/patient or of his whole "type." Quite unconsciously we may turn away from him or from considering alternative—perhaps less satisfactory but more feasible—ways in which to deal with his problem.

What seasoned helpers have long known experientially has in recent years been validated in a number of studies: that "the patient's capacity for interpersonal and object relationships is significantly predictive of therapeutic outcome."[12] But here again we remind ourselves that most human service personnel are not engaged in "therapy" and that even when the help seeker's relationship capacities are limited, there may be many ways in which his life circumstances and his basic functional capacities still may be improved.

Those signs by which capacity for "good" or at least adequate relationship (adequate, that is, to the problem to be worked on) is detected are readily recognized. Roughly: the person shows, by what he says, by his responsive reactions, that he is taking in the helper; that he sees and hears him. His initial reserve (appropriate in a new situation) begins to be lowered as he perceives that he is being given an attentive and responsive hearing, that the questions asked of him rise out of concern to understand his problem. He gets and connects with the helper's empathy, and he responds with some further deposit of his feelings in the worker. He seems relieved, to some degree, by his sense that he is developing an alliance, a burden-sharing agreement, with an interested and apparently competent helper. Taken just this far, one sees the essential trust, reciprocal responsiveness, and the balances between self and other, between mind and feeling that mark the beginnings of sound and appropriate relationships.[13]

Wistfully, we dream of client/pupil/patients who are bright, articulate, motivated, trusting, eager for our help. And then we roll up our sleeves and resolutely go to work with the whole range of people we encounter, keeping ourselves alert and responsive to both their limitations and whatever coping powers they have that may be strengthened, not toward "cure" but toward "better" rather than "worse"; and always with respect and caring for the potential humanness in even the least of them.

4
But Can You Love Everybody?

BUT. Is it possible, actually, to respect and care genuinely for everybody? For every one of the different human beings who present themselves (or are presented) for help? Is it possible to "love" all one's clients or patients? Are there not some (dare one say it?) who by their appearance, their attitudes, their actions turn off the usual wellsprings of sympathy or liking and caring?

These are uncomfortable questions that have been side-stepped and/or unattended to by those who have written on relationship. This lack of attention has several explanations. One is that much of the writing on relationship has come from those helpers whose clients or patients have been fairly easy to empathize with and feel akin to. They have reached out for help voluntarily. As has been said, they know and feel their problem, and they want their hurt to be erased or eased. They have had considerable faith in the helper's healing or change-producing powers along with some hope and trust that he will be *for* them and *with* them.

It is not hard to like and to care genuinely for such applicants for help. Their felt and recognized suffering excites spontaneous responsiveness; their wanting help bespeaks goal-directed motivation, their belief and trust (fluctuating though it may be) is the very yeast ferment for relationship, needing only the responsive demonstrated evidence that the helper is indeed competent and trustworthy. These are "ideal" client/patients. Happily

in many human welfare agencies—social, clinical, educational—
they are numerous. True, there are differences among them,
too, enough to make for differences in the genuineness and
consistency of the helper's warmth, empathy, caring; but on
the whole they want, seek, and try to use the help proffered
them.

A more subtle reason underlies our ignoring of the "unlik-
ables." It is our own discomfort at finding ourselves lacking,
somehow, in the virtues we value and are supposed to have.
Those of us who choose to be people helpers carry within us,
implanted long ago by parents or teachers or friends who have
significantly influenced us and developed as part of us, ideas
and ideals about "loving people," about "brotherly love,"
about the intrinsic worth of every human being. Social workers,
doctors, psychologists, teachers of all kinds are "supposed" to
be warm, empathic, caring about each and all of the people who
need their help.

And then they encounter the person who looks and smells
dirty; the person who, without apparent cause, vibrates with
open hostility and suspicion; the person who looks one straight
in the eye and tells blatant lies; the person who sits sullen and
silent; the surly man who has beaten his baby into unconscious-
ness; the bedraggled woman who locked in her three hungry
children while she sat at a neighborhood bar. Can one genuinely care for such persons? We face this question uneasily, even
guiltily. "Thus conscience doth make cowards of us all," and
we dodge answering it by all the small defenses by which
we habitually cope with unpleasant truths—avoidance, projection—it is the other, not I who is at fault, and this unlikable
person becomes the untreatable person. Or at least the un-
treated one.

Every human service profession has its unliked and unlikable
client/patient/applicants, persons who have needs yet are resistant, people who are often referred for but are unwilling or
seem unable to use the aids necessary to their adequate functioning. Physicians have patients who bring their symptoms but
fight medical recommendations all the way. Teachers encounter

children who are "unreachable," defiant, or withdrawn, as well as their indifferent or hostile parents, who shrug off their rightful responsibilities. Psychiatrists, especially those in large hospitals and clinics, are assigned patients whose paranoia, uncooperativeness, lack of trust or insight, and other deterrents to relationship make them "unreachable"—thus unlikable. Probation officers often find themselves being conned or manipulated by the very delinquents they are trying to help go straight. Counselors, caseworkers, volunteers, paraprofessionals in social agencies that carry family and child welfare functions repeatedly have referred to them persons who have been given up on by many others and who are openly or covertly pitted against both recognizing their problems and the person offering services.[1]

Perhaps social workers and their aides get more than their share of difficult, resistant, nonvoluntary help needers (not help seekers) because they are, in a sense, society's court of last appeal, to be utilized to persuade, engage, involve, motivate people in order to avoid the use of some form of coercion. When, for instance, the hospital physician cannot get a patient to follow his recommendations, he calls for the medical social worker. When the psychiatrist is ready to discharge his schizoid patient and yet knows what perils to the patient's frail recovery lie on the outside, he calls in the mental health social worker to deal with returning the patient to his family or community. When a teacher has tried to cope with her pupil's unacceptable behavior, and polite notes sent to his parents have been ignored, she calls in the school social worker. When, in response to neighbors' reports, the police have established that children are indeed being neglected and/or abused by their parents, they call in a child welfare social worker. It needs repeating: while social case and group workers in many kinds of human welfare agencies deal with applicants who want their counsel and/or services and thus are responsive to a supportive relationship, still many social workers—often those least prepared and trained— are daily faced with persons who distrust them and everything they (are thought to) stand for.

Why bother with such people? It could be argued—indeed, it

has been argued by some—that since there are not enough social workers, counselors, therapists of the several helping professions to deal with the many social-psychological and emotional-behavioral problems of the many people in need in our society, why not use the scarce resources for those who are best able to benefit by them? For those with whom empathy is swift and sure and who, in turn, want and can use a helping relationship? As for the others? One is reminded of H. G. Wells's solution to the problem of criminals and other deviants in his *Modern Utopia:* they were to be shipped to far-off islands, all of them together—thieves, drunkards, murderers, vagrants, all—and left to their own devices. Out of sight, out of mind—and Utopia would be peopled by those who exercise their rights and enjoy their freedoms along with personal and social responsibility.

There are societies today that have their islands—their Siberias or Outer Mongolias for persons who deviate from social norms of one sort or another. Even more permissive societies must isolate persons whose actions have been dangerous to the lives or rights of others. But there remains in societies such as ours the belief in man's improvability if conditions and opportunities and personal attitudes and understanding can be improved. Thus the existence in our society of the tremendously large and complex network of human service programs and provisions. Thus the societal concern that the people who plan and man those programs be charged with extending themselves in reforming old and inventing such new social resources as may enrich human life. Thus the parallel concern that each human being should be empowered to realize himself in ways that are both personally satisfying and socially acceptable. (We need not fear ironbound, pinpoint conformity in this perspective. "Socially acceptable," or "adequate," or "normal" behavior runs along a very wide and long continuum in today's society.) Thus society's employment of thousands of human beings in the human service professions ready to work at improving the quality of human life, in one or more aspects, both in individual instances or in the community at large.

What are the alternatives? Islands; coercion; or let the devil take the hindmost. The trouble is—even the cynic must agree—that self-destructive people are not encapsulated. They live in relationships with others. What they do, or fail to do, may have many widening ripple effects. Society must be concerned with them not simply for themselves but because their sociopsychological deficits and deformities often drive deep into the lives of others, particularly those of young, impressionable children. Their problems are often far more crucial, far more crippling to both body and spirit, far more damaging to those whose lives they touch than are the problems brought to counselors and therapists by the readily relating, voluntary help seeker. They are parents who through cruelty or neglect scar and deform their children; they are persons who are repeatedly self-destructive; they are persons so disoriented and/or alienated, so resourceless, whether of supporting persons or means, as to require being sought out, drawn in, accepted with all their limitations, nourished insofar as it is possible. They may need to be protected from themselves and/or those who would cut off their potential for greater comfort or growth. This, in part, is the argument social workers have put forward for reaching out to the hard to reach.

It is this kind of caring and concern, in fact, which makes all human service professions, and certainly social work, the benign arm of our society. Without such outreaching means to protect, to nurture, to prevent, a society would operate at only two extremes: to provide social and psychological services only to those who want them and have enough ego capacity to seek them out and use them or, at the opposite pole, to use forms of coercion to force the conformity of others. Because we care about individual rights and their concomitant responsibilities, because we believe in each man's improvability and growth potential, because we are concerned (even with all our society's lapses and deficiencies taken into account!) that children should have every possible chance for physical and psychic well-being and growth, society's representatives in the helping professions must care too, deeply, genuinely.

Enough of preachment, and agreed. But the hard to reach are often hard to love—or even to like. One may "care" about them in the mass, out of moral values or humanitarian beliefs, and make rhetorical pronouncements. Surely *somebody* should be responsible for their well-being! When that somebody is you or I—can we feel and be empathic enough, warm enough, genuinely concerned enough to invest ourselves in trying to form a working relationship? Even though we may not like this one or that and may find that our best efforts are met with antagonism or suspicion? It is a real problem that will not go away, and therefore we must face it directly and honestly.[2]

It is honestly not possible to like everyone. If we have been brought up to value certain qualities of character and mind (and which of us has not?), if we have standards (as which of us has has not?) about what is "bad" and what is "good," what better and what worse, what is harmful and what is not, if even our aesthetic sensibilities are assaulted by filth or stench or disorder—then we are likely to recoil from rather than to reach out empathically to the person whose behaviors run counter to those we value, who is most *unlike* us and thus is not spontaneously likable. Honesty with oneself, honesty in facing one's own prejudices, biases, attractions, or revulsions, is the first step in attempting to form a working alliance with another. Otherwise one's own resistances arise. And in the often unconscious, skillful strategies of our psychological defense system, we defend ourselves in several ways. One is by intellectualizing, making a quick evaluation of "untreatability," for instance. Another is by withdrawal, pulling in behind a mask of "professional" detachment; being cool, reasonable, uninvolved. Yet another is by rationalization, one seductive form of which may be to say, "*I* cannot deal with this kind of person, but perhaps someone kinder or nicer than I can." With the frequent result that the person in need but unlikable is shifted from pillar to post, or he falls between the cracks of helping organizations and is attended to by none.

"Caring" in the sense of "concern for" or "concern about" may be genuinely felt when the situation seems to hold clear and present danger for the person himself and/or those others he vitally affects. He may be a victim, yet he may also, even if unwittingly, victimize others. So we are concerned to modify or mitigate the effects of his behaviors. Only occasionally can he himself be detoured. Usually one must work with or through him or at the very least with some lessening of his effects and influence upon the lives of others. So there is nothing for it but that we must try to care for him, too.

Can one "learn to care"? Can one come to care about persons one doesn't really like? There is practice evidence from helpers who have worked with abusing parents and the hard to reach that it can and does happen; further, several research experiments give encouraging evidence of the possibility of increasing one's empathic capacities.[3] Supervisory, in-service training with special concentration on the modification of helper feelings and attitudes are excellent motivations and supports of such attitudinal and thence behavioral change. And it is also possible to be a do-it-yourself learner.

It begins with one's openness and willingness to understand.

It is a common experience that, as one lends himself to wondering about and then to learning what human needs and fears and psychic hungers underlie a lot of socially unacceptable or intractable behavior, one finds arising in himself some basis for empathy and genuine acceptance of the difficult person, if not of his behavior. When, for instance, one understands that this alcoholic is driven by his need to escape painful internal discomforts, one finds some spark of feeling with him (for who among us has not wished at one time or another for escape?). Such understanding changes what may before have been righteous moral censure. When one understands that this adolescent girl is brazenly promiscuous because (among other reasons) it is only when she has sex that she feels she has some worth, one's feelings of shock or disgust may shift to compassion and concern. So one can receive and relate to her more compassionately. When one recognizes that this neglecting mother is herself mostly a bewildered child in a grown-up body, or that abusive wife and child beater is alternately torn between rage at his life circumstances and guilt at his failures, that he did not by conscious intent decide that he was going to be a hellion—that "he" and "she" and "they" are their own destroyers—one begins to feel, in varying degrees, how much hurt may lie beneath facades of anger, cruelty, or indifference. One does not "forgive all"; that is neither our function nor our right. Stemming, rather, from our greater understanding is some flow of empathic feeling with and for the person.

There is much, then, to be learned and understood about how and why people get to be the way they are when we encounter them. Sometimes the client will explain himself insofar as he is able; sometimes his behavior is as much a mystery to him as it is to us; sometimes we can only guess at what is behind the behavior we see, making "educated guesses," based upon theories and studies of personality development and social behavior.

A tremendous body of knowledge—some theoretical, some strongly supported by research, some accumulated by years of careful clinical observations made by generations of people helpers—is available for the seeking and reading. It explains how and why people get to be the way they are, how their characters are formed by past and present potent life experiences, and the purposes or meanings of even crazy and self-destructive behavior. That knowledge and that understanding cannot be gobbled up by a student or a beginning helper all at once. Indeed, it can scarcely be mastered in a lifetime of study, and since it is continuously in the making and remaking, each helper by his own careful observations of people can be a contributor to it. But there is no substitute for a continuous awareness that all behavior has purposiveness (often unconscious); that the purpose is always to bring the behaver some sense of gratification or to lessen some psychological pain; and that, since much self- and other-destructive behavior seems to undermine these purposes, there is the continual necessity for the would-be helper to try to understand, "How and why is this? What possibly drives this person to act in ways that make things worse rather than better for him?"

If you will look back across just the last few years of your life, you will probably see that some of your feelings and attitudes have changed in one way or another. If you ask youself how so, you will discover that one powerful change agent has been some change in your *understanding* of the thing, person, or situation to which you had some emotional reaction. Knowledge, explanations, insights, all affect our feelings (and vice versa, of course, because of the continuous interplay between mental and emotional processes within us).

In preparing to be a helper—and continuously in the course of being one—our "natural" feelings (if we are aware of and able to face them) may be modified by the growth of our educated understanding. By "modified" I do not mean that the helper becomes cold, emotionless, normless, or that anything goes. He remains keenly aware of and concerned with deviance and norm violations. But he develops greater internal tolerance of them. His focus expands from *what* the person is or does to include *why* he is or does, and then to *how* this might be changed. In the mature caseworker there seem to develop some shock absorbers that allow for the reception of ugliness or deviance, not by dulled response but by some greater capacity for resilience and perspective. So knowledge and understanding temper our impulsive reactions.

By this same means it becomes more possible to accept the person truly in the ways that have already been discussed. Perhaps one aspect of "acceptance" and "respect" deserves a bit of further notice. We need to remind ourselves that people who come to us in trouble—even those who *are* the problem—may have more to them, more in them, than their trouble and their inability to deal with it. One of the meanings of "acceptance" and "respect," it seems to me, is that the person is received as one who has some potential capability and potential willingness to take some small part in such changes as are necessary in his situation and/or his actions. He is received as being potentially responsible, not for his past mistakes and misfortunes (though that may surely be the case) but in regard to his "now problem" and in regard to "from now on." This attitude is part of the expectation element in relationship. As has been said, that expectation needs to be honed to our careful assessment of the person's manifested capacities and responsive motivations. At the very least, the expectation is that the person does not relish the situation he finds himself in and that he would like to get out of it—to which aim the helper offers aid.

There are some further things that require our understanding. They inhere in the anticipated and realistic situation of the nonvoluntary application.

When a person has been pushed or prodded to seek help, has been all but taken by the scruff of his neck to the helper, when it is "take help or else," it is not hard to understand that he senses danger. Some person who is in authority (his child's teacher, his parents, his probation officer) or whose favor he dares not risk losing (his wife, his doctor, his "relief worker") has persuaded or ordered him to appear. He encounters a helper—you—but since he often not only *has* a problem but *is* a problem (or so he has been told), he fears you will be aligned *against* him, will require him to surrender his rights, his autonomy. He may not think in exactly those terms; but he *feels* that the helper is bad news.

The situation of referral and application, then, is a threat, and it calls up all sorts of protective defenses. It is often hard for us to remember this, because we may be eager and overflowing with goodwill and concern for him. So we are likely to be taken by surprise—and maybe to feel hurt, too—by sullen or openly hostile or monosyllabic responses to our proffered assistance. It is only "natural," again, that we should react in self-protective ways—all the way from becoming stiff and crisp and "business-like" to acting as if we had not noticed his negative or defensive behavior at all. It is natural, but it is not useful in forming a relationship alliance. When one understands and can feel with the fears that are bound to arise with the intrusion of an unwanted helper, self-protection becomes less necessary, and professional concern takes its place, concern that the person needing help should be brought to wanting it.

Still another common reaction will be found among people

who have been pressed to appear at social agencies or clinics or the school principal's office. When people have had a lifetime of feeling like outcasts—whether because of poverty or race or lack of educational or other opportunities—they tend to approach the "ins," the people who seem to them to have made it, with suspicion and animosity.

This is hard for the helper himself to recognize because here he is, ready and willing to be *for* and *with* this person in need. Yet the fact is that many people coming to organized sources of help have had many unhappy, frustrating, and often denigrating experiences with representatives of health, education, and welfare services that have meant to serve them well but have not always done so. Thus "negative transference" rises up to blur the person's perception of the new would-be helper. You may be seen in the image of someone else, in some other place at some other time, who was mean or impatient or who made the person feel like a fool. "They all look alike" has been said in a denigrating way of foreign or racial groups. It is often thought and said of social workers and psychiatrists and teachers and psychologists and nurses, especially when they work in large and bureaucratic settings—"They all look alike—they all act the same." (What an assault on one's specialness! Not unlike the assault an applicant feels when he believes he is seen as just another of the socially unfit, a problem carrier, rather than as a particular person who feels and suffers his commonplace problem as if it were his alone!)

Thus, for the helper of a person who by his personal qualities or problematic attitudes and behaviors rouses dislike or antipathies, there is an additional barrier thrown up: resistance to the helper and his help. This is understandable and natural, but it complicates communication and the development of a working relationship. Some ways in which the would-be helper may diminish such resistance and raise the sense of trust and connectedness will be dealt with in the chapter to follow.

"Understanding" is an unfolding process. It rarely comes all at once, all of a piece. Because of this, and also because there are people and situations that all but defy such understanding as is compassionate, there are times when one must act "as if" one cared. I know, I know—that is anathema; it is not genuine; it is something one is "not supposed" to do. So I plead to be borne with while I try briefly to explain. First an example. Then I will point up the rationale.

The case in point was transferred to me when another caseworker left the agency—Mr. and Mrs. Brown and their four children, aged three to nine. It was a family that excited everyone's concern. The childrens' teachers called our agency periodically to report how tattered and tired the children seemed; the family's neighbors whispered hoarsely into the telephone about how filthy the house was, how "crazy" the parents (but, no, they did not want to reveal their own identity); the school nurse said the children were undernourished and had nits but that the mother would not come in to talk with her. Mr. Brown was absent most of the time, supposedly on the road buying or selling job lots, earning occasional and uncertain "commissions" with which he would pay off past debts or bring home strawberries in January. He was a strikingly handsome man, who spoke in cultivated and orotund cadences of his love for his wife and his children. He probably had a high IQ and was, I think, a borderline schizophrenic with mild paranoid trends. His wife and children idolized him, and his appearance and verbal competence and the freshly washed, anxiously adoring faces of his four little ones had quite won over the juvenile court judge to whom the previous caseworker had appealed for a court order for placement of the children. Appeal denied—because Mr. Brown promised eloquently. . . .

At the start it was Mrs. Brown who was my client. She had probably once been very pretty. Now in her thirties, most of her teeth were gone, and she was bedraggled, dirty, smelly. Her basement apartment was barren except for a few rickety cots and mattresses, two chairs, and a table. Furniture that the previous caseworker had scrounged up for the Browns had disappeared, piece by piece, probably sold to secondhand dealers for rent and food money. Piles of filthy clothing lay about, bottles of soured milk, half-empty cans of food. The children were pale, scrawny, and scared. What they were scared about was their mother's hysterical behavior, her threats of killing herself, or all of them, her running from the house at times and locking them into their dark and hungry solitude. They clutched your heart. Each was potentially beautiful, once you looked beneath the dirt on their faces and under their tangled hair. The three who went to school (when they were not sick with colds or stomach-aches) were reported by their teachers to be unusually sensitive, very bright, eager to learn. It was not hard to imagine what attractive and productively involved youngsters they could be, given half a chance—say, in a good foster home.

Mrs. Brown, fearful and hysterically disorganized, could not give a straight account of anything. She evaded answers, whether on important or unimportant details. Whining, wheedling, she talked only of her need for more money to buy food, while the many half-used cans standing about gave mute evidence that the money given her had been used with no sense of cost or nutritional value. When I had pushed open the door to her "Come in!" her little three-year-old was toddling about whimpering, his soiled diaper rags falling away from his scarlet bottom, while Mrs. Brown lay on her cot straining to read a tattered Russian novel. It was hard to care for or about Mrs. Brown.

What was my purpose there? I had to remind myself often. Ah yes!—it was to try once more to engage these parents in wanting to improve their care of the children. Failing that, we would make another attempt at placement.

"To improve their care" involved, of course, a myriad of small goals. It was easy to set down an impressive list of the material aids and services that could, in fact, be provided. But it was quite another thing to figure out and work at how to get the Browns to want what could be given them and to use it con-structively. Even placement of the children would only hold if the parents were at least partly convinced of its desirability. It was, I grumbled, a case that was a case load.

My first reaction to Mrs. Brown was a mixture of censure, disgust, indignant incredulity. Had I acted in line with my true, "genuine" feelings, I would have conveyed this in attitudes or words. With what effect? Probably to drive Mrs. Brown even further into retreat and heighten even further the children's worry and protectiveness of her. So I deliberately and severely disciplined myself to act "as if."

But wait. There was no "as if" in my genuine concern. That was for the children, not for their mother. But it was real enough to motivate me to *act* as if my concern were for her.

I attended to *her*—to how *she* was, to how hard things were for *her:* how helpless she must feel; how much she really loved her children and wanted the best for them; and yet how awfully hard it was to manage; what it was she wanted for them—and for herself too; and so on and so forth.

It was not long before I knew in my head—but it had begun to creep into my feeling too—that Mrs. Brown was herself only a child, a scared child with emotional needs. What I became aware of, over a number of weeks, were two somewhat surprising things: that my understanding of Mrs. Brown began to affect my feelings about her and that my feelings had begun to match up with my deliberately assumed actions. How was this? The several possible explanations I offer bear on what may happen to any one of us when we set about to try as best we can to relate to an "unlikable."

First is the most obvious. When what we do brings us some desired response, we feel rewarded, reinforced, encouraged to repeat or extend that behavior. In small ways Mrs. Brown's responses were rewarding. Hungry for attention, she poured out much about herself—her utterly disorganized, overindulged childhood, her romanticized dreams of the future—all heavily freighted with emotion, all deposited in my apparently willing ear with grateful release. She was pleased with all the "trouble" I took for her—that, for instance, I took her and all four children by taxi to the pediatric clinic, stayed with them, and carefully went over with her the meaning of the doctor's findings and recommendations; and I promised to get her the money for ice and extra milk—and kerosene (for nitty heads). Or when, for instance, I brought her a cheap hand mirror so she could look at herself together with me and come to decide that she could still be a pretty woman if she would submit herself to dental work. In a few months she even allowed me to take the older boys with me to a community center, and because she was a "good mother," she let them enroll and take part in after-school activities that were "good for them." At times she addressed me as "little mother." It was not all forward progress by any means, but there was enough responsiveness to sustain my effort and to modify my feelings toward her.

Second, as discussed earlier, when we understand the reasons for, the causes of a phenomenon, big or small, we "reasoning" and "reasonable" human beings seem better able to allow it emotional houseroom. We seem to respond with some greater measure of acceptance and toleration to what makes sense, especially when human behavior is involved. Perhaps it is because we know our kinship with others—that every one of us is shaped, well or badly, by forces over which we have so small a margin of control—and we can feel at the very least sympathetic with the person who is manifestly a victim of such forces. Perhaps, too, our conscious intention to "understand" is at once the promoter and the product of some modified perceptions and feelings?

We tend to assume that emotions shape and drive our thought and actions. There is some evidence, perhaps insufficiently pursued and attended to, that the reverse may also be true: that our perceptions (sensory, mental) trigger physiological and emotional responses, and also that our overt actions influence the accompanying feelings. Evidence for this has been put forward by physiologists, past and modern, and its theory propounded by one of the fathers of modern psychology.[4] Indeed, it was a phenomenon recognized almost 400 years ago by that master psychologist, William Shakespeare. His Hamlet gives stern counsel to his errant mother, thus: "*Assume* a virtue, if you have it not, / ... / *For use almost can change the stamp of nature.*"

If you have ever engaged in role-play you know something of this. You have experimented with a deliberate taking on of the actions, gestures, verbalizations, responses, of a person other than your own self. You have acted "as if." If you took your part sincerely, you probably became aware that you began to feel in tune with that action, that what you said and did seemed to arouse in you certain matching emotions. (This, of course, is the point of using role-play in the training for empathy and in treatment situations when the purpose is to get a client/patient to experience how something feels to another person.) The "as if" actions excite the "for real" feelings.[5]

Thoughts, actions, and feelings are separable chiefly for purposes of their analysis. In being experienced they tend to be so simultaneous and intertwined as to elude differentiation. What is clear is that there seems to be in the human makeup some persistent drive for congruence, for harmony and compatibility between our actions and feelings. When they are incongruent we experience unease, conflict, a sense of internal imbalance. And probably one of the meanings of that overused word "adaptation" is the unconscious balancing regulation that goes on within us for the purpose of bringing our external and internal behaviors into some consistency with one another. Herein lies a third possible explanation of how it is that, when we take certain actions because of our true concern about a troubling person or situation, our caring feelings may emerge.

If we cannot in truth love everybody, we can and do care about their present or potential effect upon others. That, coupled with our concern that whatever chance there is for the person's self-betterment should not be denied him, prods us to try to relate in such ways as may draw him toward using help. By so doing, and for the several reasons suggested, our own attitudes toward the unattractive person may undergo some modifications—enough, at least, to motivate us to extend ourselves to be as helpful as is possible.

That intention must be instrumented not alone by our self-management but also by those few techniques as have been developed to lower the resistances of the person who, for his own reasons, may find *us* unattractive too, to encourage in him the trust and the sense of alliance that a working relationship requires. With this the next chapter is concerned.

5

Relating to the "Resister"

A "CLIENT," in modern usage, is one who contracts to use the services or goods of another usually under explicit or implicit mutual agreements as to the purpose and conditions of their transactions. An "applicant" is one who brings his request for services or goods to a potential granter; he may or may not become a client. But we are left without a word to name those persons who neither apply nor undertake to use the goods or services of a helper but are sent or brought to the attention of human service agencies (health, welfare, educational, correctional) against their wish or will. They have had the finger of blame or shame pointed at them, have been threatened with some dire consequence unless they do something about their problem; sometimes they have been forced to make application not by other people but by circumstances beyond their control. They come unwillingly, dragging their feet and their spirit, feeling coerced, robbed of their free will by other persons or conditions they oppose. Sometimes they want help, but not the kind that is to be had or not under the conditions to be required.[1]

For want of some better name, I refer here to such nonapplicants, nonclients, as "resisters." It is only natural that their defenses should be up; it is only expectable that they should resist what they do not want or what they fear or distrust, that they should defend themselves against anticipated further blame or shame, defend against the possibility that they may lose their freedom as the price of getting what they may need. Because they see the organization and its representative (you) as the immediate danger or threat, they plant their heels in the ground, resist becoming involved in all the varied ways we human beings have learned in which to protect ourselves.*

Some of the most common ways are these—

Denial. The person claims (perhaps even *feels*) that there is no problem; or if there is, he can handle it himself; or if he can't, he doesn't see what can be done about it; so thanks a lot, or mind your own business.

Projection. The person recognizes that a problem exists but feels it is caused by forces outside himself, usually someone else, and if that someone else would lay off or act differently, things would be okay.

Antagonism. "Offense is the best defense," so the person is angry or indignant that help is thought to be necessary at all or that such help as he might consider is not available. Antagonism may be expressed by openly hostile words and acts or by stony silence and looks that speak louder than words.

Distancing. Another way in which anger may be expressed, a cool way. Distancing usually involves the person's psychological removal of himself (his emotions and sense of responsibility) from the problem: "Just leave me out of it."

None of these defense mechanisms stands alone. They frequently intertwine. They may also contain flickers of ambivalence, flickers of the person's awareness that he ought to feel responsible in some way, of some anxiousness, and sometimes even of feeling the need of help, though it may be feared. It is

*Only the resistance roused by the present external coercion and conditions will be dealt with here. There are unconscious resistances that may interfere with many kinds of help or treatment, resistances against becoming aware of anxieties, guilt, traumatic memories that had been pushed into limbo. To these psychoanalysis and psychoanalytically informed therapies have long attended. Our focus here, however, will be only upon the here-and-now resistances to what are felt to be "clear and present dangers" in the help-taking, help-using situation.

these flickers that we draw upon, of course. Their presence is part of what the person is defending himself against.

For the helper—physician with unwilling patient, probation officer with a delinquent youngster, school counselor with a student sent by the principal for repeated unruly behavior, child care worker with a neglectful mother—the challenge (a euphemism for a tough job!) is to move the resister to becoming a client. That movement can only occur by reaching for and touching his feelings, by creating currents of emotional interchange that makes an alliance seem safe.*

Where do those feelings lie? Or seethe? Usually they are involved with two immediate difficulties that are topmost (not basic) at the moment, situationally created. One: that the person has, creates, or *is* a problem is now open, known, and apparently inescapable. Such discomforts and frustrations as he himself may have experienced with his problem but brushed aside or closed his mind to are now in full view. Second, there tumble within him feelings about having been forced, whether by other persons or by his own helplessness, to take some sort of unasked for, undesired judgment, advice, direction, penalty— whatever—or to submit to conditions set by the will of another. Degrees of intensity and rigidity and mixtures of positive-negative, defensive-attacking reactions will vary, of course. But the pervasive theme of the resistive person's feeling is of rejection of the would-be helper and of the here-and-now demand that he face the problem.

*You will be aware in what follows (perhaps you have already noticed) that, while "relationship" is in the center of our attention, I often discuss what are called "techniques of treatment." Almost all of them are for purposes of touching, drawing out, receiving, responding to the help needer's feelings. The reality is that the methods by which relationship is nurtured, developed, and utilized are intricately intertwined with other means of help—whether material, intellectual, physical, or psychological. Perhaps no one has seen this better than John Dewey. "Craftsmanship to be artistic in the final sense," he said, "must be loving; it must care deeply for the subject matter upon which skill is exercised" (*Art as Experience*). Thus in the best of helping practice, skill and caring, problem-solving methods and relationship-enhancing methods intertwine and fuse.

Put yourself in his shoes, and you can feel and understand how natural this is. Even if the helper comes on gently, pleasantly, full of goodwill. What's the catch, they may wonder—what's the put-on, when I am here because I am—or somebody thinks I am—stupid, to blame, bad—and when they are here to do something to me? Pretending that such thoughts and their accompanying feelings are not paramount and festering will not melt them away. Pleasant evasion on the part of the would-be helper only rouses unease or suspicion, because the attitude is incongruent with the problem carrier's reading of the situation and with his expectations. Talking about trivialities—"The weather's awful," "The baby is cute"—or asking for such neutral facts as are needed for face sheet information harms no one, but it only puts off the evil moment and holds both parties in suspension.

There is nothing for it but to get to it. Gently, warmly, honestly, caringly, surely, but to the recognized fact and accepted naturalness of the person's unease or antagonism or even his wondering about what this intrusion or confrontation will mean to him. One of the oldest maxims of casework practice is "Start where the client is." Where is he? The resister is mired in his resistance. This is the first problem to be worked on: his feelings/attitudes/expectations of this intrusive person-place-purpose in relation to him.

"Confrontation" is a term and an idea that has often been misconstrued. Somehow it has come to be associated with an attitude that is hostile. (A like association is often attached to "honesty" in personal relations. When a person says, "I'm going to be perfectly honest with you," we brace ourselves for a swat or a blow to our egos. Why must "honesty" make us anticipate hostility?) Among its several meanings, confrontation means "to set face to face," "to present for acknowledgment," or "to bring together for examination" (*Random House Dictionary* [1973]). It is this meaning that is most useful and pertinent to our helping purposes. Such setting forth, such open presentation to another can be done with respect for him, with tentative feeling out of his acceptance or rejection of what is said, with recognition that two different people in two different positions may have two different reactions. Confrontation implies difference but not opposition; it is a presentation of what one believes to be true. Thus one may confront in any or all of the ways we hold to be expressive of our being "for" and "with" the person (or group) with whom we are in transaction.

Back now to our first face-to-face encounter with open or even anticipated resistance. Several principles may guide what we do in an effort to establish a working relationship. They speak to the feelings and through them to the mind of the resister.

If you must go knocking on the door of a person who has been reported or referred by someone else, you must, of course, say who you are and what you represent and, as simply as possible, why you are there. You know they cannot be glad to see you. ("Cursed be the bearer of bad tidings," the ancient peoples said, and sometimes they cut out the tongue of the miserable messenger. Fortunately those barbarisms are behind us. But the feeling of "Cursed be . . . " persists.) So, because it is natural that presenting yourself will rouse feelings of fear or anticipatory anger, you yourself may express the naturalness, the expectedness of such a reaction—"You probably don't really want to see anyone like me," "You must think this is none of anybody's business"—you offer, in short, some recognition of this reaction.

It is a single, momentary, passing comment. But it tends to convey a friendly acceptance of the person and lowers his sense of threat. Moreover, it may surprise him pleasantly, especially if he has felt himself to be a constant butt of blame. Surprise that a person speaks and acts differently from one's anticipations is one of those small chinks in our defensive armors. It seems to shake up habitual perceptions, to open us to the possibility of something new.*

---

*Of course, not everyone will react in the same way. One person will deny that he has any feelings about your intervention at all—"Come in, come in; I've got nothing to hide"; another may push the door firmly shut; a third may impassively and cautiously let you in, holding, waiting for you to reveal your message and your motives. Given these variants, but also confined by space limits, I shall have to hold myself to such general principles and approaches as are susceptible to the modifications that individually different instances call for.

Quick on the heels of the recognition and acceptance of antagonism (and responsive always to what you read of the individual person's reaction) must come placing before him the reason for your (your organization's) concern. He *has* troubles, or he is *in* trouble. Because we know that there are at least two sides to every trouble story, part of the reason for being here is to hear it from him, the most important person. Help *him* to say how he sees the trouble and to express how the problem hurts *him*. In our initial efforts to involve him, what we are honestly after is not that he should "come clean" or that we should "let him have it" but that we want to know from him how *he* sees and feels his situation, what he considers the problem and his needs to be.

Anyone who has dealt with defensive people knows that they may often not only unconsciously distort the obvious truth but sometimes also consciously contrive lies and evasions. For the moment one must accept these, understanding that they hold a survival value for the person. One need not indicate disbelief. Such a confrontation may be needed, but it had better come later, when a sense of alliance has been created, when the person feels you are interested in *him,* not just in his unacceptable behavior. Nor should one go to the other extreme and indicate "I believe you," unless there is valid reason to believe. It is enough to offer him the chance to tell it as he sees it, to listen—and draw him out with interest and respect, and to indicate here and there that it is "understandable" or "imaginable" that he should feel this way, or that it should seem so to *him.* That is honest; it *is* understandable that a person will have skewed or emotionally distorted perceptions about problems in which high feeling is involved. This is not to say that how he feels or sees it is "right" or "true." But corrections are best made, whether in casework or in teaching or in ordinary life relationships, when the person who is corrected or differed with feels safe with the challenger.

What is particularly important in the early stages with a resister is that he should feel your consideration of him and the understandability, even if not your agreement with, his views and his feelings.

When any one of us has a problem, whether it is owned up to or has been thrust at us, we are most eager or anxious to get to what can or will be done about it. Somewhere early in beginning contacts with prospective clients there needs to be introduced the question of the interviewee's wishes, hopes, expectations, ideas of what the solutions or, more practically, what the next steps to the problem's amelioration might be. For the resister and the voluntary would-be client alike, this is a most important area for discussion on several counts. It says to the prospective client that we want to give a hearing to his ideas, that we assume not that he is only the creator or carrier or pawn of his problems but that he is also trying to cope. Thinking about ways to cope is a necessary preliminary to action. So what has he done, tried, thought to do, thought others (like us) might do?

Second, to draw from the prospective client his ideas about ways and means of coping is our best entry into discussion with him about whether what he wishes and proposes is realistic, feasible, possible, or whether his expectations must be corrected by fact, modified by feasibility. The coming together of would-be helper and would-be client—and certainly with a resister—in some agreed-upon understanding of where we go from here and who does what and why can be firmly based only when the misconceptions and sometimes unrealistic expectations of the help needer have been aired, stipulated, clarified, and, when necessary, corrected. Otherwise, there occurs an illusion of agreements that so often end in disappointments on both sides.

The third reason for discussing what is wanted, needed, and possible is one that permeates the other two. It is that feelings and emotional investments in what is going to happen or can be made to happen are second only to feelings and emotions about the problems themselves. Continuously interweaving, then, with the facts, possibilities, limits, ifs and buts of problem-solving or ameliorating conditions and operations is the helper's responsive relating to the feelings which infuse them. He may have to differ from what the help needer thinks or wants to do, but he repeatedly shows himself to be at one with or capable of understanding what feelings drive or pull the person's thought and action. This is how help *needer* may become a help *user*.

With the resister who presents himself to you at your office—a reluctant but perhaps ambivalent dragon, many of these same guidelines hold. There are a few twists of difference.

Such persons have usually been told by someone else to apply. What they have been told, what they have heard or made of the explanation they got, we cannot know unless we ask. We tend to assume that the applying person knows exactly what we are about or that, because he presents himself, he has no questions or misconceptions about us.

It may safely be suggested that when a person comes to a helper largely against his will, two things need to happen: recognition and acceptance of his natural reluctance or even resistance to coming need to be verbalized. This tells him at once that you can understand and accept negative feelings if he is inclined to express them. Second, one needs to ask him to tell what *his* idea is of why he was sent here—What does he expect? Are his expectations valid? Here again one creates the opportunity for the clarification of actuality, the correction of misconceptions, and the expression of and responsiveness to his feelings and attitudes about the referral.

Few people have the courage to affront a person whom they see as representing authority, so they may cover up in many ways, one of which is not to express or expose any feelings at all. Here is the opportunity for your first demonstration of help: to recognize with them, aloud, how they probably (because "naturally") feel. "You probably had a lot of questions about coming here." "You're probably mad that the teacher had the nerve. . . ." "I can see why you'd think I am something like the police." There are any number of ways to convey that you know that the person's first reaction is likely to be against you. More important, to let him know by the way you say it, unaccusingly, neither teasing nor joking, that you understand and can accept his resistance. Even at times when the person makes no visible or audible response, perhaps because of fear that a trap is being set for him, your unexpected acceptance of his resentment or resistance will be registered. It is not lost on him; some time later he may reveal that it made an impression.

With this person, wary and evasive out of caution or fear, one must still find a way to tap and draw upon his feelings, since here are the threads with which the fabric of relationship is woven. If he will not admit to feeling about you and your invasion of his life, he may yet respond feelingly to the problems or troubles put upon him—the teacher's unfairness, the neighbor's nosiness, the landlord's indifference. Projecting thus, he may be all wrong—but it is *his* version, the way he sees it, and the way *he* feels it that, at this time and place, you want to hear and try to understand. Again, this is not the same as saying that you accept what he sees as true or his feelings as valid. It is only to say that you accept that this is how he sees and interprets and experiences it. If you are to lead him to some truer, clearer, more self-responsible grasp of his problem, he must feel that you are with him, attentively, caringly; that there is some emotional binding between you: relationship.

One of the most misleading ways of dealing with one's own resistance is known to us all: to deny it. It misleads both him who denies and him who accepts that denial at face value. So many of us have learned to be yea-sayers, to quash the bad or unworthy or socially unacceptable attitudes and emotions we may have. Moreover, many of us have found that seeming acquiescence is one of the quickest ways to get rid of being talked at or pushed, so "Yes," "Of course," "I'll sure try" may come readily. As for the helper, he wants so much to get on with the business of the problem that he tends too often and too quickly to accept at face value any positive attitude or averment that his client makes.

When you detect an incongruence between what the person says and what he has typically been doing, you may be sure that negative forces are in active operation. Therefore, it is necessary to help the person to recognize and to say aloud what his ifs, ands, and buts are, what the underbelly of his ambivalence is, what unreasonable or unacceptable (even to himself) feelings pull or push him in the direction opposite to that in which he ought to go.

Some examples: From a physically depleted and functionally inept young mother whose children are reported as being malnourished, sickly, apathetic: "I love my kids! No one can say I don't do for them." Yes, surely she loves her kids. And yes, she surely does the best she knows how. But it must be very hard—it's a tough job. It must take a lot out of her.

From an uneasy mother whose eight-year-old little boy has been reported by his school as being alternately hyperactive and exhausted, highly distractible, unable to keep up with the class or follow directions: "I know Jamie has troubles at school, but I'm going to get him to the doctor this week, and I'm going to ask for some tonic to calm him down—or brace him up—or whatever." That's a good idea, to have a physical examination for Jamie. But no tonic works miracles. Mrs. A. must have been having a lot of aggravation with Jamie? Certainly with the school's nagging her all the time? She must feel this referral is the last straw?

From a fourteen-year-old boy sent to the school social worker because of frequent truancy, failing grades (despite adequate intelligence), and disruptive behavior in the classroom (when he is there): "Yeah, I know why they sent me here" (eyes downcast or looking at the wall). "I know—I've gotta settle down. Yeah, I guess I hafta turn over a new leaf—you know?" How tempting it would be to shake hands on this fine resolve and sense of responsibility! But—can it be taken at face value? Surely something is eating this boy, that he is both dropping out and clowning it up? So—tentatively—the caseworker reaches out to touch the underside. "I know you know. But sometimes it's not so easy to turn over that new leaf. You've probably thought of doing it before—but it didn't happen—it didn't work." (Silence, while the boy examines his shoelaces.) "Maybe some things are bugging you—getting you down? Maybe you feel sore that they sent you here?"

The effort on the part of each of these helpers is the same: to affirm whatever positive is asserted, but to reaffirm that there *is* a problem and that its existence speaks to the probable presence of negative or pullback feelings. And to do the latter with compassionate understanding of how very human that pullback is. Denial or resistance will not always just disappear, of course, but the helper has demonstrated that he can feel with the "badness," not just the "goodness" of the person. That is a rather different and unusual response from a person who is assumed to be in authority, and, as has been said, it may open receptivity to the helper.

In the two examples that follow, you will see not the most recalcitrant of resisters but, rather, people who know they need—but are not sure they want—help. They are offered to show how what the would-be helper does at the very first encounter may promote or impair the establishment of bonds of feeling and a consequent working alliance.

Mr. and Mrs. Carmine, a middle-class couple, had first gone to the child-guidance clinic asking for help with their five-year-old Nancy. They were at the end of their rope. She was not yet toilet trained, so she could not be sent to school. In other respects, too, she was extremely obstinate and willful, unresponsive to any form of discipline. The mother reported that she had "tried everything"—from wheedling and bribing the child to hard spankings and locking her in the bathroom for hours—all to no avail. In the interchange between Mr. and Mrs. Carmine, the clinic psychiatrist had become aware of Mr. Carmine's open disgust with his wife's "total incompetence" as a mother and of her meek acceptance of his frequent sarcastic criticisms of her. The psychiatrist decided that theirs was a family and marital problem rather than a child-guidance problem (though as every clinician knows, there are few hard and fast lines that can be drawn to differentiate these!), and he advised the Carmines to make application to the family service bureau. He phoned the agency to inform them of his referral. It was two weeks later that the Carmines called for an appointment.

Two "alerts" to the probability of their resistance might have lighted up in the mind of the family agency caseworker to whom the Carmines were assigned for a first interview: the delay between the referral and their making their first move to the family agency; and the expectable annoyance or anger at a "runaround" and at being told, in effect, "It is not the child who is the problem, it is *you*." Feelings would naturally be involved, and one would hope, then, that the caseworker preparing to see the Carmines could relate right at first to where they were, that maybe they felt they'd been sent here by mistake? That they probably had some mixed feelings about whether this place was what they needed or wanted? If the Carmines chose to brush this aside, or deny such feelings, it could be passed by. But they would have heard an understanding and accepting voice.

The case record does not indicate what explanation the pyschiatrist had given the Carmines for his turndown of their application and referral elsewhere. Whatever he had said, it would have been useful to know from the Carmines themselves what they had made of it, what they heard, whether or not it seemed reasonable and acceptable to them, what help they thought the family agency could give. Possibly they might be perfectly reasonable and convinced. Then the helper is ahead of the eight ball, ready to get to the problem. Possibly, however, they had had minimal explanation, or were so disturbed that they scarcely took in what was told them, or perhaps had distorted what was said out of their rejection of the implied blame or responsibility. If any of these possibilities were the case, one would need to take the time to clear out what might be a thick underbrush of misunderstandings and churning feelings. In so doing, one would be speaking both to their emotional involvement in the problem and the emotional involvement which the help-seeking process alone created.

The record reads: "When I brought Mr. and Mrs. Carmine into my office, Mr. Carmine immediately drew a book from my shelf and seemingly became immersed in it. I asked them to tell me about their problem. Mr. C. waved a deprecating hand at his wife and said, 'She can tell you.' He returned to his reading."

(Poor caseworker! Poor Mrs. Carmine! Indeed, poor Mr. Carmine, scarcely able to face his feelings!) He protected and expressed himself at once by open passive-aggressive resistance. No words could be more eloquent than his actions. There was hardly any choice but to recognize with him openly, empathically, that he must be feeling disgusted, or . . . ? The caseworker recognized that as father and husband Mr. C. could hardly be bypassed, so she skirted his anger and asked, instead, if he would give her the necessary facts for the face sheet.

Mr. Carmine's response: "Ask her."

But suppose he had been polite and had supplied them— address, phone, ages, dates of marriage and child's birth, and so on—it would have not brought him into closer engagement with the helper. Because that is not where he was—he was disgusted, angry, resentful about the problem for which he needed help and, on top of that, about the way he had been dealt with. To have touched and drawn upon his feelings in either of these festering areas would have involved him and, further, would have provided the helper the opportunity to respond, to connect with his feelings.

Instead, the helper now turned to Mrs. Carmine to ask her first for face sheet information and then to tell what the problem was. It was Nancy, said Mrs. Carmine (obviously not too impressed by the psychiatrist's version). She went on to give a detailed account of the child's difficult behavior and of her own futile attempts to deal with it. Mr. Carmine watched her closely, intervening at points to comment cuttingly on his wife's total ineptness. To this Mrs. Carmine listened with a kind of flat composure, like that with which she told of her difficulties with Nancy.

The caseworker observed this lack of affect on the wife's part both about the child and her husband's quiet but vitriolic attacks. However (possibly because she was puzzled by it, possibly because she feared to blow up a powder keg?), she did not comment on it. It would have been possible, even helpful, perhaps, to recognize aloud that she could see that they had some considerable differences about what was going wrong—a comment in the nature of reflecting back what their words and actions were saying. And that surely such differences probably carried a lot of tension? The problem is obviously charged with emotion for them both. Mr. Carmine must have been concerned; otherwise why would he have come at all? He was openly furious with his wife and her handling of the problem. He must surely have had feelings about the child's behavior. In short, if he would not or could not be drawn into expressing his feelings about the unwanted referral and transfer, the worker's empathic comments to his occasional interruptions of his wife ("That made you feel angry," "It's surely hard to see that happening," "You've probably racked your brains to think what to do") could have conveyed to him the worker's appreciation of what the problem was doing to *him,* how it was hurting him.

The same thing would hold for Mrs. Carmine. She spoke of her problems with apparent composure. But surely she did not whip her child with composure, or bribe her or lock her up with calm? The child's behavior would naturally, expectably make a parent feel desperate and helpless. So here too, rather than just listening to what has probably been an often recited story, the caseworker might have moved in to *involve* the mother. Which is to say, to involve her emotions—by such comments that would help the applicant know that she was indeed in a difficult situation, that it would be natural to be worried—and sometimes even furious about Nancy's behavior—and that, further, she was sympathized with, that the worker felt *with* her—indeed, with them both, because both suffered this problem, though differently. Unobtrusive and brief comments that note and draw out feelings could have been used—"That must have floored you," "Anybody in that situation would feel upset," "It's only natural," "You were doing the best you knew how at the time"—and so forth. The effort would be not to affirm that what the person did or thought or felt was "right," or to correct it because it was "wrong" but, rather, to relate responsively to natural human feelings and thus to begin the business of binding oneself and the resister into a working alliance.

Perhaps Mrs. Carmine should not be called a "resister"? She *was* making an application for help. But the resistance one sees in her is against admitting her involvement in the problem; her "composure" was a distancing method by which she defended herself against being overwhelmed by her child and her husband. Subject to her husband's attacks and the child's controls, she desperately needed a voice that said, "I can feel with you—and it is safe here for you to show and express your feelings."

This would be the beginning of a working relationship. The business for which caseworker and resistive applicants meet is a problem with which the persons themselves cannot cope. If one cannot cope, one has feelings about that, too, as well as about the problem itself. Thus the *person* who bears the problem needs a sense of support. Compassionate indications of genuine concern for his hurt is essential if he is to become a client and a participant in working on his problem. This is what relationship supplies.

After Mrs. Carmine had told in some detail of Nancy's problem and what they had tried to do about it (with dry, cold inputs by Mr. Carmine now and then to correct a statement or to show his disparagement of her), the listening and (one supposes) responsive caseworker said that this was surely a most troubling situation for them. It was, however, one with which this agency had had experience and could probably be helpful. Since both Mr. and Mrs. Carmine were involved, she went on, she would need to work with both of them. Sometimes together and sometimes separately, in a regular once-a-week session. Were they agreed to this? Mrs. Carmine looked to her husband. He said *she* could come. He could not afford the time off from work. The caseworker suggested that evening appointments could be arranged. After a moment's silence, Mr. Carmine said, "All right, then," and a next week's appointment was set.

It will not surprise you to learn that the appointment was not kept, nor did the Carmines respond to a follow-up letter.

One of the reassuring things to a helper, it has always seemed to me, is that if a problem is real and emotionally charged, it will come up over and over again, though its form and content may be different each time. It is "reassuring" because there is rarely one single moment when the iron is hot. If one moment is missed, overlooked, passed by because one was slow-witted at the time, the matter that needs to be grappled with will usually recur. It can be moved back to or picked up in its different aspect at some later time. So can the drawing out of feelings from which relationship bonds can be woven. This caseworker—and she is not alone—missed dealing with the dug-in-heels attitude that was the product of the referral and application process. She glossed over, for whatever reasons, what she had clearly observed—the high tension between Mr. and Mrs. Carmine and their ways of dealing with it, along with the emotional freightage that the child's problem carried.

But she might still have retrieved relationship right at the end of the visit, by attending to the feelings attached to ongoing plans. It is a reality that a working person usually cannot take regular time off for personal reasons. Yet Mr. Carmine's total behavior in the interview, up to the moment when the helper left him no out (and again the helper *observed* his hesitance), says that his resistance had in no way been modified. Perhaps it had even solidified. He did not *want* to come, he did not *feel* like coming, he did not *believe* any good would come of it, he was too fed up—these and other attitudes remained bottled up in him. If only the caseworker had opened to him the chance to express them, had said she recognized his doubts, encouraged him to come out with what *he* wanted, felt, thought, if only about the next steps!

I do not suggest that all would have been cleared up and well. I suggest only that with this opportunity given the help needer, the would-be help giver would on her side have had the opportunity to connect with his feelings, to receive them empathically and understandingly, to indicate that she not only saw him as important in problem resolution but was genuinely concerned with what the problem was doing to him and to them. Even in making arrangements—which we helpers often tend to see as matter of fact or even routine—there may be feeling content for the applicant or client; and this may be used to support, respect, and nurture him and thence to form the lively bridge of relationship.

Here follows a more detailed case example that illustrates a number of the principles discussed thus far.

On the advice of the school counselor, the parents of fifteen-year-old Rose applied to an agency specializing in counseling and guidance of adolescents. Rose, a very bright girl, had over the past two years grown increasingly ''impossible'' at school and at home. She had gained some forty pounds in the past year, simply by greedy overeating. Despite a high IQ, she was doing poorly in her studies and had become intolerably impertinent to her teachers. She had cut herself off from her friends; she was constantly quarreling at home with her parents and younger brother. The caseworker arranged with Rose's parents that they would try to persuade her to come to the agency, in order to tell her side of the story—and that further planning would go on from there. Excerpts from the record follow (edited and condensed for brevity):

Rose came in promptly, alone. Unfortunately, since an emergency had come up for me, she had to wait fifteen minutes.

In the interviewing room she seated herself silently and sat looking at me with a quizzical smile. I said I guessed she really hadn't wanted to come in very much. I could surely understand why. [In contrast to the Carmine worker, this one relates at once to the feelings this nonvoluntary applicant probably would have about being forced or coaxed into this unwanted situation.] Rose's response was to shrug and to say rather curtly that well, she came and here she was. I said maybe she thought my function would be to scold her or tell her what not to do. [The effort is to anticipate a natural attitude and to show acceptance of it.] She smiled but did not reply.

I went on then to say I was sorry for having kept her waiting. I meet my clients on time when I possibly can. At this she burst out angrily that she had been seeing Dr. F., a psychiatrist, for several months last year, and she described how unsatisfactory that had been. When she came in to see him she would have to wait for two hours, and she hates to to wait for people. [Every caseworker will recognize this displacement of anger—it's safe to say of another person what is meant for *you*.] I laughed and said now I could really see how mad Rose must be at me for having kept her waiting. I could assure her this was not the way I operated. She went on [to tell more about how badly Dr. F. acted, how little time and attention he gave each patient, what a fraud she thought he was].... I made no comment about all this except to point out that my arrangement with clients was quite different.

[Rose talked further in disparagement of Dr. F.—venting spleen safely to an attentive and responsive worker.]

I said I was very glad Rose had come now. I knew from her mother that things were not going well at home, and I thought she probably was not happy about it. I hoped she would let me try to help her to work out things a little better. Rose's response [again] was to shrug and smile and say everything was all right. I said quietly but firmly that I knew everything was *not* all right. I was quite aware there had been considerable difficulty.... [The worker does not accept denial of the problem, though what follows shows her acceptance of the girl herself.] I could certainly understand why she wouldn't trust me or really believe that I wanted to help her. After all, she didn't know me, and this was the first time I had seen her. Why should she trust me? But I was going to ask her to take on faith the fact that I want to be of help to her. If she was willing to give me a chance, I would try. I didn't know what would come out of it, but the two of us would work together if she were willing. There was absolutely no compulsion about this ... I have no legal authority. I am not going to run after her to see that she stays in school—or that she comes back to see me. If she will try it out ... she will be able to decide for herself whether or not she wants to go on with me....

Rose had been listening. She heard the worker say that she *had* a problem—it could not be brushed off; that the worker could understand and accept as natural her distrust and suspicion; that the helper genuinely wanted to be of help to her, not just to her blaming parents and her complaining teachers; that no coercion or force would be involved; rather, that the girl herself would be free to decide whether or not she wanted to go on.

How does one know she took in what had been said? One assumes that the worker did not simply recite a spiel, rolled off as if it were a tape recording. One assumes that for each comment the worker made she attended to the girl's responses—mouth sets, eye and head movements, body positions, along with those nonverbal sounds that often escape us as we listen, our ''um-hms'' and ''m-ms.'' And that the worker moved forward empathically as she read those. If, on the other hand, a grimace or shrug or a roving eye said, "I don't believe—or like—what you're saying," one would hope that the worker would stop to take note of it with the resister, to suggest that this wasn't cutting any ice with her, to indicate that she could understand that the person might have doubts or reservations.

The proof of the pudding is in the respondent's reactions. What this record then reveals is that, having listened, Rose now began to talk. She told first, eyeing the worker closely, about all the bad and unreasonable things she did to other people. ("I dare you to like me now," she was saying in effect. Self-recrimination is a fine defense. If I say the worst things that can be said about me, I disarm you completely. You can only rise to reassure me!) The caseworker listened to her account attentively and without censure, but also without protestations of a reassuring kind. Finally she interrupted to ask Rose how she would like things to be if they could be made different. What do *you* want that we can try to make happen?

Now Rose launched, with high feeling, into what changes she would want *others* to make—her father, mother, brother, teachers. "I am blameless" was the defense. It was obviously too early in the relationship to confront her, even gently, with the recognition that by her own account she had been a provocateur of many of the conflicts she had with others. The bond with her was still too tenuous. The issue of whether Rose had a "right" to feel hurt or put-upon by other people had to wait in the wings until she felt safe, felt that the helper was with her and for her. The caseworker, then, listened to her expressed grievances, but at the same time that she was with the girl in understanding *how* she felt, she remained uncommitted about whether how and what she felt was realistically called for. The first problem to be worked on—as with every resister—was to get this angry (and hurt-feeling) person to want to involve herself in changing her situation—and perhaps even herself.

As the time for ending drew near, the caseworker moved to arrive at some working agreement. "Could Rose tell me, in one sentence or so, what she would want us to help her with?'' She replied that she wanted one of two things from her family: either they give her more attention or else leave her alone.

I said it sounded like Rose and I would have much to talk about in further interviews. Would she want to do so? She nodded assent. I told her of our usual regular weekly appointments, and she said that would be quite all right with her. I then said I would undoubtedly need to talk to her parents further and maybe later one or two of her teachers, too. I wanted her to know, however, that I would not repeat what she had told me in confidence. To this latter, Rose's reply again revealed her defiance. ''Tell them whatever you want to,'' she said, ''I'm not afraid to let anyone know how I feel about things.'' The next appointment was agreed upon.

It was kept. As were a series of succeeding interviews, in which Rose reveled in the attention she had been hungry for and was getting from the helper. From this base of support and understanding, she was able fairly soon to lower her defenses and to take in and think about the caseworker's questions and comments that pointed to the self-destructiveness of much of her behavior.

One may look at these two case examples, the Carmines and Rose, and recognize their many differences from one another—differences in the personalities involved, the nature of their needs, their manifest problems, and so forth. But they have many similarities in regard to engaging themselves in a help-seeking, help-taking relationship—and thus, for all their differences, they challenge the would-be help giver in some like ways. They came to the helping agent not of their own free will, having been pushed or persuaded to do so by others and also, perhaps, by the internal urgency of their recognized problems. They came, then, with some ambivalence, wanting help of some sort but mostly resisting it. That resistance is likely to be a mixture of many defenses—against facing the problem with its attendant feelings of fear, guilt, or anxiety, against the place to which such people come with their often incorrect assumptions about its powers or requirements or modes of operation, against their first impressions of the person who represents that place—you—against involving themselves in who knows what uncomfortable personal changes or commitments.[2]

For the would-be helper, then, the task is essentially the same: to ally himself with those natural, expectable, simply human feelings that a nonvoluntary help needer is bound to have. You get started where the help needer *is*. But the course of relationship, like that of true love, rarely runs smooth. So it will happen that relationship snags or rifts will be encountered even when initial resistances have been overcome. The client must do something or is (caringly) prodded to think about and consider some things in some unfamiliar or uncomfortable ways, and his forward movement with you comes to a halt, a resistive barrier arises between you. The signs are not hard to detect. A courageous (or impulsive) client may simply come out with it—"I don't see any point in talking about it any more"—or he will indicate that he has gone as far as he can go, done as much as he can do. A less open client may simply drop out, breaking appointments with or without excuses, or he may be present in body but drop out in interest or engagement, lapsing into monosyllabic responses or silence.

The same principles of dealing with resistance hold: that the helper, rather than blindly pushing against the barrier, must stop with his client to take a look at what seems to be happening, what is the working and/or relationship problem that is blocking them, and why. One thing we helpers must recognize, however. There may be some considerable gap between our goals for a client/patient and his own. He may be satisfied with less; he may be unwilling or feel unready to extend himself to reach as far as we would like him to—and it is a decision of his that must be respected, once it has been openly discussed. Many clients want only to be helped across a crucial time. When the peak of their crisis has subsided, they may choose to resume what we may consider a less than effective mode of functioning but they consider satisfactory. Once the pros and cons have been discussed, the choice is theirs.

For the resisting and the voluntary help needer alike, there is one ultimate motivation that governs decisions about what they want and how they want to get it. It holds for every one of us. We are moved toward what will give us most gratification, least discomfort. What is the payoff, we want to know? What is the expectable outcome in terms of rewards and gratifications? Or punishments and dissatisfactions? This is the basic and consistent question that a would-be helper must place before his client/patient, especially before him who is resisting the help he is held to need. ''What's in it for *you* if you do—or if you don't? How will you feel if this rather than that occurs? What will tomorrow feel like and be like for *you* (or for those who are part of you) if you decide to do this or do that?'' Here too attitudes, reactions, and feelings cluster and permeate considerations of alternative choices and their plausible outcomes. Here too, then, is soil for the sharing of the concerns and conditions that bind two or more people in a working relationship.

6
Some Myths and Misconceptions

IN EVERY PROFESSION there are to be found small dark pockets of residual ideas or rigidified practice that somehow escape exposure to the light of recent thought or revisions of earlier beliefs. The human service professions are no exception. On the subject of relationship there are to be found a number of misunderstandings that deserve reexamination. There are kernels of truth in almost every one of them—as is the case with all myths. But those kernels—some now dwindled and dried and some blown up disproportionately—need to be combed over and carefully reconsidered. From among them I have selected those that follow because they seem to me to be most frequently found in—and to muddy up—the use of relationship in the human service professions.

A Helping Relationship Is a Helping Relationship Is a Helping Relationship

Gertrude Stein might have put it that way. (Then her alter ego, Alice B. Toklas, would have been heard to murmur that it would take Gertrude ten years to understand what she had said!) It is a fact that in the extensive literature on relationship in the helping process it is spoken of as if it were an undifferentiated, monolithic model, set and pat, the same for every man, for every season, for every problem.

If there is any validity in speaking of *the* helping relationship, it is to designate two constants within it: its purpose and its basic ingredients that appear to promote that purpose. Its purpose is to support, enable, and facilitate the help seeker's work on the problem(s) for which he seeks assistance. Its makeup is an emotional bond that brings one human being into alliance with another in personally and socially enhancing ways.

That is *the* relationship in general. But as soon as one moves from the general to the individual case, the cloth must be cut to fit the need. Relationship quality, quantity, emphasis, centrality, primacy—these and other differentiations will arise from the helper's assessment of the specific situation. In the wide range of personalities, of individual needs and capacities that we encounter, the varying kinds and complexities of problems brought for help, the resources present or absent from the help seeker's own milieu, the solutions and services required and/or wanted, available, and suitable—within this range there must be continuous assessments and then adaptations in the relationship between helper and the helped. What the client wants, what he needs, what he can actually get, what he can use, what he can do, what burden of emotional freightage his problem or its resolutions carry for him—all these determine to what extent relationship supports and stimulation are necessary. That is what "individualization" or "personalization" or "humanization" of helping means.[1]

The "therapeutic relationship" has had most attention, discussion, and research within the several helping professions qualified to give counseling, guidance, and psychological healing to persons seeking help with their personal and interpersonal conflicts or malfunctioning. Such problems tend to be heavily charged with emotion, are created by or create interpersonal difficulties, are often the expressions and/or the inciters of relationship disturbances. It is not hard to see why a dependable relationship with a caring and presumably powerful helper may be central to such changes of feeling and behavior as are sought. Yet, as even a superficial review of present-day therapies reveals, there is no unitary model of one kind of interchange even here. Beyond holding assurance of "love" and "power," the therapeutic relationship too will vary in its expressions, duration, intensity, frequency, and so forth. It will vary by the help seeker's age level, intelligence level, class, and cultural background; by his motivation and capacities; by the chronicity or recency of his problem; surely by the "fit" between him and his helper; and surely by his helper's system of beliefs about what is good or bad for the patient—and so on and so forth.

So "a relationship is a relationship" is true only in the sense that to every person in every case the sensitve, responsible helper brings himself ready to recognize and respond to the help seeker as a sentient human being and to be genuinely concerned that the help needed may be found and made available to him in ways that support or even increase his personhood.

When the Client's Request or Need Is for Material Means or "a Tangible Service Only," Relationship Is of Minimal Importance

This is an expectable corollary of the erroneous proposition that a relationship is a relationship, undifferentiated or chiefly for use in therapy.[2] It is a position that has been encouraged by the determined movement (touched on in Chapter 1) toward making unmistakably clear the primacy of concern with people's actual physical and social-economic deficits and thus the necessity that helpers attend to such needs first and foremost. That latter can scarcely be argued against.

What has been bypassed, it seems to me, is this reality: the experience of needing and not having, of asking and being subject to the will of another, of getting but not liking, of not getting, of waiting, of being required by reasonable or unreasonable conditions—all these commonplace experiences that helpers may come too quickly to take for granted—are charged with feeling in the help seeker. He feels them, deep within. He feels them *in relation to* the person with whom he must deal. Therefore, willed or not, a relationship bond is in formation. It may be ignored by the helper who considers what he is doing a matter of course. Or it may be recognized and responded to in receptive, understanding ways. I argue here that a responsiveness on the helper's part that is warm, empathic, concerned, controlled by agreed-upon purposes, is a vital and an enabling condition for the provision of any services on an individualized basis.

Several realistic considerations support the importance of relationship in such transactions.

Nothing takes the place of concrete help when that is what is needed. When a person applies for help to get a job, for rent money, for medical care, that is what he wants. Not a relationship. But the bitter fact is that there are many real and tangible needs for which there simply are no quick, ready, or personally acceptable prescriptions or aids. Very few helpers, for instance, have a job in their pocket for the man who insists that a job is all he wants. Most of them are able only to make some suggestions about applications or perhaps to make training referrals. The tangible aid wanted and needed is plain to be seen. It just is not to be had. And that same thing is true of many of the other kinds of help of a practical and essential nature that people need and ask for and that they feel strongly about when it is not available to them. A helpless helper in that situation has one of several alternatives. He may stonewall it—in part to protect himself from his own frustrations or from the difficulty of bearing the disappointment of his applicant. Or he may connect with the understandable feelings of the help seeker, recognizing and receiving his hurt, worry, anger—whatever. In the first instance he has dealt the aid seeker just one more experience of an uncaring society; in the second the applicant has felt himself understood, accepted, at the very least. Such relating on the part of the resourceless helper is in no sense a sop or substitute for the unmet need. (Anyone who thinks it could be suffers a delusion!) It is simply a proffer of human bonding at a moment of human helplessness.

A second frequent circumstance occurs in what is too readily disposed of in the phrase "delivery of services," that calls for some degree of the emotional alliance inherent in relationship. The help applicant asks for something that may indeed be available and readily provided. But he may not be able to use it prudently or profitably. The rent to forestall the eviction is given him—but he is driven by impulse to use the money for something else; the prescription is filled and the medicine provided, but the patient has his doubts about taking it; a special training class has been found for the neurologically damaged child, but his mother fails to get him there. It is simply not true that, as is often said, "the client knows best" what he needs and wants. No one of us always has the necessary knowledge or balance to "know best," and certainly not when we are overwhelmed by stress, pushed by desperation, racked by conflict, or simply ignorant of probable consequences. Moreover, while it may be all very well to say that we must take the consequences of our self-chosen decisions, those consequences may seriously affect the welfare of others—our children, for instance.

So to "deliver services" may be only part of what is needed. Many people may need to be helped to see the value of the service offered, to cope with its limitations or conditions, to make the most of its possibilities, to manage their own impulses or ambivalences involved in its use. When this is the case— when clarifying, advising, persuading, educating, weighing, and choosing are necessary accompaniments to the *use* of services, when the recipient's mind set or attitudes may have to be changed in even small ways, the helper will need to speak to the client's feelings and reactions, not simply to his reason. Relationship is the name of that effort.

First You Establish a Relationship, Then You Get to the Problem

Relationship, good or bad, begins at the first eye contact between helper and help seeker. Indeed, it may even begin in the latter's precontact mental anticipations of what the helper is going to be like. But this immediate experience of the other is an impressionistic and superficial one. If it is true, as has been proposed, that meaningful relationships begin with and grow on the expressed, shared, empathically responded to emotions of one-to-other, then the trouble the person brings, the problem he suffers, must be the center of attention—the problem along with what it does to the person, the hurts, angers, fears that it creates in him. Relationship is not a prelude to helping. Never. It grows out of some interchange with the help seeker about some piece of his pressing problem, about what hurts him, bothers him, pushes him to need and ask.

As has been said, it may be the problem of having to come for help at all that is uppermost, or of having been treated in certain ways by the receptionist, or the annoying procedures that preceded the interview, and so on. With some help seekers there may be hesitance about expressing such feelings. Still others come ready to tumble the whole thing out, facts and feelings jostling one another in the outpouring. The help giver relates, as has been repeatedly said, to the person; but it is to the person who is *in* trouble, who *has* trouble(s), or *is* troubled. He is not asking for "a relationship." But he will be fortified and freed if he finds that the helper connects with the feelings that are excited by being in trouble, needing help, and making the effort and compromises that are so often involved in using it.

Not long ago I experienced an amusing and telling example of a young doctor's well-meaning efforts to "first establish a relationship."

Running late to class, I hit a pavement hole and fell. So badly battered and bloodied was my knee that I dragged myself into the emergency clinic of a nearby hospital. Bleeding, swelling, annoyed at myself for not having noticed that broken sidewalk, I nevertheless sat obediently filling out the elaborate face sheet that a girl at the desk had handed me. It asked for all sorts of data that my reason told me were essential to a big hospital's records and research but that my feelings said were "absolutely absurd." After about twenty minutes (feeling sorry for my fellowmen and women who also waited with "emergencies," but mostly for myself) I was called into an inner office by a rosy-faced young man whose stethoscope in the pocket of his white coat established his identity and professional authority.

"So!" he said pleasantly, scanning not my face but my face sheet. "You are —————" (my name).

"Yes," said I.

"Hm," he said. "You are —————" (my age).

"Yes," said I.

"Do you have children?" he asked.

"Yes," said I. "One."

"Good!" he said approvingly. "Is he married?"

"Um hum," said I.

"Do you have any grandchildren?" he asked. This was followed by several other socially innocuous and totally ir- relevant (to me and my throbbing knee) questions.

Suddenly I caught on. In this good teaching hospital this young aspiring doctor had probably recently had a lecture either to the effect that a doctor should "relate to the *person* and not just to the disease" or that "first you establish a relationship with your patient, then. . . ." But it had not been made clear to him that, when the person comes suffering with the disease, it is this *combination* of the problem and its personal hurt that must be the simultaneous, interwoven focus of any caring inquiry.

(In all fairness, I must add that he *did* get to and help my knee, finally.)

There Is No Time to Develop a Relationship When You've Got Too Much to Do

Here speak the overworked, time- and task-pushed nurses, caseworkers in welfare agencies, interns in emergency clinics, teachers in crowded classrooms, and others. There is just no denying the reality of their job pressures and the frequent exhaustion of their energies. Nor can it be denied that, in the short run, looking and listening and touching upon or drawing out problem-created hurts do take more time than a business- like approach to the problem itself and its possible dispatch by advice, prescription, promise of forthcoming aid. (One says "businesslike" and is at once aware that modern businesses, commercial and industrial, are increasingly concerned with "humanizing" their relationships both with customers and employees. With all due recognition of their altruistic motives, there must, as well, be some conviction on their part that such attentions pay off.)

As has been said, the need to strive toward developing and deepening a working relationship will vary. It must be a selective decision made by the helper, determined by his appraisal of what the person's problem seems to be, how much the person himself is part of the problem or is emotionally involved in it, even if only temporarily, and what means will have to be used to deal with it. Such selection allows, then, for the brief but warmly courteous attention that may be given to a person whose apparently intact personal capacities or whose natural support system appears to give him the security to utilize whatever material means or directions or information he needs in order to deal with his problem. These are occasional instances.

Several less easily disposed of considerations have already been mentioned. If the business at hand is emotionally freighted for the person himself, some sort of relationship will develop willy-nilly. It might be mostly antagonistic, with the person resenting the lack of attention to himself. It might be positive if the helper stops to look and listen. That does take more initial time. But actual time saving occurs not in the short but in the long run. Relationship development saves time in any situation that can be expected to require ongoing cooperation and participation between the helper and the help seeker. If the latter feels understood and accepted, he is far more likely to do the things he must do to work on his problem. If, on the other hand, he feels unattached, seen as "just another case," there are many subtle, often unconscious ways in which he may block taking in the helper's advice, guidance, carefully laid plans.

Many human service helpers find themselves spending a great deal of time and energy repeatedly going over agreements made but not carried out, advice offered but left dangling, arrangements completed but not taken up by the client. It would be oversimplification to lay all such client resistance at the door of relationship failure, but that is certainly a powerful factor. So the minutes given over to empathic response may save later hours of frustrating running in place.

You Have to Be One to Have a Good Relationship with One

A variation on "You have to be one to know—or help—one," and there is a modicum of truth in this assertion. Surely there tends to be a swifter, more immediate leap of understanding between "likes" than between "unlikes." And to have experienced "the same thing" (being poor, having had a mastectomy, being marginal or outcast from the majority society, parenting a retarded child) is to assure an immediate bond of both interest and feeling. Based on such likeness and shared concerns, all sorts of human groups form and operate for political, social action, social support, and self-help purposes. Indeed, it is the commonly felt problem that is the basis of most groups formed by professional helpers for problem-solving, educational, or therapeutic purposes.

But there are often too facile assumptions about "like" relating best to "like." Beneath a skin-deep likeness between two or more people, one may find that they do not actually feel the same way at all about even the same type of problem. One woman on relief may be extremely hostile to her counterpart down the block for behavior of which she disapproves. Past their shared sorrow at having retarded children, this particular mother feels she must "sacrifice anything" to care for her retarded child, but that particular mother feels she must at any cost get some place or some other person to care for hers. In short, likeness, like-mindedness, like feeling may be more apparent than real, more immediate than steadfast, more superficial than deep-rooted.

One of the dangers in the sleek cliché that you have to be one to help one is that spontaneous relatedness is taken for granted. The possible uniqueness of the person's sense of his experience may not be paid attention at all. Rather, he may be tucked into a category by the nature of his problem, not by the nature of his special complex of feelings and attitudes. Thus one of the positives in *un*likeness is that it becomes imperative for the helper to be aware of the special need to get through the barrier that first reactions may create. It means that he must consciously, carefully lend himself to drawing out the very particular reactions and attitudes of this very particular person (including, sometimes, the reaction against the perceived unlikeness, whether of color, class, sex, age, or any of the many other differences that, on first impression, may create a sense of alienation).

There is, of course, the plain practicality that faces us, too. Even were it desirable, it would be impossible to match helpers and help seekers for their likeness, whether of particular social status or life experience.* During the decade of the 1960s, there was a strong push to use "indigenous" helpers in the human services, in the conviction that "it takes one...." Some of the success stories were widely reiterated and written about, but there is no body of evidence that such helpers were more effective or efficient or more humane than those who had entered the human services as a vocation. There *was* indication (again anecdotal rather than systematically gathered) that an "indigenous helper" very quickly lost his amateur standing and became a "professional," not in the sense that he had acquired the necessary knowledge and training but in the sense that he

----

*More than 2,000 years ago Plato in *The Republic* grappled with this issue. He opined that the "most skillful physicians are those who from their youth upwards have combined with the knowledge of their art the practical experience of disease; they had better not be robust in health and should have had all manner of diseases in their own persons." (How many of us who have been patients have wished that our physician knew "what it feels like"!) "But," Plato goes on, "with the judge it is otherwise...." He should not have associated with criminals or committed crimes since "the honorable mind which is to form a healthy judgment should have had no experience nor contamination of evil habits...." The judge should have learned to know evil not from his own soul but from late and long observation of the nature of evil in others ..." (Benjamin Jowett, trans. [New York: Random House, Vintage Books, 1955], bk. III). In other words, knowledge should be his guide, not his personal experience. Plato's differentiations are worth some rumination as we argue for or against likeness as a desideratum.

began to identify and to be identified with the program for which he worked. Thus his likeness to those he helped became expunged in their eyes, and usually in his own, too.

There are "naturals" among people with no training at all and also among highly trained professionals. There are those persons, trained and untrained, whose characteristic warmth and genuineness of concern for others, whose interest in the individuality of each person, enable them to spark and develop good relationships spontaneously. And vice versa: there are persons whose professional trappings only serve to bolster their personal and relationship uncomfortableness, and those whose apparent likeness is scarcely a substitute for their lack of compassion or tolerance of the other's differences.

Love—or being at one, or the heartfelt desire to be helpful— is not enough to ensure effective help. To these must be added knowledge broader than one's own necessarily limited life experience; good judgment based on such knowledge, self-awareness, and self-controls; and, attuned to the possible differences between oneself and the other, a readiness to lend oneself to seeing with the eyes of, speaking in the tongue of, feeling with the heart of that other.

Finally, recent reports on psychotherapy with economically and educationally disadvantaged persons offer support to the conviction expressed here that with modifications in the attitudes of the professional helper and with the tailoring of treatment means to recognized cultural and educational differences, therapeutic as well as material gains may result.[3]

Too Caring and Concerned a Relationship May Contribute to the Help Seeker's Dependency

True. Too much or too little of anything is by definition undesirable in some way or degree. Leave out that qualifying "too," and let's look at that mixed bag we call "dependency" and then at how its excess may be avoided.

First, we must differentiate between economic and psychological dependency. They tend to be lumped together in the public mind surely, but they are two separate states. A person may be economically dependent for a very long time (as, say, a woman with young children and no husband) and yet be psychologically self-reliant, able to carry all the responsibilities involved in her daily roles (as when a mother takes good care of her children, gets them off, fed and well, to school, keeps her house and financial affairs in adequate order, and so on). At the other pole, a person may have economic independency, a private income, say, and be bottomlessly dependent on others to do for him, to decide for him, to keep him trussed up emotionally. He is usually not classed as "dependent" because he can buy the means by which to escape or disguise his needs for heavy supports from outside himself. In between these opposites there fall a number of persons who may be chronically both economically and psychologically dependent and those who, like most of us, have periods or phases of either or both.

Come to think of it, how did we—you and I—become the splendidly self-reliant, self-directed, self-dependent persons we often believe we are? Was it because no one took care of us? Was it that no opportunities were offered us? Is it that in our waking hours of work and play we find no need for the material means and services or the psychological supports from other human beings?

The answers are obvious. Self-confident and competent people (differentiated from aggressive, anxiously pushing people) are usually those who, over a long period of childhood-into-adolescence-into-adulthood dependency upon the love and caring of others, were fed two messages: "You can depend on being accepted and treasured because you are *you*. You are at the same time expected to be able and willing to exercise your muscles and brain and heart feelings in doing (what you are capable of) and in give-and-take transactions with other people and tasks." When dependency has been allowed but combined with expectations and opportunities for exercise of one's own small or big powers, and when that exercise has (for the most part) yielded satisfactions, a big step toward self-esteem, self-confidence, and self-dependency has been taken. Somewhere along the widening way a further big step is taken when all at once or bit by bit we recognize the fact that it is *inter*dependency that must be the essential characteristic of human life. In a moment we will turn to the application of this common human development to the helping situation.

First, two points in defense of dependency:

Dependency means the need for and reliance upon another. It is, then, essential in all love relationships. A person who believes himself to be sufficient unto himself, needing no one, either is unaware of the many ways in which he draws upon material and psychological sustenance from others, or he has walled himself off from relationships that have wounded and scarred him. A certain amount of dependency—which is to say, need for another person or what that person is assumed to have—is essential to any helping relationship. We need not fear that.

It is expectable that the more resourceless and helpless a person feels, or actually is, the greater will be his need to depend on someone outside himself. That undermining experience of resourcelessness and helplessness is what the helper's presence and support attempts from the first to counteract. Yet we must recognize that there are some life stages and circumstances when a considerable degree of dependency is normal. The very old, the chronically sick or disabled, the mentally disturbed or retarded persons (children too, of course—but we tend to "allow" children to be dependent) are often so drained of such energy and hope or so little able to perceive and cope with themselves in relation to people and circumstances that their heavy dependency upon others must be understandingly accepted. Of course, they should be given every encouragement and every means to do for themselves, to work at tying a shoelace or using a prosthetic device, or even just talking with someone about a television program they have seen. But full recognition and compassion they must also be given for the depletions and losses of mind and body competences that inevitably create dependency.

There occur also those acute crises that drain formerly able

people of their capacity and flood them with feelings of
helplessness. The death of a beloved person, separation from
familiar people and places (as occurs with refugees or migrants),
lack of communication means or interpersonal skills due to
ignorance of language or rules or customs—all these losses and
lacks rouse feelings of need for the aid and powers of another.
Such feelings are temporarily quite appropriate, and if someone
steps in to help in whatever necessary ways, the normally
self-motored person will not fall into or lie long in the slough of
dependency.

There are safeguards that may be utilized by professionally
responsible helpers against the temptation that may arise in
helpless and hopeless people to lean too long and too heavily on
the powers of another.

The first is a temptation the helper himself must be aware of.
(Will I never let you off the hook?) It is that he may forget that
"caring" must be combined with exercising the help needer's
own powers, however minuscule they may be, that acceptance
must be accompanied by expectation, support by stimulation.
He may forget it because of his own good heart, because of his
spontaneous "feeling sorry for," or because of his own need to
be needed. (As the example of Mrs. Green and her naive
caseworker revealed, some pages ago.)

Following on the helper's self-possession comes the recognition that the antidote to excessive dependency in any of us is
to be active or activated, to be up and doing in regard to what
must be done. There is a problem(s), to which, as has been
indicated, there is rarely a swift and single ready solution. There
is a person(s) who must be seen and helped to become an active
participant in coping with that problem. "An active participant" means that he will be encouraged, aided, expected,
not only to tell about it (and thus lay it in the lap of the helper)
but to figure it out, to review the things he has tried to do about
it (so that he can see himself as one who tried, even if
unsuccessfully, to cope), to think together with the helper about
what he needs and what he can get, how he will try to act—for
each piece of his difficulty. The point is, this is work. It is

thinking work, considering work, planning, going out to try something, coming back to talk over how well or rottenly it turned out to be (whether it was looking for a new apartment or getting meals-on-wheels, or trying not to nag the children). What is at work is the person's will (faltering, sometimes) whatever resources of mind he has hold of that may be put to coping. Underpinning his willingness and capacity to work (both within the interview and at-home work, too) is the support of the relationship. To this there is now and again added the recognition of him as a striving-toward-coping person (not a dependent) and the satisfaction (or at least the lessened strain) when he and his helper have filled in some deficit, met some need.

By such means the help seeker may come to know his own strength, even if in small portion, and thus dependency is held to the level required for a trusting, caring interchange between two people.

Even when the needs of the help seeker are largely those created by economic deficits, and material means of various sorts must be given over a long period of time, we need not fear the development of psychological dependency when the person who is helped in tangible ways is kept at work (thinking, feeling, decision making, doing) on at least some small piece of his problem and in carrying his daily life tasks with reasonable adequacy. Dependency on another is diminished not by adjurations that "you are or should be on your own" but, rather, by the accretion of self-confidence through exercising one's own powers in ways that bring both social recognition and self-satisfaction. Relationship offers the temporary supports for such exercise.

The Purpose of a Helping Relationship Is to Enable a Person to Grow

True in part, and only partly true.

One of the problems in grappling with this statement is that even among those who most cherish it, the concept of "growth" has never been clarified. No specificity attaches to it, so it is hard to know what is meant by it or how it is to be discerned.

First of all, not everyone who comes to a helper needs to grow. To us come many people who are quite adequately grown for their age and life stage. What needs to be attended to are those deficits and disturbances in their inner and/or outer lives that are currently undermining their psychosocial functioning. In such instances, we may assume, once the stress level has been reduced and equilibrium of the person/situation restored or reinforced, that their natural development (is it always growth?) will be resumed. To encounter a problem with which one is unable to cope at a given time need not at all be a sign of immaturity, of not being able to act appropriately to one's age. Mature as one may be, it is possible not to know the ways and means or not to be able to command the persons and circumstances necessary to a problem's solution.

Second, the person who comes for help, even one who voluntarily brings himself to a therapist, does not ask to be helped to grow. While he may indeed recognize that his reactions and behavior bespeak immaturity, or that he has childish fears or fixations, he wants to be helped to feel better and act better in his everyday transactions with other people, his work, his studies, his role-task interchanges. He wants help in order to be able to *be* and *do* in more satisfying, less uncomfortable ways. He wants to come to feel more at ease within himself, to have and to hold more "meaningful" relationships, to overcome fears of failure, to be less emotionally dependent on parents or spouse, to know more surely what he wants to get out of life—and so forth and so on.

"Well, then!" you or my other self may say. "That's just a way of describing growth. He may not *ask* to be helped to grow. But that's what he's really after."

Perhaps—which is why I started by giving a "partly true" to the "misconception." The trouble is that the concept misleads both helper and help seeker in a number of ways.

One is its ambiguity, its lack of focus. What is the specified problem, work on which is to yield growth? Every aspect of the client/patient's life? The one aspect that has been the last straw? The several that exemplify the same problem? Or?

If the problem is not to some extent identified and specified in its manifested forms, there results not only a lack of focus but also, expectably, a lack of clarity and understanding between helper and client about goals. By what signs will our accomplishment of growth be known to us? That you will feel better all over? That I feel you have grown as far as you can? That you will feel better in at least some respect? That you have gotten a new job or a new love and need me less? Or?

Very often the problem brought to counselors or therapists (of whatever helping profession) is one of interpersonal relationships—conflict or a sense of misfit between marriage partners, between parents and children, friends or work mates. The dilemma posed by working on growth for the complainant is that his marriage, his parenting functions and behaviors, his interactions with friends simply will not stand still and await his growing. His person-to-person, person-to-group transactions continue. Not only may it be necessary at times to involve his significant other, but it is necessary and desirable to give the person who suffers the problem most acutely some usable means by which he can deal with those difficulties that continue to fester in his real-life situation here and now.[4]

Obviously this means that some part(s) of the larger problem, some typical ways in which it manifests itself and is dealt with, must be focused upon; and that in the interchange between helper and patient/client there must occur some work to feel, think through how the client may deal with that here and now that refuses to wait until he grows up. Such ways may need to be chiefly self-protective, supported by the helping relationship. More desirably, they might be small strategies of planned behavior (again underpinned by the internalized helper) in the nature of tryouts at coping in some small area but in different from usual ways. If they fail, the helper is there to try to put the pieces together again in some other way. If they work, the client feels that self-enhancing sense of having been able to do a little something about his troubles beyond talk. Growth may then be given a forward push. Just as important, however, is that the vicious circle of the problematic interchange has been slowed up or jarred out of its usual track.

Still some further problems inhere in this notion that helping is for growth. Physical growth can be measured. Psychological growth can only be inferred. It is inferred from the person's externalized behavior—he is acting more effectively, at less psychic cost to himself and/or his significant others, with better, more satisfactory outcomes—and/or from his verbal testimony that he feels more able, more confident, less anxious. That combination is a splendid testimony to change in the person. But has the person whose outcomes are less positive grown less? Or are there explanatory circumstances outside him that have contributed to his progress or its lack? "Change" can be specified and evidenced in the person's attitudes, views, values, feelings, actions, and/or the living environment with which he transacts. "Growth" eludes such specification.

Is growth uniform—that is, are we grown equally in every part of ourselves at the same time? Certainly that is not true physically. Is it true psychologically—that if one has learned to deal more competently with one's studies or work, then one has also learned to deal more satisfactorily with one's marriage? Or one's children? If it is not true—has the idea of growth expressed what the helper and help seeker were after?

And when is the ending time if the goal is "growth"? Could such a vague goal contribute to the kind of deepening, mutually dependent relationship that was exemplified in the Green case? One struggles not to give up the ideal we all hold: that somehow human life should be an unfolding, enhancing, expanding experience from birth to death; and that until the time when malignant growth sets in (growth of all those decrements and disease processes to which the human flesh and mind is eventually heir), we should be growing in healthy and satisfying ways. It is an ideal worth cherishing because it prods us to strive to be better people. But the fact is that, while we grow fast and fully in childhood, by adulthood both physical and psycho-

logical growth is a slowed-down and limited process. If only for
that reason, if only to avoid the vague disappointments so
common among helpers because they have not reached their sky
blue goals, "growth" should be recognized as a hard-to-reach,
hard-to-recognize goal in any time-limited process.

My plea here is for some more modest, more realizable, more
measurable goal. What most help seekers are after and what
most human service helpers can provide is help to cope with
some identified, recognized, and felt present-day problem.
Whether that problem is the result of a long entrenched personality difficulty or is due to some crisis for which the person
himself cannot marshal the resources, what will seem real to the
help seeker is that his present problem should be at the center of
attention. He will be motivated to work on it by a supportive,
caring, safe-feeling relationship. His own capacities to perceive,
consider, choose, try out, will be exercised within that relationship's nurture and dependable backup. He will know whether
he "feels better," "is doing better," "finds things better," as
he and his helper see and assess how and what he does with the
people and circumstances involved in his problem, and what
outcomes their joint active efforts yield. Change in him will
occur as a result of rewards both from his helper (that is, recognition, approval, reassurance) and, more importantly, from
evidence that by what he has done some desired change in the
problem situation has occurred.

He will, then, have set out not to "grow" but, rather, to cope
with an identified problem or some piece of it. Relationship will
have sustained and facilitated his effort. If "growth" or a sense
of having "grown" seems to have been promoted, it will be as a
by-product of both his efforts and his helper's nurture, affirmation, and guidance. It may be considered a special bonus.

7

Relating to More Than One

"Two Is Company and three's a crowd" was probably first said by someone who recognized (and maybe resented) the effect that the presence of even one "other" has upon a one-to-one relationship. And someone else, apparently welcoming such presences, said, "There is safety in numbers." It is with the differences in the nature and uses of relationship when small clusters or groups of people are "the client," rather than one person, that this chapter deals.

The helper of a group—whether it is the twosome of a marital pair, or a whole family, or a group purposely formed for working toward some common goal—is clearly in a relationship situation different from that of a one-to-one transaction. He "belongs" to everyone in the group. He is expected to accept and to "care" for everyone equally, to respect and guard each member's equal rights and to be fair to each. It is an ideal devoutly to be striven for! But as anyone who has worked with groups knows, it is an ideal difficult of achievement and sustainment.

Here sits an open-faced group member ready and eager as a baby robin about to be fed; and there sits a frozen-faced member, half turned away, suspiciously eyeing both the leader and his fellow members.

Here sits the tearful mother and there the thundercloud father, and in between them their gum-chewing, sprawled-out, blank-faced adolescent son. And in the next hour's interview with a marital pair, the wife is clearly a nagging Xanthippe and the husband no Socrates but a wordless Casper Milquetoast.

Here, in this hospital group, are three patients trying their best to "discuss," but a fourth one only wisecracks, a fifth remains silent and distant. And there, in the infant welfare center's group of adolescent unmarried mothers, there is a sudden rallying of the group in a silent (but loud and clear) support of one member who has expressed hostile opposition to the group leader's suggestion.

With whom does one just naturally empathize when one person seems to be clearly "in the wrong" and the other clearly "right"? With whom does one try (discipline oneself) to empathize? With which of the several or more persons does one ally oneself, to create a bond? Who is "the client"—the group? The member who needs most help? The member who gives most help?

Work with a group has yet further relationship intricacies. From the first, and certainly as the interchanges among group members go forward, there are roused positive and negative relationship feelings between and among themselves, as well as between each one and the group leader. Coming together to be helped by a presumably caring and concerned person, a presumably effective person, may often excite transference reactions. There often springs up instant (usually unconscious) rivalry with others for the helper's attention and favoritism. Even in a classroom of goal-directed people this phenomenon may occur, as every teacher has observed. It takes no subtle insights to see in this the revival of sibling jockeying for parental love and attentions. (How natural and how ancient a rivalry this is!—How much each of us wants to be related to as Isaac rather than Ishmael, as Jacob rather than Esau, as the beloved Joseph rather than as one of his less loved brothers!) There may be negative transferences, too—distrust of parental power; the fear of being pushed about by one's siblings; the conviction, probably induced long ago in the family situation, that one is the least liked, the least favored.

However, a group also operates to keep reality clear, including the realistic perception of the helper. The reason for this lies in the actual presence and activity of other group members and the (gratefully or reluctantly perceived) indications that the helper is for and with the group as a body. That recognition serves to dilute the intensity of feeling that is more likely to occur in the cocoon of a one-to-one relationship. Furthermore, alliances within a group are formed not only with the helper but also—and more enduringly at times—between one and another group member. Relationship is shared with others. It is shared, along with the sharing of a common problem and the sharing of some agreed-upon common aim. For the group member who has some sense of at-oneness with his fellows, not just with the helper-leader, there is security in his sense that all his eggs are not in one basket. (This happens in families, too. Siblings are not only rivals; they are often supports.) He may dare to differ or to withhold himself in some confidence that he has the backing of at least one other ally.

For one person, then, the group may provide the opportunity for multiple social connections; for another it serves as a shelter (if one *must* work on one's problem!) where he can remain at the margin if he chooses, protected against having to come into too close a relationship with anyone; for yet another it feels like an intervening obstacle between him and the helper he would like to claim as his own. How to treat these various human reactions and wants "equally"? Essentially the question is what variations are called for in the helping relationship when one works with groups, and what are the relationship qualities and operations that hold constant for its problem-solving efforts?

Except for teaching, social work is the profession with the longest and most varied experience in work with natural and formed groups. Its literature strongly affirms that the qualities of person and of communication between a group helper-leader and group members are quite the same as those held to be desirable in one-to-one helping: acceptance, warmth, empathy, caring and concern, genuineness.[1] It is agreed, further, that the basic principles that govern management of the helping relationship in a professionally responsible way hold for work with groups as in work with individuals, to give it substance, boundary, and direction. Our concern here, then, is what is the specialness in helping relationships with more than one, specialness of purpose and of management.

The groupings to be discussed in what follows will be limited to those most commonly worked with by human services personnel. They are families, where two or more members are involved (on their own initiative or the helper's) in working on a jointly recognized disturbing problem. They are small-sized associations of individuals who want a place where they can get together and a person who can help them with the knowledge and material means they need to fulfill their educational, recreational, or socializing interests. They are small conclaves of persons brought together on the initiative of a helper because they have an immediate and like problem to be solved.[2]

Examples of family groups: a husband-wife dyad when marital conflict is the problem; a two-parent and one (or more) child triad (or larger group) when parent-child difficulties are the problem; a couple and aged parent when some less tensional adjustment among them is sought; a whole family, or its key members, which needs to be prepared to receive back into the home a long hospitalized and still disabled member. Note that the problems are for the most part those of interpersonal relationships. Some have been long in the making and have come to a head. Many, however, are sudden disruptions in habitual and previously unchallenged family relationships caused by some new circumstance that demands new adaptions and alignments. The return home of an invalid, the mental breakdown of one family member, the pregnancy of an unmarried adolescent daughter, the death of a parent—all such crises create situational changes but also, and indeed crucially, create interpersonal relationship changes.[3]

Examples of voluntary associations of individuals are long known to neighborhood centers. Typically they are groups of youngsters seeking friendship and recreational opportunities, oldsters seeking the warmth and security of friendly peers and staff, along with "something to do"; adults of all ages seeking the stimulus and means for leisure-time, educational, and interest-expansion activities. Note that in all such groups there is a reaching for relationship, whether with other people or by experiencing the self in relation to some sort of activity or interest.

Examples of groups formed by the helper on the basis of some immediate, commonly held, clearly specified problem: patients in a mental hospital about to be discharged, afraid to reenter the outside world; mothers of diabetic children, anxious about what they must do and what to expect; children hospitalized for surgery or for onerous medical workups whose fears must be assuaged and whose sense of safety and security must be shored up; immature pregnant women who need to be prepared for childbirth and, beyond that, for taking on the role of mother. In most of these groups there is a manifest transitional problem that confronts each member. Yet that problem may feel less individually threatening when there is a sense both of its being shared with others and of being allied with others in learning to deal with it. Of which more further on.*

As is true in work with individual clients, there will be relationship variations determined by the group membership, its purpose, its goals, the often covert needs and wants of its individual members, and so forth. And as is true with individuals, it is also true in work with groups that the helper-leader must have some basic understanding and comfortable acceptance of what grouping is for, what benefits are assumed to accrue from bringing people together for joined work on the problem that is in the center of their concern. The working relationship will inevitably rest upon such understanding. As soon as a person becomes a member of a group, and certainly if his wish is mostly to remain a part and participant in it (to work out a better marriage, to restore family harmony, to continue to be with the company that misery is said to love, or just to have a

*Excluded from consideration here is that tremendously variegated and proliferated "group" of groups formed for instant or prolonged therapy per se for each individual. Whether they are led by responsible and professionally competent and prepared group therapists or are fly-by-weekend operations, they are omitted here, since therapy lies outside our particular focus.

good time with acquaintances), there is a tacit expectation that almost always needs to be made explicit: that the rewards being looked toward or experienced here and now must be for most of the persons in the group. "We" must supersede "me". *I* want to be gratified, or I expect things will work out better for *me*, but that cannot be at the expense of the others with whom I am allied (at least in regard to this problem or purpose). The greatest good for the greatest number is generally the rule that governs group transactions.* But there must be *some* good for me. One part of this may be the reward of having been instrumental in making something the group holds to be "good" to happen.

Here in the little world we create when we bring people together in a group is to be seen the nuclear conflict that has plagued philosophers and the thinkers and planners for social betterment for centuries. It is a conflict inherent in all human transactions—the tension between the individual and the group, between striving for selfish ends versus social ends. In every utopian blueprint of a good society and in every socialist experiment the individual has been valued chiefly as he contributes to the total social good. He is expected—even required—to suppress all self-seeking behavior in the interests of the group. It is assumed—and he is indoctrinated to believe and even feel—that social approval and recognition will be his gratifying reward. It often is. Yet in every utopian experiment (except for a few where religious belief and authority exercised iron controls) and certainly in the postrevolutionary societies that exist today, there has repeatedly occurred the breakout of individuals striving for greater personal freedom, greater self-realization, more opportunity for nay-saying.

On the other hand, in societies where individualism is valued, not only does there tend to emerge that socioeconomic

*Exceptions spring to mind. Sometimes, in a family group, an alliance among and efforts by several members is frankly for *one* of its members in most need, and even in formed groups there may be spontaneous joining among members to help a distressed or helpless individual in the group. But the fact remains that such altruistic efforts have only brief staying power unless the sacrifices made result in some form of personal gratification.

self-seeking called "rugged," in which each man for himself may undermine the social welfare of many, but there arise and flourish cults of "selfness," in which personal gratification is held to be the greatest "good." It may masquerade under such euphemisms as "self-realization" or "self-actualization," but its characteristic manifestation is a drive for "me" and an obliviousness to such socially binding and somewhat old-fashioned qualities as obligation, responsibility, duty, mutuality.*

This man-and-society duality is as old as man's history, sometimes an undercurrent tension, sometimes erupting into open conflict. Work with groups reproduces it in microcosm. (Not, it must quickly be added, that the one-to-one working unit is free of this conflict. Any socially minded helper of an individual person must also keep in the forefront of his mind and frequently place before the help seeker the questions "Good for whom?" and "At what consequence or cost to others?" However, in groups it is continuously in open playout—"me" or "we," separate or cooperating.)

In our struggle to sustain and perfect a democratic society, our thinkers and social planners have placed great value upon both the individual man and man-in-society (different from man *versus* society), upon the individual's pursuit of happiness in diversified ways but always in some balance between rights and responsibilities, between being owed and owing, claims and obligations. The questions of how to realize such values, how to enable man to be both giver and receiver in his interdependencies with others in his society, have been answered in part by certain learned and valued operations—participation, joined consideration and decision making, cooperation, collaboration, conciliation, compromise. All of them involve reciprocity between and among people; all include considerations of both individual and group interests; all rely upon gratifications for both individual and group in reaching some

*At this writing one of the bestselling books on the market, bought in hundreds of thousands, deals with how to get for Number One, yourself, what you want. It is flanked and competed with by a number of other best-sellers that place self-promotion and self-pleasuring on the top rung of the value ladder.

jointly desired goal; all involve some modification or relinquishment of some wants in favor of others.

Group work in this country began as a "socializing" means. It aimed to socialize people by providing them with certain kinds of educational and recreational opportunities and enabling them to learn how to relate well to one another, how to work (or play) together with others, how to take responsible part in group action, how to cooperate toward common goals—in short, to learn the skills of interpersonal relationships toward personally and socially satisfying ends.

Even groups formed for "fun and games" had as their underlying rationale the idea that here lay the opportunity to demonstrate and practice those group interpersonal relationships that led to cooperative, collaborative, interdependent decision making and activities in a common cause. "What we're going to serve at our party," "whom we shall invite," how to divide and share—all this seemingly trivial stuff was recognized by professional group workers as the commonplace materials from which ways of relating, of cooperating, and of participating with one's fellowmen toward social consensus and decisions could be taught, demonstrated, and learned. The greatest good for the greatest number would be served at the same time the individual's rights to dissent could be respected and the individual's right to informed consent or informed choice supported. He was offered the opportunity to choose whether he would become reconciled and compromise with the majority of his fellows and gain its accompanying rewards of belonging, of being in union with others, or whether he would exercise his right to be a minority of one. This latter right is part of a democratic society's valued right of self-determination. Like any self-determining action, it is most fully "free" when it is exercised not blindly but in full awareness of the self-to-other and when the social as well as personal consequences of choice are considered.

A long overture. But it is a complicated score and orchestration, this business of helping people in groups, and the leader needs some perspective on the inevitable tensions that exist and the choices that may have to be made between individual and group. At points where conflict erupts between individuals within the group, the basic question may need to be put for reconsideration by all: What are we together for? What is our held-in-common aim? What good are we to one another? What are the ways in which we can help our single selves and most of us together, too?

It may be said, then, that the main purpose in helping people with their problems via the group method is to achieve a dual goal: to enable them to cope with some difficulty they are experiencing and/or to gain some opportunity they are reaching for; and to do so by such means as will develop their interpersonal relationship competences, their abilities to connect emotionally and collaborate with their fellows. That is a global statement of the helper's purpose. Yet in the miniature world of each small group, it may be reached for.

A group is a kind of "relationship laboratory." Bound together by a common concern, people talk, act, react not only about the issue or problem at hand but always in relation to one another. And the helper-leader keeps his bifocal perceptions and his bifocused action upon both the substantive problem and the ways in which group members are dealing with it and one another.[4]

That latter concern is to the ideal aim of improving, even in small ways and in small units, everyday human relationships. But ideals often have their practical side, too. The practical reason for our concern that interpersonal relations should be gratifying to most of the group members most of the time is this: there is considerable evidence that, even when people are drawn together because of a like felt problem and are bent upon investing themselves in its solution or mitigation, they have difficulty in holding to their task and purpose unless they are sustained and nourished in their group relationships.

If you have ever worked in committees or cause groups you know this. You know how readily issues can be lost and intentions dissipated by failures in interpersonal communication or by communication that speaks clearly to antipathies among group members. So, to keep group members wanting and willing to work on the problem or aim for which they are gathered together, it is essential that they should be helped to talk with one another, to listen to one another, to lend themselves to trying to understand and feel with each other; that they should learn to respect differences and how to accept and work toward compromise, reconciliation, cooperation.

One further practical offshoot of developing good relationships among group members. In discussing one-to-one relationships, it was suggested that the helper attempt to strengthen the client's natural relationship ties, to enable him to connect more firmly and satisfyingly with relationships in his natural milieu. Within many kinds of groups (not all), members find new friendship relationships that provide company and support outside the group or after the group is a thing of the past. This is most likely to occur when they have shared not only a like problem but also a like feeling about it.*

How does this relationship learning occur? In one-to-one helping the helper must by and large deal with what the client/ patient reports of his relationships with others—what he said, what the other did, and so forth—and while the helper also is continuously observing the client's typical responsiveness to *his* inputs, they are different by virtue of the client and helper roles and relationship. Moreover, what the client tells may be unconsciously laundered or consciously selective. The group, on the other hand, is a "laboratory," as has been said, in the sense that what is said and done is on the spot, here and now, played out live. It is thus subject to immediate response that reveals its effects, and both cause and effect are there for the handling, whether by the helper or by others in the group.

By and large, the group helper-leader "teaches" by repeated and consistent demonstration and modeling. What is taught (in

*Mark Twain once said that to share a problem is to "halve it." The emotional supports people find in sharing their problems with others who have the same sort of difficulty, who, beyond this, have found ways in which to deal with them, and who share both their anguish and their encouragement is never better seen than in the recent development of self-help groups. Parents of retarded children, alcoholics, and others find solace combined with motivational power in their bonds with fellow sufferers—and fellow copers.

concert with knowledge that may need to be supplied, controls held, and problem-solving processes engaged in) are the attitudes and behaviors that make for good communication and bonding between people.

Briefly: the helper demonstrates acceptance and respect. He encourages the members' expression of feelings and attitudes so that they may be received and responded to supportively and shared and identified with by others. He shows how to disagree or question without hostility or derision. He accredits people's intentions and the humanness of making mistakes. He listens closely and often asks others to join in with the speaker in expressing their reaction, pro or con, to what he is saying. He encourages the expression of ideas, suggestions, plans. He draws whatever empathic indications there are by asking feeling-expressive questions: "How would you feel—or act—in such a situation?" "Can you imagine what that would be like?" "Has any of you ever had a feeling like that?" He affirms the positives, but he opens breathing space for the negatives, too (for reasons we know by now). He puts in suggestions of his own (if they are not forthcoming from the group), related, for example, to the need for compromise now and then, for giving as well as taking. And so on. The extent to which "relationship work" is practiced will depend, of course, on the makeup of the group, its purposes, its anticipated duration, and so on. Meetings with more than one that by plan are to be short-lived will have to focus more directly upon the task to be done.

How the group member learns to cooperate with his fellows is identical with how the help seeker learns in one-to-one relationship, except that his mentors may include other persons in the group, not just the group leader. The learning occurs by identification, imitation, and incorporation of ways he has observed that he admires, finds congenial, or sees as successful. Such partly conscious learning may be more firmly secured when what has been modeled, demonstrated, and experienced is lifted up into his conscious awareness and understanding. When some action, response, or interchange between or among group members has worked, has resulted in social acceptance or agreement or relaxation of tension, and also when the opposite occurs and some conflict flares high or a stoppage occurs, it is useful for the group leader to stop and place before the group the question of *why*. "Why do those funny human beings called people—that's us—respond better to this rather than to that approach?" "What happened here that made us swing over to this side when we started on the other?" "Nobody wants to talk about this—how come?"

"Reasons why" provide a learner with some guiding principles that he may transfer from this one specific situation to others. Reasons why lift what is amorphously and nonverbally experienced into being analyzed and understood. What we understand we are more capable of dealing with ("more capable," not necessarily "fully capable"!). Thus in working with people, whether one to one or in groups, the helper lifts up what is experienced to be thought about, so as to enable the person to "make sense" of it.*

Down now to some of the specific details in the group helper's forming and furthering of relationship when he deals with more than one.

First and always is the need for the helper's self-awareness, his honest facing up to the fact that his liking and empathy with one group member will leap up in him spontaneously, as will his dislike or discomfiture with another. He may want to examine the whys of his reactions (while munching his lunch or tossing in his bed at night, since there is rarely time or mind space to do so when he is on the job) and to separate out what his own transferences are and what the actual reality encounter provokes. But the important thing is that it is only with their owner's recognition that subjective reactions may be truly possessed and controlled.

*This lifting to conscious awareness in order that it be subject to conscious management of relationship skills occurs (or should) in professional preparation for any of the human services. It likewise occurs in the teaching of relationship skills by enlightened parents to their children when now and again the parent stops to explain how come or why something the child did brought a heartwarming or a hurtful response from another person, child or adult.

Then purpose: "No wise fish would go anywhere without a porpoise," said the Mock Turtle to Alice. Neither would a group leader. The purpose for which the group was formed or for which it seeks guidance is the glue that binds all together. It is the determinant of what we talk about and try to do together, where we're going, how best to get there.

The group leader desirably will have had an initial and separate interview with each prospective member to individualize him and to engage his interest in the group. But at the group's first meeting, when the individual finds himself one of several, there is need for some recapitulation of our purpose and how we might start off. As in beginnings with the individual client, it is useful to draw out from the group members their version of what they are here to deal with. (It is surprising sometimes how different that understanding may have become from what was agreed upon in the preparatory interview, due to what the individual heard or shut out, his subsequent considerations of it, or his suddenly different perspective occasioned by the presence of others.)

The question is, What can we agree upon as the problem to be worked on, or our common interest, and what do we—you— and you—and you—see as the point of our getting together on it rather than each of us going at it by ourselves? The group leader may have to put in starter fuel—how he sees and understands it—but his continuous activity is to draw out from the group their reactions, negative and positive, and to move in the direction of gaining a group compact of agreements. Those agreements may, as a result of present and later discussion, undergo some changes. What is essential is that the group members come to some consensus as to their joined purpose and some beginning idea of the participation expectations. At any subsequent points of conflict, or blocking resistances, this compact may need to be brought forward again for the group's reconsideration and for regaining both its direction and its "how to." This beginning and recurrent discussion may in itself be a teaching-learning experience in participation, negotiation, cooperation.

How to enable these processes of interpersonal communication and cooperation? How provide the climate most conducive to their development? It will come as no surprise that relationship is here held to be the necessary (though not sufficient) component to keep the group involved and at work.

Take "acceptance": each group member is accepted as he is. He is as he is for reasons one often cannot even know. What we do know is that he hopes to get or accomplish something via the group. Often his motivation is heavily charged with pullback, too, with motivation to flee, fight, drop out. This too is accepted as natural or understandable. The negative emotions expressed verbally or by body signs are paid attention to, given opportunity for expression, sometimes opened for discussion. But it is also accepted that there is the other side to the coin, that there is some positive hope or value, some expectation of reward that has brought the person(s) to be part of the group. What is it? The search for the positives may extend to the whole group. As they are fumbled for, partially found, haltingly expressed, the helper affirms them, encourages the possibility that they may become real, supports the wavering hopes for "better."

Each person's expectations, his wants and needs, are given an attentive ear. But those that are unrealistic or that are unacceptable to the group and its purpose must be faced and grappled with, accepting the wish, rejecting its probably unfeasible or unconstructive consequences. "How you *feel*" is acceptable; "what you *want*" is understandable; "what you *do*" here in the group (or on the outside) may be questionable on two bases. It is not likely to bring you what you want (insofar as this can be predicted). And it subverts or runs counter to the group's purpose, to the greatest good. When limits must be placed on a group member or differences expressed, this must be done without hostility and without discomfort. "It is your right to be different—or see differently—from me—or from others. It is my—our—right to differ from you. It is our *purpose*—remember?—not power, that determines what ideas and actions will be supported."

Empathy is acceptance's most active manifestation. It is the group helper's consistent lending of himself to hear and understand feelingly how something feels to a group member. Viewed objectively, that feeling may be "all wrong," skewed, uncalled for, but if it and the person who owns it are to be influenced and if group members are, as a by-product of their experience, to learn to try to feel with their fellows, there must be demonstrated the wish to be with the other person at least to the point of understanding him. Here too one may understand and appreciate how the other is reacting and yet return to the position that there may be other ways of seeing and interpreting the emotionally charged situation. Again, group members are drawn into feeling with and for their comember even if they think differently from him.

Exemplifying the combination of acceptance and support of the individual with the imposition of controls in the interests of the group is the following vignette.

In a parent-education group of ten, one of the women, Mrs. Lavender, considerably more intellectually informed than the others, kept raising abstract, sometimes irrelevant questions, always directed to the group leader—"Do you think Freud's oedipal complex is true?" "Well, how about all this business about the IQ being due to the genes and not to the environment at all?" She also delivered small lectures on her own. "From what I've read there really isn't anything much you can do after the first five years, so I think . . .," etc.

At first the group was respectfully impressed by her apparent sophistication—which undoubtedly increased her motivation to display it—but there began to be evidences of irritation at her taking over. For a time the group leader, in the interests of "acceptance" and encouraging "active participation," tried to make silk purses out of sow's ears. She tried further to get other group members to connect with what Mrs. Lavender was saying —"How does this strike you?" "What's your reaction to what Mrs. Lavender just said?" "Does this ring a bell?" But there was growing resistance, evidenced in silence. So the leader took the responsibility for greater control in the interests of group

aims. Kindly but firmly (to Mrs. Lavender), "That's an interesting point. But it really takes us off what most of us here are
concerned about. So I'm going to ask that we pass on that." At
another time, "How many of you are interested in this question?" Only one hand up. "Let's go back then to what we were
talking about."

After several such sessions, the group leader asked Mrs.
Lavender to stop by for a minute, and she held a brief individual interview with her. Mostly she wanted to call Mrs.
Lavender's attention to—or had she herself noticed it?—the fact
that she and the others in the group were not meshing. Maybe
she was too far ahead of where some of the others were—or
maybe what she wanted to talk about was ideas, and what most
of them wanted to talk about was what to do when their kid did
this or that, and why. So maybe she wanted to think whether
the group was really for her or not. Or whether she could be
more tuned in to it? Mrs. Lavender listened with a kind of
mixed pride and indignation. The group leader repeated that
she was not saying Mrs. Lavender was wrong or the group was
right; she was saying they just weren't at the same place at the
same time. Mrs. Lavender reruffled her feathers and said she saw
what the group leader meant. She returned once, sat in bristling
silence, and then dropped out (to general relief).

Operating in this example is a complex of relationship and
management factors: the helper was aware of and worked at
managing her annoyance at this self-appointed leader (or mis-
leader?). She accepted the person, perhaps to the point of
leaning over backward; she cared enough about the person
(whatever Mrs. Lavender's questionable motivation) to offer
support and then some special attention and recognition of her
"advanced" standing. Yet her most genuine concern had to be
for the body of the whole, whose investments of time and
purpose were being impinged upon by the needs of one. So it
was necessary to establish the guiding rule that the needs of the
majority must take precedence over those of any individual.
And that the individual might determine whether or not he
wished to hold with that condition.

"I care, I am concerned that what we got together for should be achieved. That's why I hope we each can help one another, to work toward that end." This is the sense (not necessarily the verbal formula!) conveyed by the helper's attitudes and necessary controls upon the group's operations.

Another example, this time of the twosome of husband and wife in a series of interviews. Their fourteen-year-old son was the cause of their coming to the family agency. Of high intelligence, Dan had suddenly dropped out of school and had several times threatened suicide. They had finally been able to persuade him to see a psychiatrist, who, aware of their emotional upset and conflicting attitudes about the boy, recommended their seeing a family counselor while he treated their emotionally disturbed son.

From the beginning the counselor-helper took the dyad of father-mother as the "case," the unit of attention. In their anxious, tumultuous pouring out of the account of their troubles with Dan and their distress that the psychiatrist wasn't "helping enough" or "fast enough," Mr. and Mrs. Gold were at one. Their concern, to all of which the helper listened with genuine compassion and empathy, was their child's disturbance and, of course, its traumatic effects upon themselves. They were agreed that their purpose with this counselor was to talk, feel, and think through how they could behave toward Dan as his parents, as a twosome joined together in their parental roles, living and dealing with their highly volatile and perhaps pre-psychotic child.

Difficulties arose when there began to be evident considerable conflict between the Golds themselves. Discussion continuously shifted from their dealings with Dan to their many dissatisfactions with one another in many past and present aspects of their marriage—money, sex, social status, their incongruent expectations of one another, and so on. Sessions began to grow hot with bickering, with each partner vying for the helper's ear and compassion— "Who's right, do you think?" "But of course he doesn't tell you what it's *really* like," etc. Underlying their accusations of one another was that neither felt she or he had ever given the other the kind of emotional support each had hoped and hungered for. The bid to the counselor was for "me-ness," for attention to "my" personal needs. It is a need which may lie somnolent in any of us at times when life is on an even keel but is likely to flare up when we are shaken and feel helpless. To this need the helper remained warmly responsive and empathic. An individual interview was offered each partner, in which each gratefully and emotionally plunged into long past deprivations, as if to say, "Look at what a hurt person I am—at how I've already suffered and struggled." To each the caseworker gave attention; with each she accepted how natural was the wish to regress, because they were under such tension; to each she expressed her admiring support of how they had been able to cope in the past and at present. Each felt she was *with* her or him. But she held to the desirability of their working with her as a team rather than one to one.

For several reasons it was held not to be feasible that they should at this time be taken on for individual psychotherapy. One was the practical necessity with which they were jointly saddled and jointly concerned—that they had to cope as parents with the immediacy of a child in crisis. So with open affirmation of their own needs, the helper records,

> In the next joint interview I gently challenged whether they were as helpless as they were saying. They were adults and they were parents. And it was their child's problem to which at present they had to give their best efforts. I told them (again) how I understood and felt with their separate difficulties, but also I was aware of their present and pressing joint problem. Perfect parenting could not be expected of them. Just the best they could manage. I was there to help them think things through and guide them as best I could. But they would have to invest themselves in their responsibilities if they wanted to give Dan a better chance.

The Golds saw this, reluctantly, but resolutely resumed their roles and twosome alliance as parents. As they struggled forward, the helper records, "Often I would have to intervene, to verbalize what seemed to be happening between them. I would have to frankly support the partner displaying the more appropriate and mature behavior and to set limitations on the behavior of one or the other, recognizing with them the discomfort that this caused, but I also clarified its relevance to our agreed-upon purposes."

What one sees in this case excerpt is, again, that combination of acceptance and expectation, of support and stimulation, and of the bonds of alliance that jointly recognized and jointly desired ends create. Negative or destructive attitudes and feelings are received with warmth and understanding, but the positives (in the sense that they are in the service of agreed-upon ends) are affirmed. Limits are placed upon certain acted-out behaviors, determined not by the helper's own preferences but by the threesome's agreed-upon purpose. The relationship to this couple says, in effect, "I am *with you both* in your need; I am *for you both* in your struggle to cope or master."

Resistances, whether transient or recurrent, are as commonly encountered in dealing with groups as in work with individuals. They may occur among group members (as the parent-education illustration reveals) when some members feel antagonistic to one or more others. They may also arise between individuals or a group coterie and the would-be helper. As holds for work with one, so for work with several (who have become "one" in this reaction): it calls for open, honest recognition and concern that the resistance be faced and worked through so that the blockages to our work together may be removed. An invitation to "talk it over" openly may not be accepted, since even hostile people are often inhibited from expressing their feelings toward someone whom they see as having "authority." (Mrs. Lavender's retreat into silence is a case in point.) What may need to happen, as in individual interviews with resistive clients, is that the helper puts before the group what he supposes the relationship problem may be. Even if the response is deafening silence, his ideas have usually been heard and tucked away perhaps for later consideration.

A personal example of this: I had been assigned to teach the third quarter of a class that had spent two previous quarters with another instructor. This transfer was long planned, and the reasons for it had been explained to the class at its very beginning. They were reminded of it before the close of the second quarter. At a rational level, the class members all understood and accepted the change. But underneath that intellectual reasonableness one could anticipate (simply because students are human beings!) that emotional reactions were also at play. There is natural resistance in all of us to any change when we are pleased and comfortable with the status quo. And if, as in this case, there have been bonds of mutual liking and alliance woven between teacher and learners as they dealt with such emotion-laden materials as values, beliefs, attitudes, uses of self as helper and as learner, one could anticipate resistance to the severing of those bonds by the intrusion of a different and unknown person.

It seemed to me there was no way to begin productively except by facing these facts, by saying out loud to the keenly alert and scrutinizing class members what I imagined their reaction to be. It was surely understandable. It was uncomfortable for them, and for me, too. They had not only lost someone they had come to like very much (I knew this to be the case) but were now having to readjust to someone new and different—etc. Everyone listened intently. A few smiled warmly and responsively. A few drew very careful doodles in their notebooks. But most eyed me inscrutably. I looked to them, inviting comments, but met silence.

I went on after a few moments to say that maybe one of the best pieces of learning they could take out of this experience was how it feels to clients to have a valued relationship terminated by ending or transfer. More responsive faces to this. But the important thing beyond their present feelings, I suggested, was that their former instructor and I and they were all of us bound together by a common goal. That was to go forward with learning how to understand people and how to use ourselves in their needs. So we would go forward now in that joined effort.

Was there a total dissolving of the resistance at this honest recognition and acceptance of their feelings? Alas, no. Somewhat more than half of the class now looked kindly upon me and showed by body attitudes that they were ready to proceed. Others kept their safe distance. But, as succeeding weeks and discussions revealed, every one of them had heard what had been said; all had been pleased or at least relieved that I could ally myself with them even in their negativism. Some, however —as will occur in other instances of group resistance—protected themselves until they could repeatedly test whether my actions actually supported mere words. What was important, I believed, was not whether I won them over but that some vent in their resistance was opened up so that their energies and intentions could be reinvested in the purposes for which we came together.

Whether a helper in any of the human services will choose to work in one-to-one or one-to-more relationship depends upon a whole range of factors and considerations. For many years in social work, casework (help to and through one person, the applicant, usually) and group work were taught and practiced as two distinctly separate methods. Group work was used chiefly for educational/socialization/recreational purposes, and casework chiefly for the mitigation or solution of interpersonal and person-to-role-task, "psychosocial" problems in the management of daily life transactions.

Over the past two decades or so, however, as caseworkers recognized that role problems always involved at least two persons, they began to interview the groups of two or more involved in family problems. As they worked in schools, hospitals, and clinics, they grew acutely aware of the many problems that parents, patients, patient-families had in common with one another, and caseworkers began to lead parent-education groups, to meet with patients and their families in problem-focused groups, and so on.

On their side, group workers became interested in these same sorts of problem-centered groups. They also began increasingly to recognize the need for the occasional interviews with individual group members for various purposes. Now in many places professional preparation for social work includes training in both individual and group methods.

The criteria for which method is best suited to what situations remain as yet insufficiently articulated. Choice may often be made on the basis of the method in which the helper finds himself most comfortable or apt, by the availability of others with whom to form a common-problem group, by the organization's traditional modes of operation, by expedience or economy of time and effort, by the helper's judgment of what relationship experiences the person(s) most needs and can most profitably use—the list of determinants, as you can see, is a long and varied one.

Some of the examples within this and other chapters indirectly suggest that *purpose combined with relationship needs* ought to be primary salient considerations. Perhaps relationship needs (to facilitate coping with a problem) and relationship capacities (to enable the person to cope with others involved in the same problem) is one consideration that deserves further examination for determining what form of helping communication is best. Sometimes persons who most need to belong and be part of a group are least able to adapt to it without considerable preliminary preparation in safe bonding with at least one other. Rose, in Chapter 5, is an example. Her cry for "attention to *me*" was loud and clear. Isolating herself from family and friends and substituting quantities of food intake for relationship nourishment revealed that something had gone awry in the usual capacity of an adolescent to be sociable. She needed to deny caring about anyone. Had she been persuaded to attend a group, say, one on dieting, one could predict that she would be a divisive, resistant member. She needed special acceptance, empathy, caring, individualized attention by one person first in order to develop enough security to reach out again to others.

Mr. and Mrs. Gold, on the other hand, could be helped as a twosome because they had no problem of relationship to a helper. They were ready, eager, trustful. They willingly came for help in their role as parents. In their emotional distress they found themselves wanting help as hurt individuals, too. But in the judgment of the helper (right or wrong), they had to hold themselves to getting and using help together as a twosome, as parents, if they were to deal with their present-day problems with their son.

In larger groups, such as those whose members prepare for transitions in their lives—from pregnancy to motherhood, from hospital to life on the outside—or whose members want (or have been persuaded to try) to expand their understanding toward changing attitudes and behaviors, such as the parent-education group—the members enter the group with a modicum of tolerance for other people, a measure of anticipation at learning, and the security that only a very circumscribed part of their lives is to be dealt with. Perhaps these conditions are the essential ones in being able to use a group well. Perhaps they are the necessary base from which persons can begin to connect with others in accepting ways, begin to watch, listen, and learn from others' behaviors, to gain sustenance from new acquaintances and friends. I make these differentiations and raise these questions tentatively, uncertainly, to open them for more general consideration.

The common qualities that characterize a helpful relationship, whether one to one or one to more than one, have been affirmed. The differences between the fairly narrow channel of feelingful communication and bonding between helper and one person and the complicated crisscross channels between and among helper and group members have been noted. The uses of relationship in both forms of helping promote the person's sense of worth and facilitate his coping and learning.

What this chapter has emphasized in dealing with such working relationships as involve more than one other may be summed up as follows. When members of a group feel in good communion with the helper, feel nurtured by his genuine interest and responsiveness, the climate for learning is maximally good. What is to be learned will differ according to what the group is for. But whatever its manifest purpose, there inheres in any group situation the need to deal with oneself *in relation to*—always in relation to—others. How to get along; how to maintain one's own rights while taking some responsibility toward others; how to express difference without being or making others mad; how to join energies and efforts with others in some common interests or goals; how, in short, to develop interpersonal competencies that at least will serve one's immediate ends and at best become part of one's repertoire of the interdependencies that social living requires—these learned skills facilitate all social interchanges.

They are perhaps never better scrutinized, practiced, and influenced than in groups formed for or focused upon some commonly sought goal. Under the conditions of identification between group members and the helper-leader, the latter may be seen and learned from as a model. But a large part of his task is to prime and develop leadership responsibility among group members themselves so that an interchange of peer learning and helping may be set and kept in motion.

Past those essential physical survival and safety needs that must be assured for every one of us is the need for love, and just past that, perhaps intermingling with it, is our continuous lifelong need for social connectedness, for belonging to and with and for other human beings. Whatever its original ancient adaptive purposes, we seem now to carry in our very genes the need for others. In their eyes we see ourselves, in the interplay with them (whether competitive or cooperative) we come to know our worth and meaning. But absent from our genes— perhaps not yet "implanted"—are the patterns by which to gain those connections and to get along with others, the means by which to develop such modes of relationship interchanges that yield the longed-for sense of belonging and the gratifying sense of cooperating to a joined end. So there is much yet to be understood about the tangled skeins of relationship bonds within groups. It is perhaps no exaggeration to suggest that each group of two or more with which we in the human services deal offers a miniature experience in understanding and furthering the belonging and collaborating skills that are essential to the enrichment of human life.

8

Relating to Significant Others

"No MAN is an island, entire of itself; every man is a piece of the continent." So said the poet John Donne more than 300 years ago. And in this last quarter of the twentieth century it still holds. Except today, straining as we do for scientific credibility, we might say something like "every individual is in continuous dynamic transaction with his ecosystem." Say it as you will. What we recognize is that every one of us from birth onward is connected to other ones, continuously acting upon and being acted upon by them, influencing and influenced, penetrating and penetrated by the emotions, attitudes, ideas, and actions of others who create and/or affect both our reality and our sense of ill- or well-being.

They are our "significant others."[1] They are significant because at any given time, lifelong or brief, what they communicate or do has an emotionally charged effect upon us, whether upon our inner selves or upon the outer circumstances of our lives. Significant others have deeply influenced our past; significant others, real or fantasized, influence our dreams of our future; and certainly they actively infuse and affect our each day's living. They are the persons, sometimes known intimately —but sometimes unknown to us—who "matter" to us in a variety of ways, because what they do or fail to do provides us with physical and psychological support (or undermines us) with physical or intellectual or emotional gratification (or frustration).

They are, in short, a major part of what we call our "environment." Of course, environment (or, if you prefer, the more recent term "ecosystem") has many aspects that are not man-made or man controlled. But as soon as we talk about environment as "social" or "psychological," we are into the peopled environment again. Here, within the confines of our special subject matter, relationship, only one part of that living environment will be dealt with: that of your client's present, immediate significant others. Even "significant" will be reined in. The others to be discussed in what follows will be counted significant only *if they bear in some vital way upon the problem* for which help is needed or being sought. That vital way may be in one or both of these ways: *the person apparently has some* current and active *part in creating or exacerbating the problem* for which help is proffered, and/or *the person appears to have some potential power in modifying that problem* or aiding our client to cope with it.

The gist of this chapter's argument is that, since significant others are people, and since our effort must be to engage their interest (in our client), to move them (in our client's behalf), to influence them to take some actions or to change some attitudes and behaviors (that will redound to our client's benefit), then what we already know about the uses of relationship must permeate our work with them. It is possible, I suggest, that if we were to utilize our relationship skills with the client's significant others, we might experience some considerably increased success in influencing what sometimes has seemed intractable and forbidding—the environment.

That seems simple enough. But it is actually quite complicated by a number of factors. Some inhere in the conditions of our work, some in the significant others themselves, and some (it will not surprise you) in our own attitudes and expectations. So to this task of examining some of these factors and the possible explanations for them.

It seems to make such plain common sense, doesn't it?—that not only are we continuously affected by the attitudes and behaviors of people who are close to us and matter, but other human beings in one status or another pull the strings, open or close the doors, give or withhold the means by which cause and consequence in our lives are heavily determined.

This common knowledge has of late been supplemented by several careful studies confirming the potency of influence of the help seeker's immediate peopled environment. In a study of some 700 cases to search out what factors seemed most vitally to affect the client's ongoing use of family agency services, it was found that "for clients with psychological problems the important factor [in client continuance] is the attitude and behavior of other persons. . . . If other persons were clearly supporting the client's .problem-solving efforts, the ratio of favorable to unfavorable outcomes is two to one. If other persons were indifferent or opposed to the client's efforts the ratio is exactly reversed. . . ."[2] Another recent study, coming out of one of this country's most highly regarded and theory-productive psychiatric-psychoanalytic facilities, concludes, "The results of our study have not only convinced us of the vital importance of the patient-environment dimension for successful treatment and for assessing the patient, but also reemphasizes the importance of including the environment in psychoanalytic theory construction."[3]

Does it strain credulity to suggest that, if significant others or environmental involvements seem heavily to affect people whose problems are usually designated as "intrapsychic" or "psychological," their importance may be at least as great for problems where material or tangible needs are present, needs for which the resources are always controlled and conveyed by other people? And needs, furthermore, that always carry their own psychological freightage?

Yet the evidence is that the helping professions and the human services in general have given rather short shrift to the business of working with the client's significant others. Of course, there are many individual instances that are exceptions to this accusation of short shrift. And, of course, the profession that is the exception is social work, which from its inception has looked always in two directions: to the individual client and, pivoting about, to those people and circumstances affecting him. Perhaps because of its theoretical commitment to working to modify and improve its clients' environment and because of its long, if irregular, practice in it, the social work experience is the most fruitful one in which to examine the problems in interventions into the client's proximal peopled "ecosystem."

From its beginnings the guiding concept in social work has been that of "person-in-situation."[4] It has been accompanied by the term "psychosocial," to indicate the person's inner and outer realities and their interchange effects. In its early years social work called its efforts to affect conditions and persons connected with the client's problem "environmental manipulation." It was a term that had rather repelling undertones, because it suggested unwanted interference and mechanistic tinkering. To take its place came the term "environmental modification," more acceptable in its implications and certainly more accurate as a description. Most recently, partly responsive to the general interest in both ecology and in systems theory, the concept "ecosystem" has been put forward to express and emphasize the indivisibility of the "system" we call a "person" from his dynamic transactions with other systems within what we call "environment." By whatever name, the essential postulate is that cause, energy, and outcomes of action lie not just within the individual person's motivations and capacities but in the transactions between him and his significant others (persons and circumstances).[5]

It was social work's environmental perspectives and practice that brought a number of other professions to seek its collaborative services. Physicians, psychiatrists, teachers were among the first to recognize that their ministrations to their patients and pupils were sometimes not enough to bring about the changes they sought, and that the circumstances and significant others with which their help seekers lived twenty-four hours a day, seven days a week, had to be attended to if medicines and psychotherapy and tutelage were to take hold and have any sustained effects. The collaboration of social workers in these purposes has become even more widespread over the years. Today, for instance, there is growing use of them by business and industry, whose leaders recognize that an employee's productivity and morale may be signally affected by what goes on in his life outside the job.

It was in social work that there began what has now become a widespread treatment mode across several helping professions for problems of intrafamily relationships (marital and parent-child problems chiefly)—the treatment rather sweepingly called "family therapy." (See Chap. 7, n. 3.) As was noted (in the discussion of the Green case), social caseworkers in family agencies had always recognized that husband-wife and parent-child were reciprocally influential roles. So the significant other was almost always seen or contacted, for purposes of getting "the two sides of the story" and also to try to influence the behavior of the one or more others involved in the problem. In the best of child guidance clinics the significant other (the mother, usually) became the "patient" of the social caseworker, while the child was dealt with by the psychiatrist (and occasionally the social worker wryly wondered who had the primary patient and who the significant other, she or the psychiatrist).

In the early 1940s it was a social worker who first proposed that a marital problem is a problem of role transaction.[6] From this recognition interviews held jointly between the members in conflict began to be experimented with, and a whole new mode of dealing with the here-and-now interrelationships, not just with individual personality difficulties, began.*

In these several respects social work has developed and contributed a special dimension of helping to the human services: the joint treatment of the significant others involved (and voluntarily involving themselves, it must be noted) in working on interpersonal relationship problems; and the exploration and influence of those environmental forces operating upon the persons and problematic situations for which another profession simultaneously carries primary helping responsibility.

*Apropos of this, the Menninger Foundation researchers, Voth and Orth, cited above (n. 3), comment, "Therapy which aims at changing the environment to suit the patient appears to be much easier to conduct than treatment which aims at producing essential intrapsychic change ..." (p. 90).

But—and yet. It is true that family treatment remains a highly valued form of helping in social work and in the several other professions that practice it. And while in some places and at some times collaborative work with other professions has been found rewarding, it has been most gratifying when work with the patient's or client's significant others has most closely approximated work with a primary client. This needs a bit of explanation. It is to say that social workers (like every one of us) seem most to enjoy and value work with a significant other who wants help for himself (say, the husband of a woman with a stroke, bewildered by how to relate to her, what to expect, how to manage the household and children, and so on); who wants to be of help to the primary client (the loving, anxious parent of a mentally or physically handicapped child); who presents himself ready for advice and open to reason; who sees or comes to see himself in a kind of partnership with the helper; and so on. There are ideal significant others as well as ideal clients!

What is far less enjoyable, less rewarding, and has been least valued are those efforts to deal with significant others who are reluctant participants, sometimes strongly pitted against the client—and therefore against anyone who is his advocate; who are minimally responsive; who take too much time to connect with (broken appointments, innumerable telephone calls, hard to find and hard to reach); those who, in short, seem to require more footwork than headwork or who make themselves psychologically inaccessible.

So understandably, naturally, these have been turned away from. To be sure, there are often preliminary forays out to "see" this person, "contact" that resource (there is scarcely a resource that is not controlled, conveyed, or withheld by a live person), to touch all bases, or to check off required routines (although such a contact is rarely experienced as "routine" by the person being seen). But these are often done with minimal interest, perhaps with little conviction of their usefulness. There is evidence that significant other persons in the client's life or possible resources and opportunities which would have to be gotten through personal interventions are often disregarded or underutilized.[7] Yet they may be sending poisons into the bloodstream of the client's life, or he may be experiencing unnecessary deprivation for want of their support.

It is this weedy field, this as yet only sporadically tilled area of the client's significant others, that I propose we dig into together to see whether it may be more consistently and effectively managed.

Who are these persons who, at any given point in the client's problematic situation, may be considered his significant others?

They are the butcher, the baker, the candlestick maker; the landlord, the creditor; the policeman, the doctor, the visiting nurse, the social worker in one or another agency. They are family members who despite blood ties are unconcerned, who have sloughed off any emotional bonding they had; or they are family members who may indeed be concerned but are unknowledgeable either about the client's problem or about what they can or might do.

Some ordinary examples may remind you of like ones.

A landlord must be talked with. Your client, his tenant, has tried and failed. Her children have been found to have lead poisoning traceable to their ingestion of broken wall plaster. The flat owner must (by a recent city housing ordinance) have the walls scraped, repaired, and repainted with lead-free paint. One's first step, of course, is to enlist his voluntary agreement to this. Should he ignore, or put off, or resist ("They never pay the rent on time," "I'd just as soon have the whole bunch move out," etc.), one may have to take a number of further actions in regard to this noxiously significant other: report it to the city housing violation department, arrange with the pediatrician to bring like pressures, follow up insistently on the (too frequent!) delays—and so on.

The twelve-year-old boy in the family you're helping suffers cerebral palsy. His slurred speech and twisted body disguise his high intelligence and sensitive awareness, and the frequent open antipathy or even cruelty of his schoolmates (for children are often acutely uncomfortable and afraid of deviance and deal with it by giving it a wide berth or mocking it) have left him isolated. And at a time when social connectedness begins to be deeply yearned for. You learn of an after-school group or a not-too-far-off neighborhood center. To tell the boy about it, to send him there on his own, would only be to thrust him into another rejecting, hurtful experience. The significant other, in this instance, is the group's leader, a young, enthusiastic, volunteer college student. He may welcome, but not really understand, this boy and his double handicap—neurological and, by now, psychological. So he must be talked with, not pressured but, rather, consulted with, about how the boy might (or might not) fit in with the group; how he, the leader, might prepare the group to receive and deal with the boy while you, the family helper, prepare the boy himself to want to join. There may be necessary some ongoing contacts or consultations with the group leader, should problems arise. Or, in the happy event that boy and group make a good connection, how rewarding to the significant other it would be if you talked with him to convey your recognition for his efforts!

The wife and three children (ten, twelve, fourteen) of a man who has been in a mental hospital for the past four months are, obviously, his significant others. They love him. But not without ambivalence, because his past rages alternating with withdrawal and self-abnegation puzzled and frightened them. And things at home have been so much pleasanter during his absence. You are the social worker—paraprofessional or trained—whose primary concern is to see that this man, now steadied by the combination of medication, psycho-, and milieu therapy, can reenter his family world with the least amount of discomfort, the maximum of support and acceptance. You explain his needs to his wife. She wants him home, she is glad he is better, but she is also afraid. Besides, she has needs, too. So do the children —they've got to be able to have friends over, to act nasty sometimes, as all kids do, and so on. You understand—but it is awfully important. So the wife-mother goes home and tells the children that Daddy's coming back and everybody's got to mind his p's and q's—and each one quakes inside himself.

Here are a group of significant others who are going to

need—and ought to get—ongoing help. They need more than a helper's sympathetic understanding and advice. They need underpinning; standing by; the chance to express their fears, perhaps their misconceptions, perhaps their skewed expectations, their frustrations; and particularly they need to talk over the ways in which they can walk that fine line of meeting the needs of another and their own, too. These talk overs might be with one, the wife-mother, or in the family group. They might be regularly scheduled over a period of time or arranged on call. But in this and many like situations, it cannot be assumed that a client's or patient's significant others will be able to act in response to cool reason.

This last example raises few questions about why the helper needs to engage and attempt to influence the people whose attitudes and actions constitute the client's most influential environment. But the first two examples illustrate the many instances in which persons who are one-time or short-term actors in the client's problem need to be drawn in and persuaded to act as helpful or cooperative others. It is these who are often overlooked or bypassed. Or we may advise the client himself to see this person, talk to that one, contact the other. Well and good, if he can do it, if he will do it, if he has the personal competence or stature to command the eyes and ears of the other.

What keeps many of the people we must help from being able and willing to make connections and arrangements with others in their own behalf?* Many things: lack of self-confidence; lack of know-how or skill in dealing with another person; just plain not knowing what his rights are, what the resources are, what the channels are; fear that (once again) he will experience a turndown, defeat; inability to express or explain himself, often because of language problems.

Added to these lacks in himself are the mind- and patience-boggling difficulties of navigating the labyrinths of the system. Helpers themselves know these—indeed, this may be one of the

*It goes without saying that one does *for* the client only when he cannot do for himself or when, in urgent situations, one seeks to expedite service.

reasons we sometimes unreasonably hope "someone else" will do this job. The switchboard operator leaves you hanging on a dead line; you get disconnected; you are sent from one desk to another; you get different information (let's say about why the social security check has not arrived, or when Dr. X's clinic next meets) from the several people before whom you have placed your query. And you have no recourse because you are just a little person. When, on the other hand, you represent an organization, a community agency, you are more than a little person; you are to some greater extent empowered to get a hearing by your occupied position.

That last, incidentally, holds not only with large organizations. It holds with individuals, too. When your little old lady client quavers over the telephone to her nephew and hopes that he'll come to see her sometimes, he assures her he will, he will. When you phone him (since he has *not* come) and ask if you might talk to him about his aunt, he may be annoyed at your intervention, but he may be pricked into action, too, because his defection is now *socially* seen. (It is not only in China that face has its importance!)

And now, at long last, to get to the business of the helper's relationship with the client's significant others, to how relationship may facilitate or hamper our purposes with them. Those purposes may be any or all of three:

> to get information and better understanding of the problem and person;
> to give information toward the other's better understanding of the client and his problem, more often to give such interpretations as will favorably affect the attitudes and actions of the other toward one's client and his dilemma;
> to actively engage the motivation and capacities and such means as the significant other has that will ease the client's problem or enhance his ability to cope.

By now you know what comes first: self-examination, self-awareness, taking a good hard look at what attitudes and feelings in ourselves as well as what actual situational deterrents may operate to lower our effectiveness.

There are, undeniably, some practical deterrents to consistent attention to the people who affect our client. Persons who do not seek you out set their own conditions. You must go where they are (physically as well as psychologically), and that is often time consuming. Moreover, if they are to be talked with more than once and for more vital purposes than simply "touching all bases," they become both time and energy consumers. And most case load assignments simply do not take cognizance of the time space that is necessary to work with others than the primary client. Agency administrators, in line with most of us, have tended to see this work with the client/patient's environment as a kind of secondary activity, necessary but somehow not necessary enough to consider it in time accounting and to modify case load numbers accordingly. Besides, these intercessions with others have not been recognized for the kinds of skill (of which relationship skills are part) they require, and therefore they have had minimal attention. The *need* for environmental modification or ecosystem intervention is repeatedly averred. The *techniques or methods* have rarely been dealt with (exception: in community organization, but these are often not immediately transferable to work with individuals).

Except where the significant other becomes jointly involved in treatment, as in family counseling, it is all but impossible to get an account of the process by which a helper engaged the motivation and influenced the action of another in his client's interest. What is recorded are such brief notes as "I talked to the real estate agent and he agreed to...." "I called Dr. X, who was very annoyed with Mrs. Y. I urged him to see her even if she came late, and after much discussion he agreed"; "I saw Z's teacher and explained about the home situation. She will try to give Z more personal attention." But how were these agreements reached, one wonders? What happened to change an attitude or a position from being against to being for the client?

The vicious circle is clear to be seen here. If a process is undervalued, it is underattended to; underattended to, it loses quality and thus is undervalued. The possibility is that time and case loads will not be readjusted until some responsible experimental practice shows that such efforts on the helper's part have actually benefited the client. To that end, we need recorded demonstrations of skilled interviewing of the help seeker's vital others. And then there must be some systematic examination of the results of such efforts in their effect upon the client's problem or his coping.

In full awareness of these external realities, we must turn our eyes back to our own personal reactions and experiences in dealing with the important people involved in our client/patient's problems. It is, after all, over our own attitudes that we have most immediate personal control.

The persons who are short-term or occasional significant others rarely seek us out. They do not feel in need; they are not hurting. Many of them would prefer to be bypassed. For these reasons alone, we feel no spontaneous leap of feeling for them, no warm outgoing of concern or caring for them. Rather, we view them dispassionately as prospects for contributing to our "own" client's welfare, or as forces whose bad effects need to be diminished.

"Dispassionately" only sometimes. At other times, we feel real antipathy toward them. They are doing what is harmful to our client, or they are not doing what might be good for him. They "ought," we feel, to be or do in different ways. Worse still, they often are actively resistive to having any part of the client's problem, and they may indicate clearly that they prefer not to be involved. "I've done all I can," "I'm sick of the whole thing," "I've got troubles of my own," "Listen, I'm not in the philanthropy business." So we bristle, trying not to show it in the tone of our voice (on the telephone) or the expression on our face (in person).*

It's true—everybody has his own troubles. And if he is lucky enough to be in a relatively untroubled period, he would natur-

---

*All of us have, gratifyingly, encountered the understanding, cooperative, ready-to-help other, too. But what we grapple with here are resisters, the problematic ones, because it is these that pose the challenge to us.

ally like to keep it that way. We arrive on the scene and bring him a trouble. We may ask very little of him, but we do ask for his time and attention at the very least. Beyond this, we often ask him to make some change in his status quo—and that change is for the benefit of somebody else. We ask that he make some shift in his thought or feeling about our client; harder still, we often ask that he should *do* something, should take on some responsibility or take some action, one time or ongoing, that is different from what he has up to now done. So it is expectable that, unless he already has a lot of emotional investment in our client, he will defend himself, stiffen against us, our interpretations or suggestions.

Sometimes by our attitude and behavior we add fuel to his already simmering resistance. Our approach may be the very model of civility, but it tends to be an approach to his mind and not to his feelings. We expect reasonableness, somehow, simply because he is not an applicant for help. We forget that if he wants no part of us or our client he is already feeling negative and resistive. Furthermore, he may fear and resent being "used." No one wants to be considered a tool in behalf of someone else. (This is rather a different situation from that of a helper's freely chosen decision to be an instrument toward another's well-being; that latter is a self-determined commitment, the former is felt as an attempted imposition by another.)

So we often encounter in this significant other a person whose feelings are running high or whose defenses against personal involvement serve as self-protective walls. Because we helpers also are human, our feelings are roused—anxiousness to accomplish our mission quickly, or annoyance or indignation that this person has so little understanding or compassion for our client. Often we have an unpleasant sense of being personally refused—or even granted—a favor. The experienced among us know all these reactions in ourselves. To know them, to admit them, is the first step in their management and control. And now to deal with them.

As is the case in direct work with our clients, we move toward restoring our balance by reminding ourselves of our purpose.

What is the point of this encounter? And from this, how do I best go after it?

To get information for better grasp of the client and his problems is the simplest purpose.

There are frequent instances where the client/patient himself is unable, for whatever reasons—mental, physical, emotional—to state, explain, clarify the nature of his problem, its antecedents and consequences. Thus it may be necessary to get such data and explanations from more reliable or knowledgeable sources. What we plan or do depends upon knowing the facts.

Most facts have their subjective as well as objective content, especially when they are accounts of realities that have been processed through the senses and apprehensions of subjectively involved human beings. So (taking a swift detour around philosophical questions about whose reality is "real") it is desirable for a helper seeking information to keep one ear attuned to the subjective involvement of the informer. He may be strongly biased, for or against your client; he may be biased against you, or what he thinks you represent; and either or both of these will shape and color what he says. One of the most reliable ways in which to come closer to objectivity is to ask for examples that will clarify meaning. For instance, what exactly does the grandmother mean when she says, "That child has acted crazy since the day he was born"? Can she tell me how? In what ways? What does the employer mean, exactly, when he reports that the man is "absolutely unreliable"? Would he give some examples? What is the teacher describing when she says, "He is too aggressive"—an overactive child? An openly hostile child? An actively curious child? One of the things any one of us finds gratifying when we are telling about something is evidence of the listener's keen attentiveness, his manifest interest in our telling. It is the old story: few of us have good listeners any more, and everyone likes to be heard out. (One must add, within the worker's time limits and relevance consideration!)

Even before the information you seek is called forth, there are several small ways of relating (perhaps they are only courtesies that oil the wheels of social intercourse) that tend to ease the informant into communication. One is the recognition that he is giving his time. Another is a kind of "giving" to him: some brief explanation of what you hope he can offer in relation to your purpose. If you see and hear that he has emotional involvement in this situation (he seems compassionate, concerned, angry, impatient, whatever), give his feelings cognizance and accept them. This draws him toward you, and this is important, especially if there is any possibility that you may be needing to involve him further.*

When a helper sets out to give information to a presently or prospective significant other, it is usually for a purpose beyond "filling someone in." It is for the purpose of increasing that person's understanding of a situation, of conveying to him another perspective. Our hope, usually, is that what we tell him or explain may modify his attitudes toward and open his greater acceptance of our client. If that hope is to be realized, then again we must relate to the person who is to receive the information or interpretation. We cannot simply prepare a spiel, excellent in its explanatory quality though it may be, and expect that it will be taken in. Its being taken in depends on the receptiveness of the listener. This may entail drawing from him what *his* concern (or lack of it) is, what *he* would like to know, and what—most of all—his felt investment is in the particular situation, pro or con. The temporary relationship established is based upon the assumption that he has some part or place in the problem at hand. It is made meaningful by attending to his reactions, to his involvement—positive, negative, or ambivalent —and to his responses to the interpretations and explanations we give him. There would be small point in giving information about one's client if it were simply to satisfy another's curiosity.

*In a considerable experience of taking background histories in a clinical setting, I found that the most helpful accounts in explaining the patient's problem (child or adult) were those where I got at not simply what happened when but how the person and his significant others felt and dealt with the situation. It took longer than just getting dates and other such data, but I believe those of us who operated this way got far more telling clinical information and, further, established a meaningful connection with the informant that readied us for ongoing contacts when these were necessary.

The aim, rather, is to engage the other's interest and from this his possible participation in helping. So the need is to connect with the listener's reactions, not just his surface words; with his heart, not just his head.

Careful management of relationship is most essential when your purpose is to gain the active cooperation and involvement of a significant other toward doing something for or about your client. Both you and he are now highly motivated—you to engage him in agreements and arrangements, he perhaps to avoid becoming too involved or committed or having to yield too much of his own comfort or interests. In our own eagerness we need to take care not to lose sight of the signs of his dubiousness or halfheartedness. They need to be acknowledged openly and understandingly received. Perhaps his participation can be tentative, a tryout. He must not feel, when you have gone, that he has been had, because his cooperation then is likely to be short-lived. If he is openly resistive, we need to take care to act in full awareness that being our client's advocate does not mean we are thereby the other's *adversary*. Rather, our task is to try to draw him into a shared, partway advocate position. This means, then, that such annoyance or counterhostility that his behavior may rouse in us must be put on ice until later, and that our attitude must be one that expresses, "I can see how you feel, even though. . . ."

Perhaps no significant other is more likely to rouse our indignation than another professional helper whom we are trying to enlist as a cooperator and who shows lack of interest, brusqueness, or annoyance at our intervention. "He should know better!" we say to ourselves, our own annoyance and hostility rising in equal degree. Interagency and interprofessional relationships are not infrequently charged with animosity.* It is often due to causes that are quite extraneous to the specific instance for

---

*Again I hasten to affirm that just as often they intermesh smoothly, and cooperation occurs that makes for a pleasurable experience for the professional participants and, more important, a productive result for the client. Here, however, we are focused on the "prevention and cure" of problematic confrontations.

which you are seeking cooperation—such as one agency's sense of superiority over the other, one profession's low opinion or competitive attitude toward the other, the irrational possessiveness that any one of us harbors sometimes that "this is *my* case, *my* client," and so on. With the result, at times, that the client and his needs fall into the widened trench that separates the two would-be helpers.

"He should know better," and we, too. He—we—are subject to human cussedness now and then; one of us, at least, would do well to proffer some understanding of the other's position in the supposition that we both are client centered and the client's welfare is what links us. As for that temporarily shelved annoyance: if it hasn't gone away, shake it out later; talk it out to some sympathetic ear—your supervisor's or a colleague's. If, however, your cooled judgment tells you that the attitudes of the professional other are seriously and consistently impeding adequate service to clients, it should be reported to and dealt with at administrative levels as an obstacle to service to clients and an issue in interagency understandings and collaboration.

If we are to try to involve a significant other in one-time or ongoing assistance to our client, and especially if there is evident resistance in him, we must ask ourselves and try to answer what is probably a central question to understanding any motivation. It is, starkly, What's in it by way of reward? What will the person get for what he gives? Why should the landlord hold off his eviction notice? Why should the brother pay for nursery school for his estranged sister's child? Why should the father quit bringing candy and costly presents to his kids in the foster home when they and he enjoy it? What will the payoff be? It is by some prospect of a reward (or by some fear of unwanted consequences) that all of us are motivated, and unless the helper or the situation can proffer some small crumbs of gratification there is little hope that the other will be much moved. So to this question we must give some consideration in any case, before we go forth to try to engage someone in helping another.

The vignette that follows briefly illustrates the three purposes for which a significant other may be involved and touches on how emotional bonding between him and a helper may be created in even a single interview.* It raises, too, the question of rewards, to which we shall return.

I went to talk to a teacher about a hyperactive, nervous, mischievous seven-year-old boy who had been referred by the school principal to the child guidance clinic where I was a social worker. The teacher had urged that the child be expelled and "sent somewhere" because he was "uneducable." Not only had Ronald "learned nothing" in his year at school, but he was intolerable in the classroom, a continuous storm center. The principal's motivation for referral was to give the child "one last chance."

My purpose was threefold: to get further information about Ronald as observed by the teacher (I had had one interview with his guardian grandmother and one playroom session with him); to share with the teacher some of my impressions and tentative plans made in consultation with the clinic psychiatrist; primarily, however, to get the teacher to hold off pressure to put him out of school until neurological and psychometric examinations had been completed and also until we had some notion about whether the grandmother's behaviors were at all susceptible to modification. This teacher, as you can see, was at this moment in time a very "significant" other.

I had learned from some earlier failures. I had learned that when I approached a harassed and angry person full of my own good cheer and reasonableness, I often found myself up against an impervious wall. That wall might have been raised rudely or courteously—but a wall it was. So now I started by saying to the teacher that I could imagine that Ronald would drive her out of her mind. He must be a continuous disturbance to her and the other kids. She looked at me sharply—as if to say, "What's the trap?" I responded sincerely. "I spent an hour with him at the clinic—and I got a pretty good idea of what he's like."

"Well!" said she, with considerable asperity. "It's about

*This is excerpted from an interview I recorded for the purpose of field teaching.

time some social worker got some idea!'' She launched then into talking with indignation about social workers. They came to the school, always trying to persuade teachers to "individu-alize" a single child, when teachers like her had over thirty-three kids to deal with, to teach, to discipline, to bring up to passing by the end of the year. *She* had as much concern about individual kids as we did (I murmured that I was sure that was true), but handling a classroom simply was another kettle of fish, etc. I flinched inside for myself and my fellow social workers, and I wanted to explain us and defend us, too—but instead (I *had* learned) I listened attentively and expressed my sympathetic understanding of what she was mad about. That was a genuine expression on my part, because I could really feel what it would be like to be in her shoes rather than my own.

When she had had her indignant say about my kith and kin, I asked if she would give me an idea of how Ronald had been behaving in her class. She went into this at length and fervently (with some occasional flashes of humor, because there was something innocently and ingeniously impish in this child, something appealing, we both agreed). So I could both feel with her about the many difficulties he presented to her and laugh ruefully with her at some of his funny if disrupting antics. (Incidentally, one needs to be reminded now and again that all relationship bonds are not those of pain. People come to feel connected with one another through the sharing of joy and pleasures, for they, too, are part of our emotional life, and we can find ourselves at one with others around the sharing of little funny miseries as well as heavy sorrowful ones.)

So this teacher and social worker were building a feelingful alliance, the one venting her anger and frustration, and fleeting compassion, the other largely drawing it out and responding to it with genuine appreciation.

I asked, then, if she would be interested to hear what our (the clinic staff's) beginning and tentative plans were. To her nod I briefly sketched our clinical impressions and our questions about whether the child's problems were largely the product of his inhibiting—severely—overdemanding grandmother and/or were complicated by neurological factors. The latter, we thought, might be responsive to medication, but along with that we would try to modify the grandmother's treatment of the child. I told her a bit about the grandmother (whom she had tried, unsuccessfully, to get in touch with) frightening the child with stories of bogeys, threatening him with abandonment, insisting that he fight anyone who crossed him, even if he had to use a knife—but that he also had to be "good." She was obviously interested, appropriately sympathetic and horrified, cleared enough of her own pent-up emotion to be able to listen and hear.

Now, I said, we had to get to the problem for her. It was our thought that our exploratory work with the grandmother and Ronald might best be accomplished if we could hold their life situation in status quo for a while. But I knew it would be hardest on her. "You said it," said she. I gathered, though, that she would have her principal 100 percent behind her. And I also knew from Ronald himself that he wanted to stay in her class—maybe to escape his grandmother, or maybe because he felt safe with her. What was her reaction?

Well, she said, after a long silence and with a small shrug, half resigned, half hopeful, she guessed she'd be willing to give it a try. As long as she wasn't carrying this thing alone—and for God knows how long. It would be a try-and-see thing, I said. We were partners, subject to change with due notice—and I'd be back in touch just as soon as I had something, good or bad, to share with her. And she could reach me at ——— . We shook hands on this and commiserated with one another, briefly.

Question: Why did she agree to bear this burden further and to join in this temporary partnership? What was there in it for her? Of course, one can rarely know all of a person's motivation —so we can only speculate that something like the following operated.

The main purpose of the social worker was to establish a working connection with a significant other, to gain beginning cooperation in a diagnostic and treatment plan. A secondary purpose was to get a filled-in picture of the child, and the giving of information was, of course, part of the sharing that any

cooperative project requires. In all three purposes one sees relationship factors operating. They are there not because they are
artificially put in by the social worker but because two *persons*
are there, persons who are in communication with one another
about a situation that is charged with strong feeling on the part
of at least one. That feeling is roused by several circumstances:
the problem pupil who is like a festering burr under the skin of
the teacher and, adding insult to injury, her being confronted
by a peer professional who, she anticipates, may criticize and try
to lay still further responsibilities upon her. One could anticipate all this.

From the first she was related to as one who was herself
significantly and unhappily affected by the client. *She,* not he,
was the first to get attention. Before she was asked to be reasonable and objective, she was, by genuinely empathic reactions
and comments, encouraged to boil over, to vent her annoyance
and distress. Some of this was against the interviewer. It was,
perhaps, one of those small turn-of-the-screw experiences that a
surprise so often creates when, instead of defensiveness on the
interviewer's part, the teacher heard understanding and honest
acceptance of her feelings.

Because she found the social worker in accord with her, she
felt some beginning bonds of alliance rather than antagonism.
Moreover, here was someone who promised to share her burden.
Further, here was someone who wanted to listen to her side of
the story and, past this, to offer some additional understanding
of what the child's trouble might be about. A prospect of hope
was held out to her and a time-limited partnership proposed,
in which her part was recognized as necessary and valuable. Her
importance to the child was affirmed.

Several other factors probably played a part, too. That her
principal would support her—perhaps prize and reward her
sacrifice, flexibility, cooperation?—undoubtedly had its impetus. That the child himself wanted to stay with her touched her,
added a sliver of gratification. (In regard to this problem, the
principal and the child were *her* significant others.)

The question remains. How is it that these fragments in their

combination served to compensate this teacher for the self-sacri-
fice that is always involved, in small or large degree, in putting
oneself out for another?

I would speculate as follows: at base was this teacher's own
underlying commitment to children. At base was her long held
wish, fluctuating and uncertain as it might be at times, to have
some part in the growth of small human beings. That basic
motivation was revived, perhaps refueled, by the recognition
and appreciation she got, and the sense of social and emotional
bonding that grew out of the particular relationship and substance of her interview with the social worker. Her hope was
raised that in this joined effort she might indeed cause something "good" to happen in a child's unhappy life. So it was not
only what the social worker put in that mattered but what was
already there that was drawn out.

It is probably a similar amalgam that makes up the multifaceted,
subtly nuanced, exclusively human phenomenon we call altruism. In varying degree, of course, and subject to ebb as well as
flow, depending on our own sense of fulfillment, most of us
carry a sense of obligation to those less fortunate than we or to
those who, felled by some blow of misfortune, remind us that
"there but for the grace of God go I." Call it guilt, if you
will—but recognize that a certain measure of guilt has its highly
constructive social uses.

Most of us, too, want to be seen and accredited as "good" by
others, particularly by others whose opinion we respect or whose
liking we value. Our reward may be a general suffusion within
ourselves of "feeling good," at having done well, of having met
the standards of our own ego ideal. And/or our reward may be
gratification at the recognition or the gratefulness of another
human being. That "other" is always there!—whether he is a
long ago incorporated image now indistinguishable from ourselves and called our "conscience" or our "ideals," or whether
he is in here-and-now responsive relationship with us. Interest-
ingly, the word "altruism" denotes this. Its roots lie in the
Latin *alter* and the French *autre*—both "other." And it implies

not only that the "good" feeling and action of the one is for the other but that the one can only know and take pleasure in his selfness as he is recognized and responded to by the other, internalized or there in person.

Yet another reward is realized when we do a "good deed." It is part of that basic drive in us, noted and developed in the work of Robert W. White:[8] the "drive for effectance." It is that active push in us, from infancy onward, to be a "cause," to make something happen, to experience whatever potency we have by having an effect upon another person or object or situation. When what I do or say matters, makes a ripple of difference in the life of another person, and when that is held to be "desirable," "good," or "admirable" (whether by myself or by others), my sense of self-esteem and potency is expanded and enhanced. When I have been a cause in another human being's well-being, it is like a tiny taste of divinity—a sense of self-transcendence, of being bigger and better than I knew.

"We are all much more human than otherwise," said Harry Stack Sullivan, and even recalcitrant significant others may qualify. "Look," we must repeatedly admonish ourselves, "we who choose to be helpers to people in trouble are not the only ones with compassion, we are not the only ones who may be touched by human hurt, not the only ones whose still, small voices of conscience may be tapped to redirect our actions. We hold no corner on righteousness and virtue. We are not the only ones whose self-concept is heightened by the sense of having acted generously and of having had that action recognized and approved by another." We must remind ourselves of that.

9

The Heart's Reasons

IT WAS a mathematician and physicist whose experiments and theories set the foundations of several present-day sciences—it was he, not a romantic or a poet, who said, "The heart has its reasons." That was Pascal. One wonders—perhaps it is those who have most rigorously probed life's mysteries with systematic thought and the exact tools of science, who have pondered both the particle and the universe, perhaps it is they who know most deeply the imponderables in what we call man's "spirit" and who dare to affirm the realness of that which is both invisible and ineffable.

If you have come this far, you know that this is a book about the heart's reasons. It has asked that you open your awareness to them. It has asked that you seek to know them, not simply by acknowledging their presence but by engaging yourself in understanding their impelling, dynamic effects upon the mind and action of human beings. It has asked that you recognize their swift and moving drive into the relationships between and among people, and between people and their everyday tasks and involvements. All this has been asked of you because you have undertaken to be a helper, to be of service to other people. This may be an occupational commitment on your part, expressed in your nine-to-five contacts with those who are your patients or clients or pupils, or it may be a more full personal commitment, carried into the small world of kinship and friendship. Perhaps it is both. If you have come this far, it is because you are moved by wanting to be and to become more meaningfully connected with human life, that you feel and value the motive powers and the potential enhancement of personhood that inhere in emotional alliances with other human beings.

You have been asked throughout these pages to view relationship—one expression of the heart's reasons—from the angle of its uses and usefulness for the "other," for the help seeker or the help needer. The question continuously pursued and sometimes answered has been, What value does relationship, in one or all of its dimensions and expressions, seem to have in enabling a person to cope better with his problems or to enrich and enliven his capabilities?

But now, at last, I turn to you yourself. What's in it for *you?* Since helpers are also "only human" (as we say when we are about to forgive frailty), they, too, are motivated by the need for self-gratification. What do they get out of the demanding self-discipline, the self-controlled practice, the putting themselves out, the steadfast giving, the tasting and bearing of the pain of others or the slings and arrows of some of the outrageous persons and problems they encounter? The continuous awareness and practice of relationship-conducive behaviors on the helper's part take some considerable toll of him, and few of us are willing to wait for some afterlife's promise for our "just rewards." What, then, do we get out of it?

Let's at first rule out those persons who have just happened to "fall into" one of the human services simply because it was there, a job to be had. Unless they undergo some change of feeling and perspective (as some of them indeed do!), they are likely to fall out just as soon as some other opportunity presents itself. Almost at once, too, we can dispose of considerations of economic and prestige rewards. They are at best modest ones in most of the human service professions. Let's rule in those people who have chosen to become responsible helpers because they have some "feel" for it, because they have concern about easing or enriching the lives of other human beings, if only in some small ways. So we are back again to the reasons of the heart which, we must surely recognize, include our values and ideals. These are without substance unless they are cherished and heartfelt.

Several years ago there appeared a book with the arresting title *The Gift Relationship,* by the eminent social scientist Richard Titmuss. His research, in part, was to ferret out the motivations for individual altruism as it exists in highly industrialized, large-scale societies where depersonalization is most likely to occur. He chose to study as a most significant form of "giving" (certainly in its symbolic value) the giving of blood. The donors in his study sample were not paid for their blood; they gave it voluntarily and to a blood bank rather than to a known or named recipient.

Why, they were asked, did they do it? The reasons given strike familiar chords: they wanted to be of help to another human being in need; they felt they "owed" because they were privileged (to be in good health, able, secure); they felt that at some time they might need help and wanted the sense that they merited it; they felt some sense of personal "goodness" mingled with a sense of kinship with their (unknown) fellowmen.

In his conclusions, Titmuss suggests that "gift exchange has more important functions in large-scale societies than [the writings of several modern anthropologists] suggest . . ." and that "the spread of complexity has increased rather than diminished the scientific as well as the social need for gift relationships." [1]

There is food for much thought in that statement. Here our focus has been upon the giving or "gift" of relationship itself, as an experience of human concern and bonding. Relationship will not of itself save a life. And at the end of a long, hard day a human service "giver" may opine that it is actually easier to lie back for a few minutes and have blood drawn than to spend oneself over and over—eyes, ears, senses, mind, heart—attending to and trying to meet the imperative needs of face-to-face others. Still—one is struck by the repeated evidence of the sense of social bonding that supports altruism, and there is need to keep that feeling alive and vivid in our increasingly faceless societal arrangements. And when the nurture that relationship proffers is responsively received, the giver himself is warmed and fed in turn, aware that this is the beginning and the essence of lifelong reciprocations between man and his society.

This recognition anchors and secures us in our concern with relationship in the helping process. But to sustain ourselves there must be more immediate experiential rewards. In the chapter on the client's significant others, the possible gratifications for those who "put themselves out" to be of aid were sketched in. They hold for the professional helper, too, since he is in fact a temporary significant other. So they merit our review of them, this time selfishly, in our own self-interest.

First to explain ourselves to ourselves. Underlying any attraction to, interest in, curiosity about, responsiveness to other human beings who are outside our own close-in family-friendship world is some sense of kinship with all human beings. "Nothing human is alien to me," said the ex-slave Terence over 2,000 years ago. This might be put even more positively, if less elegantly: "Everything human touches me." Or "at the very least interests me." How that "feel for" or "feel with" happens, whether it is some inborn capacity or the product of early trustworthy interchanges with human beings who met our dependencies and then alerted us to the feelings, motives, and behaviors of others, we can only guess. Is it "natural" empathy —is it inborn? Inbred? Both?

Suffice it here to say that many of us who are drawn to the human service professions have known enough of small hurts or passing sorrows to resonate to them in others and thence to want to ease or heal them in others, as if once again to heal them in ourselves. We have known enough of the pleasures of small masteries or the opportunities proffered at one time or another by some helpful person to want to offer something of that sort to someone like ourselves. He is "like" not in the sense that there is necessarily an external resemblance at all but "like" in what we believe is his inner thrust or need.

Moreover, many of us have dared to look into our own internal lives and found them so complex and rich in interest that we are repeatedly intrigued by trying to fathom the infinite varieties of that "work of art" called man. By the time we have reached young adulthood we may have already lived many parts of other lives vicariously, through sharing the thoughts and emotions of people we have known and by having entered into the depicted feelings, motives, joys and miseries of people in books, the theater, and other humanistic arts. Once it has been titillated, the appetite for such vicarious experience is never satiated for long. Like an appetite for good food—whether for the palate or the mind—it recurs eagerly, repeatedly, as long as its periodic fulfillments are stimulating by their variety or nourishing to our understanding.

So it is that the helper who is open and resonant to the lives of others is himself the recipient of a variegated and expanded life experience. This is no small reward, that our own inner world becomes livened and enriched by our relationships with so many different human beings in so many different life situations. The work life of a helper in the human services can often be taxing; but it is rarely boring.

The pervasive sense of wanting to help people that young people bring to the human service professions is probably made up of a number of internalized values and ideals. One is a sense of social-personal obligation, of reciprocality. A second is an ego ideal, an offshoot of our conscience, that requires that we should be more than for ourselves alone, that we should make some constructive contribution to the lives of other people. Another is the need in us to mean something, to "matter" to somebody else, to feel our worth and potency by being the cause or source of solace or hope or change for the better in the life of another human being. We cannot always disentangle these mixed motivations.

Conscience makes more than cowards of us, Hamlet to the contrary. It makes decent human beings of us, too. However, conscience has had rather a bad time of it in the past half century or so. The severe and excessive inhibitions and guilts found in many neurotic personalities were held to be the causes of their constrictions and anxieties, and releasing people from their inner guilts became one of the dominant goals of therapeutic treatment. Today (for many reasons more powerful than such therapy) there is evidence that there is some scarcity of guilt, that too great permissiveness, not just confined to parent-child relationships but in society as a whole, has created a conscienceless race.

As is quite usual, however, it is the extremes that are noted with alarm. In between, in the wide middle range, are many people like Titmuss's blood donors, like those of us in the helping professions, and many others who have achieved some livable balance within themselves between giving and getting, between personal rights and social responsibilities. Our sense of obligation is a sense of fairness, of reciprocative debt to others, of gratitude for whatever favors life has bestowed. It was probably instilled by the words and behavior of parents and other admired or loved persons. It was probably instilled with some lovingness, with forgiveness for our "badness" coupled with expectations of "goodness." There were punishments at times, but also there was consistent recognition of mistaken intentions and consistent attention and praise for small but growing evidences of mutual responsiveness, self-mastery, respect for the rights of others.

People who grow up with such love-borne requirements and supports tend to live in fairly comfortable relationships with the still, small voices within them. They are more open and free as they grow to take in the realities and ideologies that serve to modify, expand, and deepen their sense of right and wrong, of ought or should, of social ethics, of what is worthwhile and what is worthless in human life. At a half- or fully conscious heartfelt but rationalized level, they develop within themselves an "ego ideal," which is to say, a self-image they would like to live up to in order to earn their own self-esteem.

One manifestation of maturity is the readiness to "take care of," in Erikson's phrase. Having been nurtured, one is able to turn about to nurture; having been helped with love and respect (by parents, teachers, friends), one is ready to help others with equal love and respect; having become aware of one's luck or good breaks in physical and psychological health, in self-developing opportunities, one feels some impetus to create and expand such life assets for others; sometimes, having suffered and mastered such suffering, one is motivated to "repay" and to spare or succor others.

In short, to "take care of" others may for many of us fulfill our sense of social (not only personal) obligation.

We will have disappointments. Not everyone will be responsive to our good intentions or caring acts and concerned relationships. But if a helper's expectations are realistic, that is, if they
are commensurate with the possibilities and limitations present
in the persons/circumstances being worked with, there will be
rewards to support one's sense of usefulness to another. They
may be small rewards—the trustful nestling up of a small child
who had been afraid of strangers, the warm glance and sigh of
relief of someone who has been given a much needed provision,
the lighted-up face of the bedfast invalid, the verbal expression
of gratitude from someone who believes you understand and
have been helpful, the reshouldering of responsibility in work
or school, the determined effort to behave in some more constructive ways—these are the sorts of responses and successes
that reinforce the helper's pleasure in knowing that what he has
put in has been found "good."

Happily, there are success stories, too—instances where some
combination of the client/patient's own motivations and capabilities and the helper's relationship skills, knowledge, and
access to resources may literally refashion a person's life. How
nourishing to the ego ideal of the help giver these instances are,
and with what fresh energy and hope they infuse his ongoing
work! But such eureka experiences, the swift and complete
resolution of a problem, are more rare than usual. Helpers—
whether of individuals and small groups or in larger social
change and reform efforts—must make their peace with the fact
that in anything as complicated as today's society, or even as a
single human being, change must be anticipated as piecemeal
—one part, one aspect, one step at a time. Small may or may
not be beautiful, but it is usually practical and manageable and
is the usual portion in which life's good gifts are doled out to us.

To find that one has been the cause or the facilitator of some
change for the better in another human being's life is a powerful reinforcement of one's sense of personal and social worth. It
is a common reaction we all know in everyday life. "Making
someone happy" or easing someone's physical or emotional
pain suffuses us with feelings of gratification. It even happens in

most trivial incidents—for instance, a two-minute sense of satisfaction with oneself (mingled with compassion) when one has led a blind person across a busy street. It occurs in daily small interchanges between parents and children, between friends. Why is this? one wonders. Why do I feel filled in and affirmed because I have made even a small ripple of "good" or "better" in another person's life? Is it some all but instinctive sense that my being is actualized mainly by responses to my actions that "prove" that I *am* to a valued purpose? Is it that, just as "any man's death diminishes me," so each man's rebirth of hope or relief from despair enhances me? Particularly, of course, if I feel a sense of alliance with him, and especially if I believe that I have had some part in his betterment, minute or large, temporary or enduring as it may be? We struggle again to understand and to articulate the mysteries in human relationships.

Often the knowledge that we have made something good happen is not confined to the twosome interchange between helper and helped. In our professional endeavors others are likely to hear from us about it, too—not always, but often—those work mates with whom we share our modest pleasures—our supervisor, the friends or family members with whom we talk over the woes and weals of the day (within the bounds of our commitment to confidentiality, of course!). Some among us put into print accounts of what we have done so that many eyes may see. It is a "contribution to knowledge," we say, the sharing of an experience or findings with colleagues who have the same problems and concerns. But is there not also involved in such communications the wish to have our significant others join in the chorus of approval of us, to expand our sense of "contribution"?

Is it ignoble, this wish to have our work appreciated and our effectiveness affirmed by others? Is it indicative of trailing wisps of childishness? Perhaps. But is it not also an attestation to our humanness and to our interdependency with others, that while we may each be our own man much of the time, we are yet enough related and bound together with others that we need and want not only self- but social approval, especially from those who matter to us?

One further possible gain for the help giver who learns and patiently practices the art of relationship. It is a quite personal one. It derives from the fact that the behavior that yields rewards tends to become entrenched, to be incorporated, to become habitual. It begins to feel and to be expressed as one's own, as "natural." Thus your learned and caringly practiced modes of relating become part of you and carry over into outside-of-work exchanges with other people.

This does not at all mean that in our natural relationships we must relinquish our personal needs for reciprocity of response, our need to be given to as well as to give. It surely does not mean that we must act always in the interest of the other, or that at times of personal stress we may not ask and expect supports and caretaking from those with whom we have "meaningful" relationships. (Perhaps even saints are not altogether saintly when they are off duty!) What it does mean is something like this:

You have learned to look at each newly encountered person with attentiveness to his being his particular self. You have learned to listen to what he has to say—or to draw him out—in ways that express interest and respect. You are open to trying to understand what he means, and can convey (in your own way, and in consonance with what the particular situation calls for, of course) that what is important to him—an opinion, an act, an attitude, a set of facts—is important in that it is invested with some emotion on his part, transient though it may be. So you have learned to stop to acknowledge this rather than to ignore or brush it off, and to give him some sign, verbal or facial, that you recognize that he has feeling invested. That may be as much as he wants of you—to know that you know not "all about" his feelings, or even what they are, but that you are sensitive to their presence. Then he may choose to reveal them further or to contain them further, but he is aware of someone potentially receptive to him. That is a rather arresting experience in our too hurried lives.

So much for the everyday touch-and-go relationships. For those relationships you value deeply, for those that touch the heart, you will find as you attend to the interchanges between yourself and others that your sensitivity is keener, that your capacity to feel *in* to another arises more swiftly and truly. You will become more conscious of the currents of feeling that weave between you and a cared-about other and of the variations in the balance of support and stimulation, of acceptance and expectation, that differing roles and times and situations call forth. You may, in short, have made your own a whole range of small interpersonal skills by which to draw in and hold close the people you care about, and also the means by which to navigate the rocky shoals and rough crosscurrents that are encountered now and again in the course of any vital relationship.

You will not live happily ever after. Love, too, is a form of exchange. It has its costs as well as its rewards. Sometimes it is in happy balance, but other times one party in it pays far more than the other. A person who characteristically relates with compassion and consideration for his others may find himself at times feeling drained, find himself in need of supports. Even love must be worked at now and again. But we make our choices, repeatedly struggling to find in ourselves the answer to the ancient rabbi-scholar Hillel's questions: "If I am not for myself, who will be for me? But if I am for myself alone, what am I?"

There is far more that needs to be said and thought about the humanizing powers of relationships in our increasingly technologized world; about the means by which to enhance the self-confidence and the social responsibility of the "diminished man"; about the yet to be forged linkages among us that would facilitate the sense of communion and thence of community. But perhaps there have been words enough. It is the "labor thereof" that must be got on with.

This chapter started with a seventeenth-century scientist-philosopher's affirmation of the heart's reasons. At the point of ending here I turn again to a scientist, to one living with us here and now in the twentieth century, an internationally recognized nuclear physicist, a researcher and theoretician in electrodynamics and atomic structures. I was determined, you see, to listen closely not just to those with whom I feel a ready kinship but also to one whose levels of knowledge, thought, and discourse are quite different from mine and are disciplined by the rigor and cool objectivity of the "hard" sciences.

It is Victor Weisskopf who speaks: "... One can understand a sunset or the stars in the night sky in a scientific way but there is something about *experiencing* the phenomenon that lies outside science." And, "... although science can study and explain every human experience it does not always illuminate those aspects that are considered most relevant." And yet further, "... the two pillars on which most human activities must be based: curiosity to know more about the world around us and how it works, and the *significance of compassion for the fate of our fellow men.*" [2]

The italics are mine. The heart's reasons are his—and mine, and yours.

Comments on Terms and Readings

In General: Terms, Usages, Meanings, et Cetera

At the risk of being considered as capricious as Humpty-Dumpty (you remember what he said: "When I use a word it means just what I choose it to mean—neither more nor less"), I append these explanations for terms that are sometimes misused or ambiguous or that I have drafted into serving "what I choose" them to mean.

Re: Gender

"He" is used throughout this book as the generic designation of a person, third person singular, in conformity with long established usage. The women's liberation movement has by now progressed far enough, it seems to me, and into issues substantive enough not to need wordplay as a bulwark.

Re: Nomenclature

"Help seeker" and "help needer." Since this book is addressed to a wide range of "people helpers," each sector of which may categorize their "helpees" by a different name, I have resorted to a general use of these terms as a convenient umbrella to cover clients, patients, students, all manner of individuals or groups seeking or needing the services of a helper. Differentiating "help seeker" from "help needer" is chiefly to discriminate between a voluntary, motivated applicant for service

213

and one who may need to be drawn into wanting and using help.

However, when a specific form of help or a specific human service is discussed, I have employed the designation usually used. Thus nurses and physicians (and sometimes other therapists) have "patients." Social workers, many psychologists, and other counselors have "clients." Teachers have students or pupils.

A "client" in present-day usage means "a person who employs the professional advice or services of another" (*Webster's Third New International Dictionary*). Long ago it meant a "dependent," a "leaner"; in ancient Rome, a "client" was the dependent of a "patron." Today, however, the term is used in many professions and businesses—by lawyers, architects, brokerage firms, social workers, consultants of many sorts. It means one who undertakes to use the services of someone else who is believed to have certain knowledge, expertise, and/or access to resources in the area of need.

A "patient" (again according to *Webster's Third New International*) is "a sick individual, esp. when awaiting or under the care and treatment of a physician ..." or, alternatively, "a client for medical service."

However, general usage is not fully consistent. In hospitals and clinic settings, many social workers designate "clients" as "patients," since the latter term is used by the physicians with whom they collaborate. Conversely, many clinical psychologists offering "psychotherapy" call patients "clients," precisely because they wish to break away from the idea that a person who is emotionally disturbed or distressed is "sick." Thus I have resorted at times to the use of that slash-connected designation "client/patient"; when the reference is clearly nonmedical, nonpsychiatric, to "client" alone.

"Helper." "Helper" or "help giver" is used herein for all human service personnel. It seems not quite satisfactory when it designates teachers or group workers in recreational and educational endeavors. While pupils, students, group members are given help in the sense that they are provided the tangible means and psychological stimuli by which their functional or cultural

development is to be promoted, sometimes "leader" or "teacher" may be the preferred and more accurate word.

When we come to specific professions, the variety of terms for the helper proliferates, often to differentiate special statuses and functions within a given profession. Thus the term "paraprofessional" ("para" meaning "along side of," as in "paramedic"), "dental assistant," "nurse's aide," "social work associate," and so on. Physicians tend to be identified by their specialization, as are some nurses. Social workers are identified by the special setting in which they work—"child welfare worker," "psychiatric social worker"; and confusingly, one may become the other when he moves from one agency to another, provided of course, that he has met basic qualifications for the job. Social workers are also designated by their special methodology—as "caseworker," "group worker," "community developer." Early in this century Mary Richmond, the mother of modern social casework, suggested "sociatrist" as a across-the-board name for social workers, but it never caught on; and some years ago, the National Association of Social Workers launched a contest for a title by which social workers could be more adequately identified. No one won. So there will be found herein a range of titles used when a specific form of help is being discussed, along with the generic if indeterminate terms "helper" and "help giver."

"Profession," "helping professions," "human service professions," "professional helper," etc. Strictly speaking, a "profession" has several significant identifying characteristics. It is a body of persons engaged in a "calling" or "vocation." (Note that there is implicit in those words some moral and value mission, whereas in "occupation" there is none.) A profession has as its prime purpose the provision of a public service; it has criteria and standards of education, achievement, and conduct for its members; it harbors a special body of knowledge and skill which is expected to be under continuous study and critical analysis and to be followed by appropriate development or modifications of its body of knowledge and its modes of operation.

Individual members of a profession are "professionals" in

that their conduct, knowledge, and practice competence conforms to their profession's purposes, ethics, and standards of preparation and practice.

However, loose popular usage has blurred the meaning of "profession" and "professional" by giving that designation to a motley variety of occupations that, while they may indeed require special knowledge and skills—from the "professional burglar" to the "professional mortician"—do not necessarily meet the other requirements held to characterize a profession.

How, then, does one classify the whole range of human service workers? The "human services" include some long established and learned professions, several quasi professions whose practitioners range from those who are fully qualified by the most rigorous professional standards to those who meet few of them, and an increasing number of paraprofessionals.

I was concerned that all those who had chosen to work in the human services because they had some real commitment to helping people, those who were eager to increase their knowledge and to improve their practice in the interests of the human beings they served, who were bent upon working in as responsible and self-disciplined a manner as was required of them, should feel included as a vital part of the total helping endeavor. Therefore I have taken the liberty here and there of calling that service or service provider "professional" when what is done is ethically governed, committed to human well-being, caring, and responsibly managed. This usage seeks to differentiate an endeavor from such work behavior and attitudes as are expressed in phrases like "I only work here" or "It's a job." But it is open, I know, to question. (See "Professions, Human Service," in *Encyclopedia of Social Work* [Washington, D.C.: National Association of Social Workers, 1977], 2:1097–1107).

"Therapy"/"psychotherapy." "What is therapy?" a present day jesting Pilate might well ask. Was there ever a word so batted about or used with such profligacy? Psychotherapy, physiotherapy, occupational therapy, family therapy, reality therapy, group therapy, relationship therapy, hydrotherapy, bibliotherapy, dance therapy, primal scream therapy, chemotherapy—the list is endless.

At its Greek root (*therapeuin*) "therapy" means "to attend, to treat"; also "to worship" (in the sense of praying to the gods for their healing powers?) But from this point even a precise dictionary (*Webster's New Third International*) offers little direction. It proposes that therapy is "treatment of the maladjusted ... through a program of clinical, custodial, or casework services in order to further their restoration to society"; or "a force working to relieve a social tension"; or "treatment of disease." And thus any help to a person that relieves, ameliorates, or heals his physical or emotional malfunctioning or undue psychological stress could be called "therapy." In the latest *American Handbook of Psychiatry* (ed. D. X. Freedman and J. E. Dyrud, 2d ed. [New York: Basic Books, 1975]), it is admitted that "it is difficult to arrive at an acceptable definition," and several variations are offered (5:5).

Here I have held to a fairly strict (though not unassailable) definition, limited to psychotherapy. That is the treatment of a person's emotional, cognitive, and behavioral stances and processes by means of psychological influence, on the assumption that his problems in coping derive chiefly from intrapsychic rather than external conditions.

Several reasons dictate these limits. The effort to heal or lessen emotional disturbances in a human being requires of the therapist an extensive and fully digested knowledge of the nature and development of the human personality in both its usual and pathological aspects. It requires long and disciplined practice for which competent and responsible supervision was utilized in the practitioner's early learning. It should be attempted only by those who are qualified by both education and responsibly supervised practice. Perhaps it should be added that a therapist's personal psychotherapy, while it may be highly desirable, is in no way a sufficient qualification. That these safeguards are frequently breached by all manner of self-proclaimed therapists today is a matter of concern, not of validation.

Now, many plain and practical services may indeed be "therapeutic" in their effects. They may lower stress, release energy, increase confidence and hope, and so forth. It is chiefly with the therapeutic value of such concrete and tangible aids that this book deals, particularly when they are conveyed within that nurturing climate, relationship.

However, references to "therapy" appear frequently herein, because it is about this kind of help that most of the research on relationship has been done. Many of the findings in that research have relevance and transferability to the uses of relationship in any effort to enable people to accept and benefit by the services they seek and need.

About Reading References

I have not supplied what could be a comprehensive bibliography on relationship because, it seems to me, whether for food or for learning, nothing so dulls the appetite and discourages the sampling as too many possible choices in too large portions. Instead, you will find for each chapter a few carefully selected readings, chosen on the basis of their immediate pertinence to the points under discussion and in the secure knowledge that almost every such reading carries its own bibliography which may guide your further reading. Most of the readings are from the literature of social work. The reason for this is not only the obvious one—that I am most familiar with these publications—but also that, since social work embraces such a wide range of helping services and operates in collaboration with so many other helping professions, its exposition of relationship is communicated in ways that may be readily grasped and found usable by others. The studies on relationship are chiefly from psychology which, usually operating in university settings rather than in the community at large, has had the special stimulations and resources for research and publication.

Reading references, then, are highly selective, but almost every one points to where "more" or "beyond" may be reached for and found.

Notes

Chapter 1

1. Perhaps right here is the place to stop and look at "Comments on Terms and Readings" immediately preceding. They are set down as a guide to terms and designations used here: to what is meant by "helpers," "help needers," "help seekers," "clients," "profession" and "professional," "therapy" and "therapists," and other terms that in their common usage are often unclear, ambiguous, or overloaded with meaning.

2. *Abstracts for Social Workers* (New York: National Association of Social Workers), publishes résumés of articles pertinent to social work's endeavors, articles drawn not only from social work journals but also from those in the fields of clinical psychology, philosophy, psychiatry, medicine, and a variety of other relevant sources. Between 1968 and 1978 there is no rubric "relationship." Partial aspects of relationship such as "empathy" and "communication" may be found; they appear largely in psychology journals. From several widely used books published since 1970, a few samples.

Social Work Practice: Model and Method, by Allen Pincus and Anne Minahan (Itasca, Ill.: F. E. Peacock, 1973): relationship is briefly defined as an "affective bond between the worker and other systems." Its three characteristics are "collaboration, bargaining, or conflict" (p. 73). An affective bond with a "system" seems remote and leaves much to be explicated, and the characteristics cited seem to be applicable (except in highly abstract ways) less to one-to-one transactions than to community development endeavors.

Social Work Practice, by Carol H. Meyer, 2d ed. (New York: Free Press, 1976): the author comments briefly that ". . . modern versions of social work practice demand that relationship be a tool to move the case forward and that except in special situations it not be an end in itself" (pp. 200–201). Decried here is the assumption by some counselors and therapists, dealing with problems identified as intrapsychic, that relationship may be the "sufficient" means in helping people with psychological problems. That it should be viewed as a means (it probably has never been considered an "end") to

219

movement toward problem solving is in full consonance with the proposals set forth in this book. However, how this means may be used and what variations of relationship may be called for are not developed.

Problems and Issues in Social Casework, by Scott Briar and Henry Miller (New York: Columbia University Press, 1971): the authors attempt to explicate relationship by equating it with "five prerequisites of the communication process" (p. 130). But what is to be communicated and with what purpose is more implied than specified.

Each of these authors, one must recognize, had as his major aim an emphasis upon aspects of social work which in his judgment had been insufficiently developed in professional thought and writings. Everything cannot be given equal emphasis in any book. Furthermore, as later references will reveal, relationship had had its all but overweening day in social work's treatment concerns for a long time. These examples are cited chiefly to indicate that a newcomer to the human services, whether in social work or some other field, is likely to find meager guidance in recent writings on the what, how, and why of relationship.

3. Compilations of research on varied aspects of relationship (always in therapeutic endeavors) are the following: (*a*) *Sources of Gain in Counseling and Psychotherapy*, ed. Bernard G. Berenson and Robert R. Carkhuff (New York: Holt, Rinehart & Winston, 1967); (*b*) *Handbook of Psychotherapy and Behavior Change*, ed. Allen Bergin and S. L. Garfield (New York: John Wiley & Sons, 1971); (*c*) *Psychotherapy Research: Selected Readings*, ed. Gary E. Stollak, Bernard G. Guerney, and Meyer Rothberg (Chicago: Rand McNally & Co., 1966), esp. pp. 503-95; and (*d*) *Towards Effective Counseling and Psychotherapy*, ed. Charles B. Truax and Robert R. Carkhuff (Chicago: Aldine Publishing Co., 1967).

4. A study of R. B. Sloane is cited in a recent article entitled "Behaviorism and Psychodynamics," by Arthur Schwartz (*Child Welfare* 56, no. 6 [June 1977]: 368-79): the findings on two matched groups of clients, one getting therapy from behaviorists, the other from psychotherapists, were that "successful patients in both groups rated 'the interpersonal interaction with the therapist as the single most important part of their treatment'" (p. 374).

5. One of the most careful and analytical studies of the historical development of the concept and uses of relationship in social casework remains bound in an unpublished dissertation, "A Historical Study of the Concept of Relationship in Social Casework, 1917-1960, by Carmen Couillard (Ph.D. diss., University of Chicago, 1966). Couillard's evidence from the 1940s and early 1950s signally reveals the pervasiveness of interest in and the powers imputed to relationship among caseworkers of that era.

6. *The Faith of the Counsellors*, by Paul Halmos (New York: Schocken Books, 1966), p. 58.

7. One such effort to identify and grapple with "what else?" "what beyond?" was my own book *Social Casework: A Problem-solving Process*

(Chicago: University of Chicago Press, 1957). It had been in the writing (and in my practice and teaching) for a number of years, underpinned by study of Freud and John Dewey. Its widespread acceptance was due, I believe, to its coming at a time when ego psychology had begun to be more fully grasped. One of the criticisms the book drew, however, was that it was "intellectualized," that it did not give enough recognition to people's emotional and irrational drives. Perhaps so. Perhaps the reason for its emphasis on conscious ego functioning was the inevitable Hegelian pull toward antithesis when an established formulation seems to have been fairly well drained of its generative powers.

8. For a quick overview of the changing trends in social work treatment within the decade 1955-65, see "Social Work Method: A Review of the Decade," by Helen Harris Perlman (*Social Work* 10 [October 1965]: 166-79; reprinted in *Perspectives in Casework* [Philadelphia: Temple University Press, 1971]).

9. See *The Casework Notebook*, by Alice Overton and Katherine Tinker, 2d ed. (St. Paul, Minn.: Greater St. Paul United Fund and Council, Inc., 1959), in which is set forth simply and with clarifying helpfulness the thinking and practice of the first and probably most influential project on "reaching the hard to reach." As consultant to this project, I learned a great deal from its devoted staff about the powers of acceptance and genuine caring, especially in work with distrustful and resistive persons.

10. For a good overview of present-day opinions of behavioral therapists on the potency of relationship, see "Beyond Reinforcement: Integrating Relationship and Behavior Therapy," by Michael H. Margolen and Susan Goldman (*Clinical Social Work Journal* 2, no. 2 [1974]: 96-104). In their *Social Casework: A Behavioral Approach* (New York: Columbia University Press, 1975), Arthur Schwartz and Israel Goldiamond say, ". . . Operant casework takes place within the context of an interpersonal relationship" (p. 15), and ". . . Relationship factors play a critical part . . ." (p. 270).

11. From a voluminous literature I select a few "starter" articles and book chapters, mostly by social workers who over many years attended to the development of enabling relationships that included therapy and counseling but were not limited to these forms of help:

a) *A Changing Psychology of Social Casework*, by Virginia P. Robinson (Chapel Hill: University of North Carolina Press, 1930). This was a benchmark book, opening new insights about relationship as a "constructive new environment in which he [the client] is given an opportunity to strive for a better solution." Still rich in its implications for helping people.

b) "The Mental Hygiene of the Social Worker." Written in 1935 by Charlotte Towle, this article was among the first to stress the necessity for the helper's self-awareness and self-acceptance. (In *Helping: Charlotte Towle on Social Work and Social Casework,* ed. Helen Harris Perlman [Chicago: University of Chicago Press, 1969]).

In this same volume see "Factors in Treatment" (1936), "Some Uses of Relationship" (1940), and "Underlying Skills of Casework Today" (1941). These articles, ahead of their time, have as much cogency today as when they were written. Perhaps human beings have not changed much in regard to their deepest human needs?

In 1950 Towle, social worker, and Carl Rogers, psychologist-therapist, published companion papers in the *Social Service Review* 24, no. 4 (December 1950): Rogers, "A Current Formulation of Client-centered Therapy" (pp. 442-50); Towle, "Client-centered Case Work" (pp. 451-58). Rogers, as his title indicates, focuses upon relationship factors in treatment of psychological problems. Towle deals with relationship's motivating and supportive uses in helping people within a range of physical, social, and interpersonal problems.

c) "The Worker-Client Relationship," by Annette Garrett (*American Journal of Orthopsychiatry* 19, no. 2 [April 1949]). A clear and readily understood presentation of both realistic and nonrational elements in helper-client relationships.

d) *The Casework Relationship*, by Felix Biestek (Chicago: Loyola University Press, 1957). A simply written and in many ways clarifying presentation of a number of aspects of relationship, though perhaps relationship is made to embrace too many other concepts. The citation of earlier sources adds useful perspectives to this small volume.

e) Special chapters on relationship, with bibliographies, are to be found in the following currently used books on casework: *Casework: A Psychosocial Therapy*, by Florence Hollis, rev. ed. (New York: Random House, 1972); *The Social Work Interview*, by Alfred Kadushin (New York: Columbia University Press, 1972); and *Social Casework: A Problem-solving Process*, by Perlman (n. 7 above).

Chapter 2

1. I first put this idea forward in "The Casework Relationship," in *Social Casework: A Problem-solving Process* (Chap. 1, n. 7 above). It was at a time when both Rogerians and psychoanalytically guided caseworkers were stressing "unconditional" acceptance and neutrality, and it seemed to me these fell short of providing for both the stimulus hunger and the inherent feedback that every meaningful relationship holds.

2. Perhaps the most deeply understood and compellingly presented expositions of the ebb and flow of union and individuation in every potent relationship has been set forth in the thought and writing of the so-called functional school of social work, which drew upon the theory and vision of Otto Rank. See "The Functional Approach to Casework Practice," by Ruth Smalley, in *Theories of Social Casework*, ed. Robert W. Roberts and Robert H. Nee (Chicago: University of Chicago Press, 1970), for a compact presentation and a guide to further reading.

3. This developmental description and what follows draw upon Erik Erikson's eight stages of human development, first presented in his *Childhood and Society* (New York: W. W. Norton & Co., 1950) and ramified in some later publications such as the second edition of *Childhood and Society* (1963) and *Identity, Growth, and Crisis* (New York: W. W. Norton & Co., 1968). As you read Erikson you will recognize that it is the expansion, deepening, and ramification of *relationship* capacities—to self, to other persons, to tasks, to ideas, and to ''objects''—that mark psychological maturation in human beings.

4. *Persona: Social Role and Personality*, by Helen Harris Perlman (Chicago: University of Chicago Press, 1969). See chapters on work, marriage, and parenthood for discussion of relationship requirements and rewards in common and vital roles; also see pp. 16–27, on interpersonal relationship experience as motivator and change inducer.

Chapter 3

1. These qualities of a helping relationship are most succinctly expressed in ''The Necessary and Sufficient Conditions of Therapeutic Personality Change,'' by Carl Rogers (*Journal of Consulting Psychology* 21 [1957]: 95–103). The work of Rogers, beginning with his publications in the 1940s, has focused upon relationship in its therapeutic powers and purposes. His own continuously observed and examined clinical work has been accompanied by research (his own and that of many others influenced by his thought) that has sought to capture some of the elusive aspects of interpersonal transactions between helpers and helpseekers. There is fairly consistent agreement today among counselors and therapists that Rogers has winnowed out ''necessary'' qualities in beneficent relationships. Beyond therapy, however, and for the many other kinds of helping tasks carried and services rendered by most human service workers, they cannot be considered ''sufficient.''

For an inclusive report and analysis of studies on the held-to-be-necessary attributes of relationship, see ''Research on Certain Therapist Interpersonal Skills in Relation to Process and Outcome,'' by Charles B. Truax and Kevin M. Mitchell, in Bergin and Garfield (Chap. 1, n. 3 above).

2. In his article on ''The Conditions of Change from a Client-centered Viewpoint'' (in Berenson and Carkhuff, Chap. 1, n. 3 above), Carl Rogers drops a footnote in which he says, ''It is probably evident . . . that completely unconditional positive regard would never exist except in theory . . . . [Ah, there, Mr. Rogers!] I believe the most accurate statement is that the effective therapist experiences unconditional positive regard for the client during many moments of his contact with him . . .'' (p. 77). One can scarcely quarrel with that.

3. See ''An Experimental Study of Empathic Functioning,'' by Pauline Lide (*Social Service Review* 41, no. 1 [March 1967]: 23–50), which recounts a

successful attempt to heighten empathic sensitivity in social work trainees. For an overview, see "Research on the Teaching and Learning of Psychotherapeutic Skills," by Ruth Matarazzo, in Bergin and Garfield (Chap. 1, n. 3 above).

4. If I may quote myself in connection with helping people to form and sustain their natural social bonds, "... The client cannot live off the bread of a prolonged therapeutic relationship, but must be prepared for chewing and digesting the tougher crusts of ordinary relationships" (*Persona: Social Role and Personality* [Chap. 2, n. 4 above], p. 222).

5. The "functional school" in social work first put forward the idea that time limits are useful in the helping process, through forcing focus and mobilizing the energies of help seekers and helpers both. See *Family Casework,* ed. Jessie Taft (Philadelphia: University of Pennsylvania Press, 1944), p. 14; and "Social Casework: The Functional Approach," by Ruth Smalley and Tybel Bloom, in *Encyclopedia of Social Work* (New York: National Association of Social Workers, 1977), vol. 2.

The recent interest in short-term treatment is in part a resurgence of this long-ago idea about time controls. *Brief and Extended Casework*, by William Reid and Ann Shyne (New York: Columbia University Press, 1968), reports an experiment with time controls and its effects. Highly readable and stimulating of further thought about time-limited helping relationships.

6. The nature, controls, and responsibilities inherent in professional authority, whether in social work or in any other professional or organizational services, are most cogently set forth and analyzed in "Worker-Client Authority Relationships in Social Work," by Elliot Studt (*Social Work* 4 [January 1959]: 18-28).

7. Freud first identified and examined the relationship phenomena he named "transference" and "countertransference." For the original source, see "The Dynamics of the Transference," in *Collected Papers of Sigmund Freud,* trans. Joan Riviere (New York: Basic Books, 1959), 2:312-22. For a simpler and clarifying interpretation, "Transference and Counter-Transference: A Historical Survey," by Douglas Orr, M.D. (*Journal of the American Psychoanalytic Association* 2 [October 1954]: 621-70). See also "The Transference Phenomenon," by Franz Alexander, M.D., and Thomas French, M.D., in *Psychoanalytic Therapy* (New York: Ronald Press, 1946).

8. See Truax and Mitchell (n. 1 above), in which accurate empathic understanding, nonpossessive warmth, and genuineness in the relationship of helper to client have systematically been shown to be connected with positive outcomes. Here again, however, one must be aware that the particular clientele that seek therapy tend to be motivated, relationship-seeking, relationship-perceptive persons.

A different clientele whose problems were those of environmental stress or deficiencies were studied by Ripple and associates in relation to their continuance with the family agency to which they had applied for help. Findings indicate that the "feeling tone conveyed" and "warmly positive" outreach and encouragement by the helper increased the clients' motivation: *Motivation, Capacity and Opportunity: Studies in Casework Theory and Practice*, by Lilian Ripple, Ernestine Alexander, and Bernice Polemis, Social Service Monographs (Chicago: School of Social Service Administration, University of Chicago, 1964), pp. 76–77.

The beneficial effects of teacher empathy and warmth upon student learning are consistent, as revealed in a number of studies listed on pp. 115–17 in Truax and Carkhuff (Chap. 1, no. 3 above).

9. Reported in the *Chicago Tribune* (August 8, 1977), from *Human Behavior*. A second study finds that patients tend not to sue physicians who they believe are concerned about them.

10. See "Socialization and Social Casework," by Elizabeth McBroom in Roberts and Nee (Chap. 2, n. 2 above). For an example of a "rehearsal" of behavior, see "In Quest of Coping," by Helen Harris Perlman (*Social Casework* 56, no. 4 [April 1975]: 220–25). Family-life education groups often utilize role-play and "what if" discussions where participants may learn from tryout imitations of effective behaviors modeled by their leader or by fellow group members.

11. One of the most vivid depictions of children who suffer this shallow or inconsistent affectional nurture is to be found in *The Drifters*, ed. Eleanor Pavenstedt, M.D. (Boston: Little, Brown & Co., 1967): esp. chap. 6. While this book is a description and analysis of the characteristics and work done with "children of disorganized lower-class families," you will be aware that emotional starvation or inconsistent nurture is not confined to one class or ethnic group.

12. Studies on the client's relationship capacity as it affects therapeutic outcomes appear in Truax and Carkhuff (Chap. 1, n. 3 above): see chap. 5, "The Focus of the Therapeutic Encounter: The Person Being Helped."

"The more the therapist is perceived by the client as having an empathic understanding and an unconditional regard for him, the greater will be the degree of constructive personality change . . . ," says Carl Rogers in "The Process Equation of Psychotherapy" (*American Journal of Psychotherapy* 15, no. 1 [1961]: 27–45). In other words, the client's capacity to take in what the helper proffers strongly determines the effects of the helping relationship. But—a caveat: that capacity must be tested, not snap judged.

13. Some further description of these relationship-capacity indicators appear in *Social Casework: A Problem-solving Process*, by Perlman (Chap. 1, n. 7 above), pp. 189–95.

Chapter 4

1. A study of the attitudes of over 200 therapists—psychiatrists, psychiatric social workers, psychologists, and psychoanalysts—toward a group of mentally

disturbed patients (shown on sound films) found that fewer than one-third of these therapists revealed positive attitudes toward the patients; more than one-third were negative; the rest were ambivalent. Negative reactions clustered about such factors as these: the patient's diagnosis suggested hopelessness; the patient's behavior roused moral judgments (he seemed "weak," "lax," etc.) or irritation and annoyance (*Psychotherapists in Action*, by Hans H. Strupp [New York: Grune & Stratton, 1960]). A number of other studies reveal what every professional helper knows from experience—that the attractive, motivated, likable help seeker gets the most attention and caring help.

2. There is little to be found in the publications of the helping professions on "how and why I failed." That's understandable. When we become brave enough to face and analyze our failures, we will probably find what private retrospection and some recent studies suggest: that the helper's attitudes and relationship efforts are vital in evoking client/patient responsiveness (although they will not yield success in many instances).

3. See Lide (Chap. 3, n. 3 above). For further studies on the teaching and learning of relationship competences, see Truax and Carkhuff (Chap. 1, n. 3 above), pp. 108-12. "See also "Training in Facilitative Skill," by Richard A. Wells (*Social Work* 20, no. 3 [May 1975]: 242-43).

4. William James, who taught physiology at Harvard before he shifted his interests to psychology, and Carl Lange, a Danish physiologist, each independently arrived at the conviction (James in 1884, Lange in 1885) that bodily changes are triggered by our perceptions and that emotion is the person's feeling response to such change. Their joined opinion was named the "James-Lange theory of the emotions." Relegated to oblivion for some years, the theory is currently under reconsideration and research. One interesting experiment, for instance, found that an identical physical reaction artificially created in a group of subjects resulted in antithetical emotional responses when what the subjects were experiencing physically was differently interpreted to them. See *Psychological Stress and the Coping Process*, by Richard Lazarus (New York: McGraw-Hill Book Co., 1966), pp. 250-57.

5. Drawing upon the experience and testimony of professional actors, Paul Halmos (Chap. 1, n. 6 above) concludes that "behaving 'as if' is not an act of dissembling but a genuine movement towards an ideal" (p. 56). For more scientific support of this point, see *Persuasion and Healing*, by Jerome D. Frank (Baltimore: Johns Hopkins Press, 1973), pp. 108-12.

Chapter 5

1. There is a paucity of discussion in the helping profession's literature on resistance except as it seems to stem from unconscious, intrapsychic sources. Here we are concerned with the situationally induced resistances—those that express the need to defend against recognition of open, manifest problems,

against the helper and what he is assumed to represent, against the real or imagined dangers or changes that help taking may require.

2. Another example of resistance, caused by fear and misunderstandings, may be seen in the case of Mr. Grayson, pp. 209–22 in *Social Casework: A Problem-solving Process* by Perlman (Chap. 1, n. 7 above).

These several references offer views of this form of resistance and suggestions for its management: (*a*) "The Problem of Resistance in Social Work," by Arthur L. Leader (*Social Work* 3 [April 1958]: 19–23); (*b*) "Dealing with Early Resistance," in Overton and Tinker (Chap. 1, n. 9 above); and (*c*) "Dealing with Resistance in Social Work Practice," by Judith C. Nelsen (*Social Casework* 56, no. 10 [December 1975]: 587–92).

Chapter 6

1. A close reading of the casework "models" presented in Roberts and Nee (Chap. 2, n. 2 above) will reveal the basic likenesses but also the differences of emphasis in the uses of relationship as between, for instance, crisis-oriented, family, and behavior modification treatments. Or compare differences in degree, duration, and purposes of relationship in two case citations in this book: with Mrs. Brown, for instance (Chap. 4), and with Mrs. Lavender (Chap. 7).

2. "Our folklore includes the notion that it is only through the medium of the relationship that services can be provided. Actually some clients may require and request a tangible service only—e.g. a new place to live after being evicted, or a new job after being fired, and not want to engage the worker further. For social workers to insist on developing a 'helping relationship' is to put conditions on the provision of services which may serve our professional biases but not necessarily the clients' best interest." So writes Thomas Briggs in his article "Identifying Team Functional Roles and Specializations," in *The Team Model of Social Work Practice*, by Donald Brieland, Thomas Briggs, and Paul Feuenberger, Manpower Monograph no. 5 (Syracuse, N.Y.: Syracuse University School of Social Work, 1973). I quote this example of what is to me a misconception about relationship because it expresses what is frequently implied in many discussions or passing comments on the place and use of relationship when one is dealing with material needs and "real" problems. I have puzzled over these because I cannot imagine how one might "insist on developing a helping relationship" even if one were bent upon it.

3. "Research in Psychotherapy and Behavior Change with the Disadvantaged," by Lorion Raymond, in *Handbook of Psychotherapy and Behavior Change*, ed. S. L. Garfield and A. E. Bergin (in press).

4. Children—most open, most malleable, most rapidly and totally "growing"—are probably most deeply and pervasively influenced by relationships that are loving, accepting, respectful. Yet even with children: reporting on a

recent national survey of group-treatment centers for disturbed children, Morris Fritz Mayer, himself a gifted child therapist, writes, "No treatment center assumed that ... the therapeutic sessions (alliance) alone could help the child. All stressed that the social and educational program and the success of the child in his daily life experience were of equal or greater importance" (*Group Care of Children*, by Morris Fritz Mayer, Leon H. Richman, and Edwin A. Balcerzok [New York: Child Welfare League of America, 1977], p. 82).

Chapter 7

1. See, e.g., "Psychosocial Practice in Small Groups," by Helen Northen, in *Theories of Social Work with Groups*, ed. R. W. Roberts and H. Northen (New York: Columbia University Press, 1976).

2. This decade (the 1970s) has seen an outpouring of literature on group process and helping relationships in work with groups. The most accessible and succinct articles are to be found in the *Encyclopedia of Social Work* (Chap. 3, n. 5 above), vol. 2, "Social Group Work." Especially useful to human service workers are pp. 1321–50. Accompanying bibliographies include recent and helpful references, particularly these: (*a*) *Groups in Social Work*, by Margaret Hartford (New York: Columbia University Press, 1972); (*b*) *Essentials of Social Group Work Skill*, by Helen U. Phillips (Norwood, Pa.: Norwood Editions, 1974); and (*c*) Roberts and Northen (n. 1 above).

3. Begun and carried forward in social work, family treatment has been widely taken on and developed by psychotherapists of several professions, particularly by psychology and psychiatry. The term "family therapy" has come to be more generally used than "family treatment" (see comments on "therapy" under "Comments on Terms and Readings."

Here, for our across-the-board purposes, we should note that helpers in the human services are most likely to have short-term and task-focused sessions with family members about specific, situationally connected problems. Relationships among family members are not necessarily the problem in such instances. Rather there may be needed some agreements reached about separate and combined roles and responsibilities in dealing with some recent, externally created problems, some enlightenment about the impact or consequences, some counseling and easing of problem-induced stresses, and so on.

The first formulation for treatment of the family as a group was (as far as I have been able to determine) that of Robert Gomberg, in his article "The Specific Nature of Family casework," in *Family Casework*, ed. Jessie Taft (Philadelphia: University of Pennsylvania Press, 1944): "... The client must be individualized, but certainly he need not be isolated from *his role as family member*" (p. 114). "The experience with one client must never become isolated from the experience with the other, else the *common goal may be jeopardized*" (p. 130; italics mine).

For recent, readily available, and succinct presentations of the treatment of family members as a group, see (*a*) "Family Services: Family Treatment," by Sanford Sherman, in *Encyclopedia of Social Work* (Chap. 3, n. 5 above), 1:435–40; and (*b*) "Theory and Practice of Family Therapy," by Frances Scherz, in Roberts and Nee (Chap. 2, n. 2 above). Both articles suggest further reading references.

4. In discussing family treatment Sanford Sherman points up the fact that in group discussion "a piece of family life, an incident of family interaction is thus transplanted live into the [group] session."

Chapter 8

1. The term "significant other" was coined by the social scientist George Herbert Mead, who, long before the professional community was ready for it, set forth his insights about the potency of other people in affecting each person's sense of self and of his social status, and his consequent behaviors. The term creates awkwardness in repetition, but there are few synonyms to convey the same idea.

In its use here, it refers to any one who at any point is or may become strongly influential in the feelings, thoughts, behavior, or life circumstances of another person. Almost every help seeker has one or more significant others operating within the orbit of the problem for which he seeks help.

2. Ripple, Alexander, and Polemis (Chap. 3, n. 8 above), pp. 203–4. It must be noted that this finding is for clients with "psychological" problems, chiefly interpersonal conflicts in which significant others might themselves have been part. However, for problems that were "external," which is to say environmentally induced, continuance was strongly associated with "strong encouragement," "assurance," "warmly positive affect" from the helper. In such instances the helper, he who is assumed to hold the needed resources, is surely a most "significant other."

It is worth noting that in many studies that compare improvement in troubled persons who had therapy with those who did not there seems to have been all but complete neglect of the environmental factors, including significant others, that played into improvement or deterioration of the patient/client. For a review of some studies and comments upon people's use of their significant others, see "The Evaluation of Therapeutic Outcomes," by Allen E. Bergin and Michael J. Lambert, in Bergin and Garfield (Chap. 1, n. 3 above).

3. *Psychotherapy and the Role of the Environment*, by Harold Voth, M. D., and Marjorie Orth (New York: Behavior Publications, 1973). This study reports on forty-two cases known over a ten-year period at the Menninger Foundation. "We are impressed by the fact that while the ultimate basis for psychopathology is to be found in the individual psyche, environmental factors must be taken into account" (p. 7). The research revealed that, here as

elsewhere, rather little attention was given to the patients' current environmental influences (although early childhood influences may have been noted). It is because counseling by practitioners has often ignored the environment that I note this commentary from a psychoanalytically oriented setting.

In a similar vein, and over thirty years ago, Franz Alexander and Thomas French (Chap. 3, n. 7 above), both of the Chicago Institute for Psychoanalysis, wrote, "The careful analyst ... is actively concerned not only with the analytical situation but also with the patients' other relationships ..." (p. 28).

4. More than sixty years ago Mary Richmond wrote, "... Where disorders within or without threaten a man's happiness, his social relations must continue to be the chief means of his recovery" (*Social Diagnosis* [New York: Russell Sage Foundation, 1917] p. 369).

Some twenty-five years ago, seeking to revive the recognition by social workers that "the meaningful experiences the client encounters in his social living today will be part of his psychic experience tomorrow" and to emphasize that professional interpersonal skills are required in environmental modification, I suggested that "... in order to modify clients' environment [the helper] must be engaged with the personalities that represent the environment ..." and "to modify a client's social situation ... is almost always a matter of influencing the feelings, attitudes and behaviors of [other] people" ("Social Components of Casework Practice," *Social Welfare Forum,* National Conference of Social Work, 1953; reprinted in *Perspectives on Social Casework,* by Perlman [Chap. 1, n. 8 above]).

For a survey of the persistence of the idea, if not the practice of active engagement of significant people in the client's current life, see "Environmental Modification: Casework's Concern or Casework's Neglect?" by Richard M. Grinnell, Jr., *Social Service Review* 47, no. 2 (1973): 208-20.

5. See "An Ecological Perspective in Casework Practice," by Carol Germain (*Social Casework* 54 [June 1973]: 323-30).

In her recent *Social Work Practice,* 2d ed. (New York: Free Press, 1976), Carol Meyer uses Germain's concept: "... The eco-systems approach reaches for the transactional exchange between the person and environment" (p. 201), and "... Potential interventions are viewed as located everywhere that is relevant in the life space of the client ..." (p. 200). Perhaps the concept "environment" has tended to convey some sense of stasis and remoteness? One wonders if the concept "ecosystem" carries more dynamic implications— and whether "what's in a name" might capture some fresh interest?

6. See Gomberg (Chap. 7, n. 3 above).

7. See the findings reported in "Environmental Modification: A Study," by R. M. Grinnell, Jr., and N. S. Kyte (*Social Work* 20, no. 4 [July 1975]: 313-18).

8. This concept of White's, generative in its explanatory power for the understanding of many kinds of human endeavor that are not always satisfactorily explained by concepts of libidinal and aggressive instincts, is pre-

sented in his "Ego and Reality in Psychoanalytic Theory," in *Psychological Issues 3,* no. 3, Monograph 11 (New York: International Universities Press, 1963).

Chapter 9

1. *The Gift Relationship*, by Richard M. Titmuss (New York: Pantheon Books, 1971), p. 224.

2. From "The Frontiers and Limits of Science," by Victor F. Weisskopf (*Bulletin of the American Academy of Arts and Sciences* 28, no. 6 [March 1975]. (An editorial error resulted in a reversal of the two last phrases in the article's publication. In a letter to me, Professor Weisskopf suggested the form in which I have quoted him.)

My Thanks

ONCE AGAIN, as I write the last sentence of a book, there rises up the full realization of how much I have been nurtured and enabled by my "significant others." They are legion. They are all those whose writings or teachings or everyday exchanges in talk and acts have sparked or fueled my thinking, or who have opened and extended the edges of my knowing and insights. They are my mentors past and present, my colleagues, my family and friends, my students, and surely most of the people—men, women, and children—who were my clients. For all their gifts how meager a "thank you" seems!

To those helpers and researchers who have made public their thoughts and findings by putting them into print I acknowledge my debt, at least in part, by documenting to them. To the several social workers whose cases I have used to illustrate points or principles I am both grateful and apologetic—grateful that they and their agencies were so generous in providing me with their records for teaching purposes, and apologetic because in my zeal to guard the confidentiality of their clients I so thoroughly disguised names and places that I can no longer identify to whom I owe not only my own thanks but those of the many learners who have found their examples illuminating.

Several persons have helped me in specific ways with this book. Mary Louise Somers gave me her sound advice about the chapter on work with groups; Robert Nee opened the library of Barry College to me when I needed it; Pauline Lide and John

Moore, each in separate ways, encouraged me in writing the book; Gwen Graham, calm and imperturbable, transformed sheaves of scrawled, pasted, interlineated legal pads into legible typescript; and Harold Richman, dean of my professional home, the School of Social Service Administration of the University of Chicago, by his characteristic empathic responsiveness and unfailing support has made the stern discipline of productive effort a kind of pleasure.

No one has "acknowledged" with more simplicity and truth than that great man Albert Einstein. "Many times a day I realize how much my own outer and inner life is built upon the labors of my fellow men," he once wrote, "and how earnestly I must exert myself in order to give in return as much as I have received." So it is for each of us—even when our gifts are small ones. We take and give and dare to hope now and then that what we return may be found good or sustaining to others.

Index